ABC Relaxation
Theory

Jonathan C. Smith, Ph.D., is a Licensed Clinical Psychologist, Distinguished Professor of Psychology, and founder and Director of the Roosevelt University Stress Institute. He has published numerous articles and 10 books on stress, relaxation, and meditation and has taught relaxation to thousands of individuals.

ABC Relaxation Theory

An Evidence-Based Approach

Jonathan C. Smith, Ph.D.

Springer Publishing Company
New York

Springer Publishing Company, Inc.
536 Broadway
New York, NY 10012-3955

Acquisitions Editor: Bill Tucker
Production Editor: Helen Song
Cover design by James Scotto-Lavino

99 00 01 02 03 / 5 4 3 2 1

Library of Congress Cataloging-in-Publication Data

Smith, Jonathan C.
    ABC relaxation theory : an evidence-based approach / Jonathan C. Smith.
       p. cm.
    Includes bibliographical references.
    ISBN 0-8261-1283-8 (hardcover)
    1. Relaxation. I. Title.
  BF637.R45S549 1999
  613.7'9—dc21
                                       99-25934
                                           CIP

Printed in the United States of America

Matthew Shepard
Billy Jack Gaither

Casualties of the Season

Contents

List of Tables

List of Figures

Preface

This book covers new ground. The theory has been around for over a decade—first as Relaxation Dynamics, then as Cognitive-Behavioral Relaxation Theory (CBRT), followed by CBRT-II, and now as ABC Relaxation Theory. My past theory-making has been mostly armchair speculation. The present volume is my first attempt to ground theory in research—so far, 30 studies involving 6,000 participants.

This has been a collaborative effort, involving an army of colleagues and students. Many, many thanks are due. Let me first extend my deep, heartfelt appreciation to Alberto Amutio, who showed up at my door, fresh from the Basque country in Spain, with maroon trousers and floral shirt, and more energy than I could muster in a decade. It was "hurricane Alberto" (ironically, the designated name of the big storm of the season) who pounded the pavement and visited just about every yoga, meditation, and relaxation training center in northern Illinois, assessing nearly a thousand relaxers in a few months. Alberto played a crucial role in the research that eventually led to the ABC approach. Thanks, Alberto. And the best of fortune in continuing your promising career.

I also wish to thank my students for their diligent and creative effort. These include Dan Allen, John Anderson, Pam Anderson, Les Aria, Chan Seok Bang, Sherry Clavin, Jennifer Cox, Louis Cucci III, Robert Holmes III, Amy Khasky, Kathy Leslie, Kenneth Lofland, Steve Rice, Tim Ritchie, Tiago Velho, Julian Williams . . . and many others. And of course, there are the cats, Moco and Clyde, who perched on my shoulder and studied with patient determination the scurrying of my computer cursor.

Finally, thanks to Roosevelt University for granting me a Distinguished Professorship, with a reduced teaching load so that I could explore the ideas and applications of this book and develop the Roosevelt University Stress Institute. Special thanks to Ron Tallman, Dean of Arts and Sciences, for his patient and generous encouragement and support. Without his tangible commitment to my work, I would still be mired in the eternal swamp of administrative meetings, reports, and deadlines.

To all these collaborators, I want to say that I sincerely think we have done something new, perhaps even important. If I am not mistaken, I believe we can rightly claim a number of firsts:

- The first comprehensive, evidence-based, psychological theory of relaxation.
- The first evidence-based, replicated map of the subjective experience of relaxation that, for the first time, integrates secular approaches generated in medical and psychological laboratories with approaches born of religion.
- The first demonstration of strong, replicated differences among approaches to relaxation.
- The first demonstration of strong, replicated gender differences in relaxation.
- The first demonstration of strong differences among African Americans, Latinos, and Whites in relaxation experience.
- The first demonstration of strong and replicated predictors of success for practitioners of relaxation.
- The first strong and replicated map of relaxation beliefs.
- The first clear demonstration of the relationship between personal beliefs and relaxation success.
- The first evidence-based map of relaxation outcomes.

To my colleagues and students, we can now, briefly, sit back and enjoy the R-State Mental Relaxation ("at ease, contented, soothed, relaxed, calm, rested," and above all "relieved").

JONATHAN C. SMITH, PHD

A Parable for Arthur C. Clark[1]

A wise but troubled writer called upon his most trusted advisors for counsel. They included an odd assortment of men and women of faith—a Buddhist, a Christian, a Hindu, a Jew, and a Muslim. A problem weighed heavily on the writer's mind. You see, he was not a believer; indeed, he considered religion to be irrational, a type of mental illness. But this was only part of his concern. Carefully, he explained:

"I am sincerely happy that your religion gives you peace of mind.

"Yes, I acknowledge that Western medical science now shows religion may help you live longer and healthier lives.

"However, I have a sincere and important question. Is it best to be un-sane and happy? Is it best to be sane and un-happy? Or is it best to be both sane and happy?"

The advisors thought long and hard. Some kneeled and closed their eyes in fervent prayer. Some sat, legs folded, in deep meditation. Some looked to the sky. After a few minutes, the tension grew, like the unbearable calm before a storm or earthquake. Clearly, a Great Theological Discussion was about to erupt.

And at that precise moment the wise man had his answer.

Slowly, he took a breath and paused:

"My friends. It is best to be silent."

1

The World of Relaxation

Relaxation is a world of many riches. A vast landscape of techniques extends from the heights of imagery, meditation, and prayer to ordinary health club yoga and massage. Thousands of studies have considered over 200 benefits in every realm of life, love, and leisure (see Table 1.1). And

TABLE 1.1   Attempted Applications of Relaxation Techniques

Addictions	Creativity	Panic disorder
Aggression	Dentistry	Peptic ulcer
Agoraphobia	Depression	Performance anxiety
AIDS	Diabetes	Physical fitness
Alcohol abuse	Gastrointestinal disorders	Psoriasis
Anger control	Healing from surgery	Public speaking anxiety
Angina	Hyperactivity	Raynaud's syndrome
Anticipatory nausea	Hypertension	Schizophrenia
Anxiety	Hyperventilation	Self-blame
Assertiveness	Immunocompetence	Self-mutilation
Asthma	Insomnia	Smoking
Back pain	Irritable bowel syndrome	Social anxiety
Bradycardia	Math anxiety	Somatoform disorders
Burns	Migraine headaches	Spasmatic dysmenorrhea
Cancer	Motion sickness	Stress management
Cardiac arrhythmia	Motivation	Stuttering
Childbirth	Multiple sclerosis	Substance abuse
Cholesterol	Muscle cramps	Surgery, recovery from
Chemotherapy side effects	Myocardial infarction	Tachycardia
Combat fatigue	Nausea	Tension headaches
Congestive dysmenorrhea	Negative self-image	Tinnitus
Coronary-prone behavior	Neurocirculatory asthenia	Type A behavior
Coronary heart disease	Obsessive-compulsive	Writer's cramp
Coughing	disorder	

practitioners reflect a remarkable and perhaps curious diversity—
Freudians and behaviorists, pastoral counselors and astrologers, and physi-
cians and healers of every faith and fancy. Indeed, relaxation is a
professional tool that abounds with possibilities (see Table 1.2). Yet,
surprisingly, most who teach relaxation are impoverished in what they do.

Ask typical relaxation professionals about their craft, and they will
claim proficiency at only one or two techniques. Go to a psychologist
and learn progressive muscle relaxation. Attend a yoga retreat and practice
stretching, breathing, and maybe meditation. Seek a pastoral counselor
and pray. Most of us have been taught that this is enough. Why waste
time with additional techniques when one or two work fine? Why pursue
relaxation when the symptom is cured? Why venture forth into unfamiliar
worlds haunted by cult and pseudoscience? (Or, conversely, why traverse
the arid deserts of laboratory-derived techniques?)

For whatever reason, most who use relaxation suffer from an unfortu-
nate poverty of practice. However, thousands of relaxation students, over
30 years, have taught me some important lessons. One or two techniques
are rarely enough. Symptom reduction is not an end but a beginning.
There is more, much more, to the vast world of relaxation.

TABLE 1.2   Examples of Specific Uses of Relaxation

Trainer: Clinical psychologist
Application: Therapy for phobia

Sharon is undergoing desensitization therapy for her public speaking anxiety. First she
masters progressive muscle relaxation, a popular approach that involves briefly tensing
up various muscles and then letting go so that muscles become limp and relaxed. After
learning the skill of "going limp" very quickly, she proceeds to imagine increasingly
challenging public speaking scenarios, always taking care to stop and relax deeply at
the slightest indication of anxiety.

Trainer: Sports psychologist
Application: Sports performance enhancement

Bill is learning imagery in an attempt to enhance his basketball game. When deeply
relaxed, he rehearses a vivid imagery sequence in which he mentally recreates the
physical sensations of holding the ball and making a basket.

Trainer: Social worker
Application: Day end recovery

Julia uses hatha yoga to unwind from a hectic day. After arriving home from work, she
puts on loose clothing and starts playing a simple video instruction tape. The instructor
slowly models a series of very easy and gentle stretches, ranging from bending over
and touching the floor to reaching high to the sky. Julia finds the stretches very
invigorating and refreshing.

TABLE 1.2   *(continued)*

Trainer: Counselor
Application: Dental anxiety
John used to find going to the dentist very stressful. He has learned a simple relaxation
exercise to practice while the dentist works on his teeth. He imagines that the drill is
actually a thin stream of pressurized cool water and that the pain sensations are actually
the sensations of water.

Trainer: Psychology professor
Application: Personal enjoyment
Sue enjoys her walks through the forest. At the end of a walk, she sits on a bench and
for about 15 minutes simply gazes at the beauty of nature. She doesn't think about
anything but becomes absorbed in her surroundings.

Trainer: Rehabilitation psychologist
Application: Cardiac surgery rehabilitation
Ben has just had open heart surgery and is in a rehabilitation class. Part of the class
involves learning to relax and take a less stressful stance toward life. He quietly attends
to the flow of breath. Whenever his mind wanders, he gently returns to attending to
the flow of breath. He finds this meditation deeply quieting.

Trainer: Counselor
Application: Cancer prevention
Rebecca has had surgery for breast cancer and wants to do whatever is possible to prevent
a recurrence. She has signed up for a "cancer survivors" program that emphasizes group
psychotherapy, nutrition, exercise, and daily practice of breathing relaxation exercises.

Trainer: Clinical psychologist
Application: Smoking control
Terrance is in a behavioral smoking control program that emphasizes relapse prevention.
In one part of the program, he masters relaxation imagery. Whenever he wants to, he
can close his eyes and engage in vivid imagery of a peaceful outdoor scene and a
refreshing brook. Now, whenever he has the urge to smoke, he simply tells himself,
"I do not need this cigarette" and engages in 5 minutes of relaxation imagery.

Trainer: Industrial/organizational psychologist
Application: Prevention of work-related injury
Todd is a secretary in an accounting firm. His work involves sitting for extended periods.
Recently, he has complained of lower back pain, clearly precipitated by work. He now
practices a set of stretching exercises for back pain, taught by the firm's psychologist.

Trainer: Clinical psychologist
Application: Personal growth
Grace participated in a meditation and prayer class presented at her local church by a
psychologist. She learned a simple breathing meditation exercise to incorporate in
daily prayer.

Note: The above vignettes should not be viewed as prescriptive. Scientific evidence for the efficacy
of relaxation treatments is stronger for some applications (stress management) than others (enhancing
performance). It is, however, appropriate for properly trained professionals to teach relaxation on
an experimental, trial-and-error basis, seeing what works and doesn't work for each client. It should
be assumed that such a procedure was use for each of the hypothetical vignettes.

ATTENTIONAL BEHAVIORAL COGNITIVE (ABC) RELAXATION THEORY IN A NUTSHELL

We begin with a few basic facts. Life is *effortful*. We deliberately think, plan, and carry out our actions. Life is *discursive*, ever moving and changing. We tend to our schedules, vacations, and shopping lists. And when the discursive efforts of life take their toll—wear and tear on body, mind, and soul—we relax. We pull away from the stress of life, recover, and return, renewed and refreshed.

I call my approach *Attentional Behavioral Cognitive* or ABC relaxation theory[2] (with a respectful wink to Albert Ellis). We begin with this idea: The key to relaxation is sustaining *A*ttention while diminishing overt *B*ehavior and covert or *C*ognitive activity. To elaborate, all forms of relaxation involve *sustaining passive simple focus*—the opposite of discursive effort. In everyday life, we strive; in relaxation, we let go. In everyday life our attention moves discursively from complex topic to topic; in relaxation we focus on just one simple thing. Here is a more formal definition:

Passivity involves reducing deliberate analytic and planful effort.

Focusing involves identifying a restricted stimulus, attending to it, and redirecting attention to the stimulus after distraction.

Everyone has experienced special moments of passive simple focus. You might gaze at a sunset and for an instant feel a sense of peace and beauty as golden rays burst through violet clouds. Or after reading a moving story, you might close your eyes and savor the moment, feeling wonderfully distant and far away from the cares of the world. Throughout life, all of us spontaneously encounter a rich variety of instances of passive simple focus through music, poetry, art, prayer, and so on. Such moments are part of life's treasures, but they come and go quickly. The sun sets. The story's over. The music ends. We go on with our day's work. The secret of relaxation training is to *sustain the moment*. This is a very difficult thing to do, like balancing a basketball on a calm and steady fingertip. *Sustaining*, uninterrupted, the state of passive simple focus is made easier by practicing a formal relaxation technique.

In the rest of this book we explore what happens when people learn this special skill. Here's ABC Relaxation Theory in a nutshell:

All relaxation evokes a fundamental process of healing and growth in which one withdraws from the efforts of the day, recovers, and opens up to the world. I call this the Cycle of Renewal. The idea of a cyclical renewal process has been around for several millennia and can be manifest at many levels. World religions speak of global cycles of death and rebirth, repentance and forgiveness, as well as acceptance and enlightenment. Professional approaches to relaxation involve mastering the discipline of withdrawing from everyday stress for healing and recovery, and returning to the world refreshed and restored. And each time we pause and sigh we display a moment of relaxation and renewal.

This book presents a universal, evidence-based lexicon of relaxation and renewal and proposes how the cycle of renewal works. Our lexicon consists of three basic constructs: relaxation states (R-States), relaxation beliefs (R-Beliefs), and relaxation attitudes (R-Attitudes). R-States, R-Beliefs, and R-Attitudes determine the effectiveness of all of relaxation.

R-States are psychological states of mind associated with practicing relaxation and mastering the act of sustaining passive simple focus. Those now identified include:

- *Sleepiness*
- *Disengagement*
- *Physical Relaxation*
- A thought-free state of *Mental Quiet*
- *Mental Relaxation*
- *Strength and Awareness*
- *Joy*
- *Love and Thankfulness*
- *Prayerfulness*

The effects of relaxation can be blocked by negative anti-relaxation attitudes, or "R-Attitudes" (I don't have the time to relax," "I'm afraid I will lose control," "Relaxation is just taking a nap") and enhanced through relaxation beliefs or "R-Beliefs." Currently included R-Beliefs include:

- *Optimism*: View the world with optimism.
- *Acceptance*: Accept things that cannot be changed.
- *Honesty*: Be honest with yourself and others.
- *Taking it Easy*: Know when to let go and take it easy.
- *Love*: Relate to others with love and compassion.
- *Inner Wisdom*: Trust the healing wisdom of the body.
- *God*: Trust God's love and guidance.
- *Deeper Perspective*: Put your concerns in deeper perspective.

The most effective way to teach relaxation is not to give one approach to all clients, but to tailor an individualized and comprehensive relaxation treatment package based on client technique preferences as well as desired R-States and R-Beliefs. As such, ABC Relaxation Training represents an application of *broad spectrum behavior therapy* or *multimodal therapy* (Lazarus, 1976, 1997).

Many relaxation traditions have good ideas about specific R-States, R-Attitudes, and R-Beliefs. Manuals of progressive relaxation alert trainers to sensations of Physical Relaxation ("letting go," "feeling limp"), yoga manuals emphasize Awareness, meditation texts discuss feelings of Prayerfulness, and prayer books speak at length of Love and Thankfulness. Furthermore, every year we see another best-selling volume abounding with beliefs claimed to contribute to a relaxed and peaceful life. Indeed, for many millennia, the world's great religions have been producing vast libraries of sacred books of relaxation beliefs.

However, traditional ideas about relaxation have been handed down from an expert or holy person. In contrast, R-States, R-Attitudes, and R-Beliefs are variables identified through more than 10 years of research on over 6,000 individuals. Thus, ABC Relaxation Theory is the first comprehensive approach to relaxation that is fully *evidence-based* rather than *authoritarian*, evolving from the ground up rather than the top down. As such, ABC Relaxation Theory reflects not so much the notions of a single person as, to be a bit poetic, the wisdom of a thousand voices. More on this in later chapters.

ABC Relaxation Theory builds on and goes beyond current relaxation thinking. I propose that if a relaxation practitioner does not minimize negative R-Attitudes, cultivate R-Beliefs, and experience R-States, he or she will not benefit from relaxation, no matter what the technique may be. Furthermore, different approaches to relaxation are associated with different R-States, R-Attitudes, and R-Beliefs. Different R-States, R-Attitudes, and R-Beliefs may be appropriate for different therapy and training objectives.

SIX APPROACHES TO PROFESSIONAL SELF-RELAXATION

To understand ABC Theory, we begin with the raw material of professional self-relaxation, the six approaches used most in clinics and consulting rooms around the world. First, it is important to recognize that many activities can trigger R-States and contribute to the development and expression of R-Beliefs. *Unstructured casual pursuits* are the most common and include leisure and recreation—listening to music, sunbathing, taking walks, stroking pets, listing to music, and the like. To these we can add *structured nonprofessional activities*, formal disciplines taught by experts outside the health professions. One might learn art appreciation at school, hiking from an Eagle Scout, and prayer from a priest.

Professional relaxation techniques are formal approaches developed, perfected, and taught by educators and health professionals. Unlike casual or nonprofessional activities, professional relaxation techniques must stand up to the rigors of professional ethics and scientific inquiry. In this book we consider the six approaches to self-relaxation most popular among psychologists, social workers, counselors, nurses, and others in secular behavioral professions. We will examine their history and consider how each has a unique approach to the central attentional task of sustaining passive simple focus.

Progressive Muscle Relaxation

Progressive muscle relaxation (PMR) is perhaps the most widely used professional approach to relaxation in America. For years it has dominated textbooks and relaxation research, and even now we see the term "progressive relaxation" used interchangeably (and incorrectly) with relaxation itself.

Early in the 20th century, Chicago physician and psychologist Edmund Jacobson began work on relaxation as a doctoral student at Harvard in 1907, prompted in part by his desire to cure his own insomnia (Jacobson, 1929). In 1926 he joined the Department of Physiology at the University of Chicago and conducted research on the knee-jerk reflex (the "kicking reflex" evoked by gently thumping an area just below the knee). Jacobson developed a private practice, often making use of relaxation procedures. At first he used reductions in the knee-jerk reflex as a sign of relaxation and a tool for refining relaxation techniques. Later he enlisted the aid of scientists at Bell Telephone Laboratory (today's Lucent Technologies) and invented the integrated neurovoltmeter, essentially a biofeedback device capable of measuring tension-related action potentials from muscle groups and nerves. Such a tool fit well with Jacobson's bias that all stressful worry had neuromuscular manifestations and that reducing these manifestations would in turn reduce stressful worry.

Minimal PMR

Jacobson's (1929) approach (which I term "minimal PMR") involved training subjects to detect and recognize increasingly subtle levels of muscle tension and remain relaxed throughout the day. In each session a client would focus on a body part (e.g., the hand), generate the smallest amount of tension possible, and let go. Jacobson felt it was very important to avoid suggestive patter, fearing it might introduce what he felt were the confounding effects of hypnotic suggestion (ironically, some hypnosis scholars consider Jacobson's approach to be a form of hypnosis [Edmonston, 1986]). Subjects would learn to relax two or three muscle groups per session, eventually covering 50 groups for the entire body. Training required 50 or more sessions that could last from 3 to 6 months to a year.

Illustration of Minimal PMR

> *Quietly attend to your right hand. When your mind wanders, simply return. Gently begin to tense up the muscles in your right hand, very very slowly. The moment you notice the slightest increase in tension, let go. Relax.*

Overt and Covert Abbreviated PMR

Jacobson's minimal method was cumbersome and not widely used. In 1958, Joseph Wolpe (1958) introduced the first abbreviated version of progressive relaxation. Earlier, Wolpe had found that a conditioned fear reaction in cats could be eliminated by evoking a response incompatible with fear concurrently with a feared stimulus. Progressive relaxation could work as such a "reciprocal inhibitor" and became a part of Wolpe's well-known desensitization treatments.

The abbreviated approach of Wolpe and others involves overtly creating a considerable level of relaxation, starting in the first session. One effortfully "tenses up" for about 5–10 seconds and then "lets go," attending to the release of tension for 30 seconds or so. Often up to 16 muscle groups, rather than 1–3, are separately targeted in each session. As training progresses, muscle groups are combined until eventually one can simply detect and relax tension without first overtly creating tension. In the most abbreviated format, termed conditioned relaxation (Paul, 1966) and cue-controlled relaxation (Russell & Matthews, 1975), one covertly thinks of a relaxing cue word, such as *relaxed* or *calm*, immediately after practicing progressive relaxation. In time, thinking of the cue itself is sufficient to evoke relaxation. Alternatively, in covert PMR one simply lets go without first tensing up.

Illustration of Overt PMR

> *Quietly attend to your right hand. Tense the muscles in your right hand now. Keep the rest of your body relaxed. Notice the tension grow in your*

right hand. And let go. Let the tension flow away. Notice the sensations of relaxation. Can you tell the difference between how your hand feels now and how it felt when you were tensing it?

Illustration of Covert PMR

Quietly attend to your right hand. Let go of any feelings of tension you may feel. There is nothing you have to do but let the tension flow and dissolve away.

Autogenic Training

Autogenic training is a popular European approach to relaxation that has had modest impact in North America. Its roots can be traced to authoritarian hypnosis of nearly a century ago. In the late 1890s, a hypnotist might, after an induction ritual, directly issue any of a variety of command-like hypnotic suggestions, such as "Sleep," "Your eyelids are so droopy you cannot keep them open," "Your arms are so heavy you cannot lift them. Now try to lift your arms." Berlin neurophysiologist Oskar Vogt developed a less authoritarian and directive approach that involved gently hinting at what he wanted a patient to do or perceive. His wish was not to disturb the patient's freedom of will. In addition, Vogt introduced a step-by-step approach, the "fraction method," in which a patient would be repeatedly hypnotized for a few minutes and then wakened. The effects of each brief hypnosis would be ascertained and used to adjust subsequent suggestions (Loewenfeld, 1901). Finally, Vogt made the important observation that a number of his hypnosis patients were able to induce their own hypnotic-like states (Schultz & Luthe, 1959) and that these states, when evoked a few times a day, appeared to have relaxing, therapeutic value.

Around the same time, a dermatologist, Johannes Schultz, shifted to neurology and psychiatry and began practicing hypnosis. Schultz (1932) made use of the notion that thinking of physical sensations related to relaxation can often evoke physical relaxation. Importantly, he was convinced that hypnosis was not something imposed on a patient by a domineering hypnotist but an inner ability that patients permitted to unfold. In the 1920s and 1930s, Schultz introduced autogenic training, a relaxation-based system of therapy based on his notion of "self-generated" (autogenic) healing. Central to this idea is that the brain has powerful self-healing potential, which can be activated through what Benson (1975) later termed the "relaxation response." During the course of his career,

Schultz published more than 400 articles and several books. His system became widely known in Europe and was introduced in the Western Hemisphere by Wolfgang Luthe (1965).

Standard and Organ-Specific Exercises

Traditional autogenic training is a highly structured sequential program (Linden, 1990; Luthe, 1969–1973). It begins with six standard exercises that involve mentally repeating verbal formulas targeted to heaviness, warmth, cardiac regulation, respiration, abdominal warmth, and cooling of the forehead. Emphasis is placed on "passive volition," that is, repeating formulas passively while maintaining complete indifference about the result. A beginning client might be instructed to let the phrase "hands are warm . . . hands are warm" repeat in his or her mind, quietly attending to the words much as one might attend to the slow repetition of an echo. One exerts no effort to regulate the pace or volume of the repeated words. Indeed, one attends with complete indifference; the exercise is considered valid even when the suggested somatic effect is not perceived. After mastering beginning warmth and heaviness exercises, a client progresses to phrases targeted to the heart ("heartbeat strong and even"), respiration ("it breathes me"), abdominal warmth ("warmth radiates from my stomach"), and forehead ("forehead cool and calm").

Illustration of Autogenic Standard Exercise

Gently let these words float through your mind, like echoes. "Hands and arms, warm and heavy. Hands and arms, warm and heavy." There is no need to deliberately try to conjure up these feelings. Just let the words float through your mind like a meaningless nursery rhyme. When your mind wanders, gently return to repeating the words "hands and arms, warm and heavy."

Once the standard exercises are mastered, a variety of special exercises may be introduced. Organ-specific formulas tailor the standard exercises to the particular needs of the patient. For example, a backache patient may use the phrase "My back is warm"; a headache patient, "My forehead is cool," and so on. Intentional formulas are phrases targeted to behavioral change objectives ("I will study more, drink less").

Autogenic "Meditation"

Next a series of seven "meditative" or, more accurately, imagery exercises are presented. One begins with an imagery preparation exercise that involves attending to vague retinal sensations that spontaneously occur with eyes closed in relaxation (visual phosphene activity). Such sensations might include faint and formless clouds of light, spots, and so on. Once a trainee can sustain attention on such phenomena, he or she graduates to increasingly challenging images, including colors, then simple shapes (square, circle), and concrete objects (chairs, vases) until they can be produced and modulated on demand. The most advanced images include abstract constructs (truth, justice, friendship), emotional states, and other people. Eventually, exercises are directed toward seeking "answers from the unconscious," that is, asking questions ("What is the source of my frustration?") and passively waiting for a spontaneous answer to emerge in the form of a change in image (an answer spontaneously appearing on an imagined blackboard or TV screen).

Today, autogenic training more or less in full form is popular in Europe and Canada, whereas highly abbreviated forms (usually targeting "warmth and heaviness") prevail in the United States. In addition, abbreviated variations have emerged with highly specific suggestions targeted, for example, to individual cancer tumors, the immune system, and so on (Simonton, Matthews-Simonton, & Creighton, 1978).

Breathing, Yoga Stretching, and Meditation

The histories of breathing, yoga stretching, and meditation are intertwined. We begin with two oriental religions, Hinduism and Buddhism. Hinduism, one of the ancient religions of India, has incorporated a diverse assortment of yoga stretching, breathing and meditation exercises for thousands of years. In the second century B.C., such exercises were codified in the yoga aphorisms of Patanjali (Eliade, 1969; Prabhavananda, 1963). Patanjali emphasized an eight-step path for cultivating a meditative state of mind conducive to spiritual insight. The steps included various initial ascetic practices, yoga postures and stretches, breathing relaxation exercises, and finally meditation. The easiest of meditative practices, often called concentrative meditation, involved withdrawing the senses from troubling and distracting influences of external stimuli, memories, and so on, and concentrating on a single point.

Through the centuries, numerous divisions of Hindu thinking appeared, some emphasizing devotion to a Christian-like God and others an impersonal nontheistic absolute. This latter position, associated with the 8th-century Indian philosopher Shankara, was eventually to form the basis of most Western forms of Hinduism, yoga, and meditation, including transcendental meditation (TM). Currently, health professionals teach a variety of secular forms of concentrative meditation, all involving attending to a simple stimulus, such as repetition of the word *one*, the flow of breath, a visual image, and so on. The most popular is transcendental meditation, an approach that involves focusing on a mantra, or mental repetition of a Hindu Sanskrit syllable or word.

The second major oriental religion, Buddhism, gave birth to Zen, one of the most popular approaches to meditation in Japan and to some extent in the West. Around 500 B.C., Buddhism emerged as a reform offshoot of Hinduism (Conze, 1959; Layman, 1976). Buddha taught that existence is permeated with suffering caused by self-centered thought. Selfish thought could be destroyed by following an "eightfold path" of right motivation and conduct, eventually culminating in a passive focusing exercise, meditation. In the 6th century, Buddhism was carried to China and appeared 600 years later in Japan as Zen. Unlike concentrative meditation, Zen is an open technique that involves calmly attending to the flow of all stimuli, not a continuous single stimulus. One does so without thought or analysis. Today health professionals outside the Buddhist tradition teach simple Zen awareness techniques, often in combination with stretching, breathing, and other concentrative meditation techniques.

Illustration of a Breathing Exercise

Gently take a deep breath. Pause. And slowly exhale, slowly letting the air flow through your lips, as if you were blowing on a candle flame. Attend to the flow of breath. Notice how it quietly moves in through your nostrils and down into your lungs. Follow the flow of breath in and out.

Illustration of a Yoga Stretching Exercise

Stand in a comfortable, upright position. Let both arms hang to each side. Slowly swing your right hand and arm up, tracing a circle in the air to your side. Do this very slowly, smoothly, and gently, as if you were balancing a feather on your fingertips. Gently attend to the smooth and graceful movement. Let your hand and arm easily move higher until it is pointing straight up into the sky. Continue attending to your hand and arm as you slowly, smoothly, and gently return it to your side.

Illustration of a Meditation Exercise

Let the word "one" easily float through your mind, over and over. There is no need to force it to repeat at any speed or volume. Just let the word gently repeat again and again. All you need to do is attend to the word "one." Whenever your mind wanders, gently return to attending to the word "one" as it repeats over and over.

Imagery

Imagery has scientific roots in both hypnosis and autogenic training and antecedents in 19th-century religious and self-help cults. Images often form an important part of hypnotic induction, and the production of hallucination is a frequently suggested hypnotic response. Advanced autogenic exercises incorporate a graduated series of simple and complex images. It should be noted that yoga and meditation traditions have their own imagery exercises, although these are rarely employed in the West. Focal stimuli can be as complex as circular-patterned mandala artwork or simple as a candle flame. Kundalini meditation, a form of yoga, involves attending to sensations and images associated with various internal "chakras," or somatic energy centers, such as the heart ("attend to the feelings of warmth in your heart"), throat, spine, and center of the forehead

Although imagery is often used in psychotherapeutic traditions as diverse as psychoanalysis and behavior therapy, we are concerned with imagery used in relaxation. Such relaxation imagery involves creating a cognitive or mental representation of a real or imagined relaxing activity or setting. Most forms of imagery can be divided into three categories. Narrative imagery involves attending to a simple and somewhat plotless relaxing story, for example, walking through the woods, floating through the air, riding a horse, and so on. One attends to simple relaxing sensations (sights, sounds, feelings, smells) that arise while completing a relaxing activity. Sense imagery is simpler: one passively attends to sense stimulation without fantasizing about an activity. One might imagine a beach and attend to the waves, sky, sounds of birds, and so on. Finally, insight imagery begins with a simple preparatory story (walking through a special forest to find the magic pond) and ends with an utterly simple focus. One presents a question related to relaxation and meditatively and nonanalytically attends to a designated source of insight (a mirror, pond, "magic door," etc.) and passively waits for an answer to spontaneously emerge. For example, one might attend to a reflective pond, waiting for words or an image that address the question "what is truly relaxing for me at this time in my life?"

Illustration of an Imagery Exercise (Sense Imagery)

In your mind's eye, let yourself enjoy a fantasy about a pleasing vacation spot on the beach. Involve all of your senses. What do you see? The blue

sky above? The green trees? The clear blue water? What do you hear?
Perhaps the gentle rustle of trees or the splashing of waves. What do you
feel touching your skin? Perhaps the warm sun or cool breeze. And what
relaxing fragrances are there? The clean scent of water? Flowers? Let
yourself enjoy this image with all your senses. Whenever your mind wan-
ders, gently return to your image.

A Diversity of Techniques

It is a bit misleading to claim that there are only six approaches to
professional relaxation. The true diversity of relaxation becomes apparent
if we perform a small conceptual experiment. Frequently, both clinicians
and researchers isolate one specific exercise from a broad tradition and
present it on its own. For example, suggestions to mentally repeat the
relaxing phrase "hands warm and heavy" are often selected from the
autogenic sequence; TM mantra meditation is taken from a yoga tradition
that integrates stretching, breathing, and meditation; and PMR tense–let
go exercises are often taught apart from a full sequence of overt PMR,
minimal PMR, and covert PMR. Something interesting happens when we
isolate every plausible and usable component exercise from its broader
tradition (while taking care not to go too far by isolating exercises by
target organ (arms, legs, back, heart) or theme (health, nature, spiritual
expression). We discover an array of more than 30 distinct relaxation
techniques (see Table 1.3). The profusion of relaxation exercises calls for
a unifying model. In the chapters that follow we consider one such attempt.

RELAXATION AS AN ATTENTIONAL ACT:
SUSTAINING PASSIVE SIMPLE FOCUS

We can now return to our attentional definition of relaxation as sustained
passive simple focus. Each approach to relaxation accomplishes this task
in a different way. For all variations of PMR, the simple focal stimuli
are the kinesthetic sensations resulting from evoking and releasing striated
muscle tension, that is, one attends to tensing up and letting go or simply
letting go. Passivity in PMR is deliberate, the letting go, or tension release,
phase of the relaxation cycle. And passive somatic focus is deliberately
sustained, made easy by continuous trainer instructions to proceed from
muscle group to muscle group.

TABLE 1.3   **Thirty-two Common Relaxation Techniques**

Specific Technique	Typical Specific Exercises
Autogenic "answers from the unconscious"	"What is the source of my frustration?"
Autogenic imagery preparation	"Attend to the vague visual sensations you see with eyes closed."
Autogenic intentional formulas	"I see myself studying more."
Autogenic meditation	"Visualize colors and shapes."
Autogenic organ-specific formulas	"My headache is lifting."
Autogenic standard exercises	"Warm and heavy."
Breathing (active)	"Take in a deep breath as you reach up and stretch."
Breathing (passive)	"Attend to the flow of breath."
Contemplative imagery	"Attend to the candle flame. Let enriching thoughts and images come and go."
Imagery (insight)	"Imagine finding a secret box. Inside is an important message."
Imagery (narrative)	"Imagine playing a good game of golf. Imagine a perfect swing."
Imagery (sense)	"Imagine a peaceful forest, the leaves, wind, sun, and grass."
Meditation (on internal energy centers)	"Attend to warm feelings of energy in your abdomen."
Meditation (on external stimulus)	"Attend to the candle flame."
Meditation (on internal image)	"Attend to the point of light you see with your eyes closed."
Meditation (rocking)	"Gently rock back and forth. Attend to this movement."
Meditation (walking)	"Slowly walk, attend to the movement of each foot."
Prayer (expressive)	"Say your feelings and wishes."
Prayer (receptive)	"Listen to the object of your prayer. What is it telling you?"
Progressive muscle relaxation (abbreviated overt version)	"Vigorously tense up; let go."
Progressive muscle relaxation (covert version)	"Let go of tension without first tensing up."
Progressive muscle relaxation (original "minimal" version)	"Tense up very slightly; let go."
Tai chi	"Slowly move your arms in front of you, as if you were swimming."
Transcendental meditation	"Passively attend to your TM mantra."
Yoga stretching (active)	"Slowly and gracefully stretch to the sky."
Yoga (passive)	"Passively and slowly, let your head fall forward, gently stretching your neck."

TABLE 1.3   *(continued)*

Specific Technique	Typical Specific Exercises
Yoga (postures)	"Calmly stand on one foot, focusing attention on your posture."
Zen meditation (breath counting)	"Count 'one' with every outgoing breath."
Zen meditation (breath awareness)	"Attend to the simple flow of breath."
Zen meditation (*hara*, meditation on energy from solar plexus)	"Attend to the warmth and energy radiating from your abdomen a few inches above the navel."
Zen meditation (on a simple paradox or koan)	"What is the sound of one hand clapping?"
Zen mindfulness meditation	"Attend to the flow of all stimuli."

For autogenic training, the simple target stimulus can be seen as either the suggested standard phrases ("hands and arms warm and heavy") or the actual physical sensations resulting from the exercise. Traditional autogenic trainers minimize the importance of actually experiencing the suggested effects; others direct clients to these very sensations. Passivity is maintained as a clear instructional set: "Do not try to deliberately evoke these sensations . . . let the phrases 'warm and heavy' float through your mind . . . you are nothing more than a passive observer." And again, this passive somatic focus is sustained.

Breathing and yoga stretching exercises provide a clear simple target stimulus, sensations associated with the flow of breath and the slow moving and stretching of joints and striated muscles. Passivity is indirectly encouraged. Forced, effortful breathing, panting, or holding of one's breath are to be avoided. Practitioners of yoga avoid rapid or extremely effortful stretching. In addition, many yoga stretches can be achieved by ceasing deliberate effort (letting one's head hang to the chest rather than forcing one's head down). Again, passive focus is sustained by presenting a sequence of somewhat varied exercises.

For imagery, the target stimulus may seem to be complex and effortful (enjoying a fantasy walk through the woods). However, the task is focused and passive relative to everyday discursive efforts. One has a simple imagery theme, a vacation spot, for example; in everyday life, thoughts and activities are often more diverse. Meditation is the most passive and focused approach to relaxation. The target focal stimulus is utterly simple, a candle flame, a word, a simple repeating sound. And one exerts no effort but simply attends.

NOTES

1. Fashioned from an observation by Authur C. Clark, the final passage of the final footnote in his book *3001: The Final Odyssey* (New York: Ballantine Publishing Group, 1997):

   Finally, I would like to assure my many Buddhist, Christian, Hindu, Jewish, and Muslim friends that I am sincerely happy that the religion which Chance has given you has contributed to your peace of mind (and often, as Western medical science now reluctantly admits, to your physical well-being).

   Perhaps it is better to be un-sane and happy, than sane and un-happy. But it is best of all to be sane and happy.

   Whether our descendants can achieve that goal will be the greatest challenge of the future. Indeed, it may well decide whether we have any future. (p. 274)

   To avoid confusion, please assume that Mr. Clark is not the "troubled writer."

2. This is a theory, not a hypothesis or model. Hypotheses and models are simple things, identifying one or two variables with a relatively simple relationship. Theories are complex, identifying many interacting variables and permitting numerous complex, often unidentified hypotheses. Compare the frustration-aggression hypothesis with Freud's theory. Most relaxation researchers appropriately refer to Benson's (1975) relaxation response *hypothesis* and the cognitive-somatic specificity *hypothesis*. This book presents the first true psychological *theory* of relaxation.

2
The Physiology of Relaxation

We have briefly introduced the six major approaches to self-relaxation most used by health professionals and educators. How do they work? What are their effects? One way of looking at this question is to consider the physiology of relaxation, a perspective that has had a profound impact on how relaxation is understand and taught, by both the general public and health professionals. Indeed, it has defined the field for over 20 years.

STRESS AROUSAL

Most people think of relaxation as the opposite of stress. To understand the value and limitations of this view, we begin with a quick overview of the physiology and neurology of stress. We will deliberately gloss over exquisitely complex processes, focusing on those most often mentioned in the stress and relaxation literature.

The Brain, Nervous System, and Endocrine System

The three body systems most involved in stress are the nervous system, endocrine system, and, when considering the impact of stress on physical health (not a focus here), the immune system. To review the basics, the nervous system is divided into the central nervous system (CNS) and peripheral nervous system (PNS). The CNS includes the brain and spinal cord; the PNS is divided into the somatic and autonomic nervous systems. The somatic nervous system is sometimes termed the musculoskeletal, or "voluntary," nervous system because it is primarily involved in voluntary muscular activity (walking, gesturing, deliberate facial expressions). In contrast, the autonomic nervous system regulates physical functions over which people have relatively little control, including breathing, digestion, and regulation of blood flow.

The autonomic nervous system is in turn divided into sympathetic and parasympathetic branches, which, as we shall see, are very much involved in stress arousal and relaxation. Finally, all nervous system activity, including stress and relaxation processes, is modulated by neurotransmitter substances, including acetylcholine, norepinephrine, serotonin, dopamine, GABA (gamma-amino butyric acid), glutamate, and the endogenous opiates, or endorphins. These substances regulate communication between nerve cells, or neurons, throughout the body and are associated with a wide range of states associated with stress and relaxation, including anxiety (GABA); general pleasurable and reinforcing states (dopamine); positive mood, sleep, and pain reduction (serotonin); arousal, excitement, and wakefulness (norepinephrine); and pain reduction and feelings of euphoria (endorphins). Many man-made psychoactive pharmacological agents (Valium, Prozac) occasionally used to reduce stress and evoke relaxation work through their impact on various neurotransmitters.

In tracing the physiology of stress, it is useful to begin with the brain, specifically, the forebrain and hindbrain. The forebrain is most responsible for complex and highly developed human mental functions and contains three structures: the cerebral cortex, the diencephalon, and the cerebrum. Most people have heard of the cerebral cortex, the brain's outer "bark," an advanced structure that controls a wide range of functions, including language, thought, and perception—all of which are involved in the process of appraising what is stressful or relaxing. Still in the forebrain and beneath the cerebral cortex are the diencephalon and the cerebrum. The diencephalon includes the thalamus and hypothalamus, two deep structures involved in emotion, fundamental drives, and sensation. The cerebrum contains the amygdala and hippocampus, which are involved in emotion and memory. As we shall see, functions of the diencephalon and the cerebrum—emotion, basic drives, sensation, and memory—are all involved in stress and relaxation.

The hindbrain resides deep inside and near the back of the skull and is actually a continuation of the spinal cord. Two salient features are the medulla and the reticular activating system (RAS), both involved in the transport of incoming stimuli to the brain. The medulla is involved in many autonomic functions associated with stress and relaxation, including blood pressure, heart rate, and breathing. The RAS begins at the core of the brain, ascends to the cortex, and is interconnected with many of the sensory pathways that bring information to the cortex. As such, the RAS is involved in altering and moderating the activity of the entire brain, specifically contributing to arousal, attention, wakefulness, and sleep. When stimulated (e.g., by incoming sensory or muscle stimuli), the RAS arousal stimulates and readies the rest of the brain and endocrine system for stress. Indeed, continued stress activation of the RAS can contribute to chronic state of stress-related activation of other components of the nervous and endocrine systems.

To summarize, it is through the brain that we recognize when something is stressful or relaxing; experience emotions and motivations associated with stress or relaxation; maintain a ready and alert state during stress (or invigorating relaxation activities); and let go, relax, and sleep when stress is over. But there is more. Once the brain is ready and awake for an impending stressor, how does the body take appropriate action, and how does it relax when action is no longer called for?

The Stress Arousal Response

Each of us has a stress arousal "fight or flight" response that automatically awakens and energizes the body for emergency action. A constellation of changes occurs, including he following:

- Fuels, in the form of glucose sugars, fats, and proteins, are released for energy.
- Additional oxygen is breathed in so that the fuel can "burn" through metabolism. Breathing rate and volume increase.
- Fuel and oxygen must be efficiently carried to where they are needed—the muscles of the arms and legs that will do the fighting or fleeing. The heart beats more quickly, and more blood is pumped with each beat, blood pressure increases, and blood vessels to needed muscles dilate.
- Metabolic rate increases as body fuels are burned. Excess heat is carried away through breathing and perspiration.
- Functions not needed for emergency action are reduced: stomach and intestinal activity are limited, and blood flow to the skin, stomach, and intestines decreases.
- The body prepares itself for possible injury. Surface blood vessels constrict, reducing the possibility of serious blood loss. Clotting substances are dumped into the bloodstream, easing the formation of protective scar tissue. The immune system increases activity in anticipation of possible infection or reduces activity to minimize the

potentially damaging effects of infection and to conserve resources for fighting and fleeing.

- Natural pain killers, endorphins, are released by the brain, to help us keep going in the face of considerable discomfort.
- And finally, the body readies itself for active involvement with the outside world. Muscles tighten, pupils of the eye enlarge to let in more light and enhance vision, palms and feet become moist to increase grip and traction when running, and brain activity increases.

Two things about the stress response are important to recognize. First, it is adaptive, supplying quick energy for fighting off or fleeing attack, quickly responding to unexpected physical assault, and so on. Second, the response is automatic. One does not have to plan for increased stress arousal, as one might deliberately prepare the proper stance for striking a golf ball or running a race. In times of severe crisis, our ancestors in the jungle needed automatic, quick energy. To understand how all of this takes place, we begin in the center of the brain, with the hypothalamus.

The hypothalamus mediates this stress arousal response in three ways. First, it can more or less directly activate the sympathetic nervous system to quickly arouse key organs. The brain tells the heart to beat more quickly, the lungs to breathe more rapidly, and so on. The hypothalamus can also stimulate the adrenal glands (residing above the kidneys) to secrete a variety of stress hormones, notably epinephrine and norepinephrine. When acting as hormones (they can also function as neurotransmitters, as we have seen), these substances have an effect very similar to that produced by direct sympathetic nervous system arousal, except that is delayed by about half a minute and lasts an hour or longer. Third, the hypothalamus secretes corticotropin-releasing factor (CRF) into the blood, which in turn causes the brain's pituitary gland to secrete adrenocorticotropic hormone (ACTH). ACTH then activates the adrenal gland to release stress hormones, primarily the fuel-producing glucocorticoids. Hormones released through this hypothalamic-pituitary-adrenal (HPA) pathway can take even longer to act, and their effect can last for days and weeks. It is important to understand that much of the stress response is a massive combined response of hundreds of physiological changes, some of which are immediate and short-lived and some of which can persist for weeks.

This constellation of responses is ideally suited for coping with the threats our ancestors may have faced in the wild. They had little time to think about how to awaken and energize all body organs to deal with an attacking wild bear. However, the stress response is also triggered by many

20th century challenges—deadlines, arguments, school exams, alarms, worries, physical problems, studying this chapter—the list is endless. As a result, we are often subjected to chronic high levels of stress arousal. Indeed, our sympathetic nervous system may become chronically oversensitized and aroused through a chronically activated RAS. This is called *ergotropic tuning* (Gelhorn, 1970). Excessive ergotropic tuning can contribute to a wide range of illnesses, inhibit healing and recovery, and impair performance at work, school, and play. Such excessive stress subjects the body to excessive wear and tear, contributing to system and organ damage and breakdown. In addition, it can suppress or interfere with the immune system, impairing the body's ability to resist and recover from illnesses ranging from flu to cancer and AIDS.

THE RELAXATION RESPONSE

In the early 1970s, Harvard cardiologist Herbert Benson (Wallace & Benson, 1972; Wallace, Benson, & Wilson, 1971) found that practitioners of transcendental meditation show a constellation of physiological changes suggesting deepened relaxation. These include reduced heart rate, blood pressure, respiration rate, brain wave activity, and so on. Benson's research was not only partly responsible for increasing public and scientific interest in meditation but also popularized a definition of relaxation as generalized reduced arousal, the *relaxation response.*

The idea underlying this arousal reduction hypothesis is simple. The relaxation response is the mirror image of the stress response. It is mediated primarily by the parasympathetic system and automatically results in a protective reduction in arousal. The body more or less pauses for rest and recovery.

Benson's popularized notions are actually preceded by the work of W. R. Hess. In 1925, Hess began an ambitious exploration of the diencephalon, a project that won him the 1949 Nobel Prize. His experiments (Hess, 1957), performed on 350 cats, localized various autonomic functions such as blood pressure, respiration, elimination of waste, and sleep. Hess discovered that electrically stimulating different areas in the hypothalamus consistently resulted in either stress arousal of the sympathetic nervous system, an ergotropic pattern we have already described, or an opposite restorative "trophotropic" reduction in arousal mediated by the parasympathetic nervous system. All relaxation techniques result in reduced sensory input that, when processed by the reticular system and thalamus, trigger the hypothalamus to reduce ergotropic activity. As Lichstein (1988) summarizes, "Trophotropic functioning emerges by default as ergotropic signals subside" (p. 23).

Processes Contributing to the Relaxation Response

Various "microhypotheses" have emerged that isolate specific physiological processes augmenting the global relaxation response. For example, autogenic theorists claim that physiologically targeted relaxation suggestions promote isomorphic physiological changes. Entertaining a fantasy about sucking a fresh lemon readily evokes salivation. Similarly, thinking the phrases "hands warm and heavy" can evoke increased skin temperature in the hands. Indeed, it appears that any physiological process that can be brought into awareness can eventually be brought under such control (Schwartz, 1995).

Jacobson (1938) speculated that skeletal muscle stimulation maintains cortical and autonomic arousal; clients with tense muscles are more likely to worry and remain upset. In contrast, reduced stimulation from skeletal muscles in turn lowers cortical and autonomic arousal. Various physiological mechanisms can easily be invoked to support Jacobson's idea. Striated muscle tension can directly arouse the cerebral cortex, which in turn can contribute to HPA-mediated stress arousal (a client, seeing manifestations of muscle tension such as fidgeting and muscle aches, begins to worry, which in turn enhances arousal). Through the RAS, muscle tension can maintain arousal throughout the brain. As we saw in the previous chapter, Jacobson's progressive muscle relaxation directly attempts to reduce arousal my modifying changes in skeletal muscle tension. Although little support exists for Jacobson's hypothesis as a sole explanation of relaxation, reduced skeletal muscle tension is quite likely one of many interacting factors in augmenting the relaxation response (Lichstein, 1988).

Changes in breathing also can contribute to changes in overall arousal. To understand breathing, it is important to note three muscle groups involved in inspiration and expiration: the intercostal muscles (connecting ribs), the trapezius (upper back and shoulders), and the diaphragm. The diaphragm is a flat, muscular, drumlike sheet that stretches from the backbone to the ribcage and separates the chest from the abdomen. At rest, the diaphragm forms a dome, arching upward into the chest cavity. When constricted, the diaphragm flattens out, pressing more toward the abdomen. Stressed breathing tends to involve the intercostal and trapezius muscles (note the heaving chest breathing of joggers or the inflated chest of pumped-up boxers). Such breathing involves additional expenditures of energy, producing increased internal stimulation and contributing to autonomic arousal.

Relaxed breathing involves greater movement of the diaphragm. When inhaling, the diaphragm constricts, pulling air down into the lungs; when exhaling, the diaphragm relaxes, pushing up into the lungs and expelling air. As breathing becomes more relaxed, internal stimulation and arousal lessen.

The relationship between breathing and the relaxation response goes beyond reducing internal stimulation associated with stressed breathing. Slow, shallow breathing, often associated with relaxation training, may contribute to relaxation through increased blood carbon dioxide (CO_2) levels. Carbon dioxide is a by-product of metabolism, expelled primarily through the breath. The level of CO_2 in the blood is an important factor in regulating blood pH, or acidity. Too much blood CO_2 is termed hypercapnia, a condition that can lead to diffuse analgesia, convulsions, and unconsciousness. Too little blood CO_2 is termed hypocapnia, a condition can be induced by rapid deep breathing, or hyperventilation. Hypocapnia is associated with dizziness, possible anxiety and panic, and eventually unconsciousness. Although extremely high or low CO_2 levels can be anything but relaxing, moderate CO_2 elevation can contribute to general relaxation by reducing heart rate, dilating peripheral blood vessels, depressing cortical brain activity, and contributing to a general sense of "mild somnolence" (Lichstein, 1988). Indeed, early stages of sleep, when one moves from wakefulness to drowsiness, are associated, in part, with mild hypercapnia.

Additional breathing-related processes may contribute to general relaxation. Hirai (1975) has speculated that the up-and-down motion of diaphragmatic breathing causes the abdomen to gently stimulate the vagus nerve. Others (Lichstein, 1988) have suggested that relaxed movement of the lungs may induce similar stimulation. The vagus nerves consist of motor fibers that lead primarily from the medulla in the brain and innervate the muscles of the pharynx, larynx, heart, and thoracic and abdominal viscera, as well as sensory nerves that lead from these structures to the brain. Because of its involvement with numerous internal organs associated with arousal, it is plausible to speculate that stimulation of the ascending vagus nerve (from the viscera to the brain) may have an impact on the trophotropic response.

Regardless of how arousal is reduced, Benson (Benson & Friedman, 1985) argues that *all* relaxation techniques are equally effective in evoking a relaxation response. This perspective has become something of a worldview of relaxation, a standard hypothesis that has profoundly influenced the course of relaxation training for half a century. Consistent with relaxation response perspective, most graduate programs and textbooks in psychology, social work, nursing, and counseling teach only one technique, usually progressive muscle relaxation (PMR). Today it is rare to find a psychologist, social worker, counselor, or psychiatrist professionally trained in more than one technique.

Limitations of the Relaxation Response Hypothesis

It is useful to elaborate some of the limitations of the arousal reduction hypothesis. Many have questioned whether arousal reduction can be characterized as a global, undifferentiated response of parasympathetic dominance (Poppen, 1998). There are parasympathetically mediated functions, such as digestion, that do not play a central role in relaxation. And some parasympathetic processes may not operate consistently in response to all relaxation procedures (Hillenberg & Collins, 1982; Holmes, 1984; Qualls & Sheehan, 1981).

Furthermore, contrary to what is nearly universally believed, research has *not* demonstrated technique equivalency in reducing generalized somatic arousal; at best, the jury is still out. Studies have compared a handful of techniques, including autogenic training, mantra meditation, self-hypnosis, and progressive muscle relaxation (Lehrer, Carr, Sargunaraj, & Woolfolk, 1994). We simply do not know if yoga stretching, diaphragmatic breathing, mindfulness meditation, and the dozens of other techniques available to health professionals have similar global effects. I strongly suspect some do not.

Even if we provisionally accept the proposition of technique equivalency, the relaxation response perspective has problems. It cannot readily explain within-modality treatment differences, paradoxical "relaxation-induced anxiety," or why people continue or discontinue practicing (Smith, 1985, 1990). It offers no insight concerning the long-term course of relaxation and the generalization of relaxation to life at large. It has no implications for practical training issues such as managing relapse, fostering outside activities conducive to relaxation, identifying and controlling attitudes and behaviors incompatible with relaxation, selecting appropriate relaxation reinforcements, combining techniques, determining when a technique should be abandoned or changed, or deepening relaxation.

One consistent finding points to what may be the most serious limitation of the relaxation response perspective, one that is perhaps the most significant paradox of relaxation research. People not in psychotherapy can generally reduce cognitive or somatic arousal in a month or two (Borko-vec & Sides, 1979; Lehrer & Woolfolk, 1993; Lichstein, 1988). Once arousal is reduced, the relaxation response hypothesis has little to predict. Yet people continue to practice, change, and grow in relaxation for months, years, and even decades. People continue to claim that the nature of relaxation itself changes over the course of long-term practice. If relaxation is only reduced arousal, this cannot be.

SPECIFICITY HYPOTHESES

Specificity hypotheses claim that specific types of relaxation can reduce specific arousal symptoms. Everyday examples reveal that, to some extent, this is obviously the case. A typist stretches his fingers before work, a jogger rubs his legs after a run, a motorist stretches her shoulders after a long drive, a teacher rests her feet in a pan of hot water after a day of standing at the blackboard, and so on.

The Somatic Specificity Hypothesis

Highly targeted somatic relaxation training reflects what we might term the *somatic specificity hypothesis*. For example, autonomic symptoms (cold hands, palpitating heart, elimination problems, dry mouth, watery eyes, digestive problems, migraine headache, Raynauds syndrome, colitis) might respond well to autonomic techniques, including breathing exercises, autogenic standard exercises, autogenic organ-specific formulas, and organ-targeted kundalini exercises. Skeletal muscle symptoms might respond to muscle techniques, including all variations of PMR, stretching, and some active breathing exercises.

Research suggests that the greatest specificity can be achieved when a symptom precisely matches the specific goal of an exercise. Thus, for someone suffering from tense shoulders, PMR, yoga stretching, or an autogenic shoulder exercise ("your shoulder muscles are relaxed") would be appropriate. Similarly, one could match breathing exercises for those who suffer from shortness of breath, autogenic hand-warming exercises for cold hands, and so on. Davidson and Schwartz (1976) have proposed that such specificity may be superimposed on a generalized relaxation response; once clients have mastered generalized arousal reduction, they may target specific areas of tension.

Global Specificity Hypothesis

The *global specificity hypothesis* suggests applying relaxation techniques according to global symptom modality. Stress researchers frequently speak of three types of subjective stress symptoms: somatic, cognitive, and affective (Smith, 1993b). Somatic symptoms include all subjective reports of psychological complaint, including those we have just considered. Cognitive symptoms of stress have not been well differentiated, and can include forgetfulness, difficulty in concentrating, and distortions in thinking and perception. Of these, relaxation researchers have focused on simple cognitive arousal, or worry. Self-report indicators of worry include "unwanted negative thinking," "difficulty keeping troublesome thoughts out of mind," "bothered by negative thoughts," and so on (Weinstein & Smith, 1992). The three categories of negative affectivity most frequently mentioned are anxiety, depression, and hostility (Smith, 1990). In addition, there as been less systematic attention devoted to shyness and frustration.

According to the global specificity hypothesis, cognitive techniques such as meditation and imagery should work for worry, or cognitive arousal; and somatic techniques, such as PMR or yoga, should be best for somatic symptoms. Although affective relaxation techniques have not been clearly identified, breathing exercises might be a good candidate, given the close connection between breathing and emotion. Most research has focused on a restricted variation of the global specificity perspective, Davidson and Schwartz's (1976) cognitive/somatic specificity hypothesis. Evidence is conflicting. For example, cognitive techniques such as meditation have clearly somatic effects, and somatic techniques such as progressive muscle relaxation can have cognitive effects.

Multiple Modality Specificity Hypothesis

Lehrer et al. (1994) have additionally proposed what might be termed the *multiple modality specificity hypothesis*: Techniques involving multiple response modalities (e.g., cognitive plus somatic) should have a broader range of effect than more narrowly focused methods. Such complex treatments should work better for symptoms with complex etiologies. For example, generalized anxiety has somatic, cognitive, and autonomic components. It might respond better to a combination of yoga stretching, breathing, and meditation than to stretching alone. Similar combinations might be appropriate for many forms of pain, depression, and substance abuse. One limitation of this hypothesis is that most symptoms have multiple and complex etiologies, suggesting that combination treatments may often be the intervention of choice. Also, the multiple modality specificity hypothesis does not suggest which exercises to include in a combination treatment or how to combine them (which come first, which should be emphasized, etc.).

Superstitious Specificity Hypothesis

There is a serious potential for confusion concerning the specificity perspective. A client may have a rather precisely defined problem, perhaps a benign tumor or an allergy that affects breathing. He or she may wish to apply a relaxation technique that, on the face of it, appears targeted to the problem, perhaps visualizing the tumor melting to nothing or breathing away an allergy. Although such strategies may have no specific somatic effect, they may well contribute to reduced generalized arousal, the relaxation response, and thereby contribute indirectly to symptom reduction. What the client then perceives is apparent confirmation of a strategy of targeting specific strategy to a specific problem. Of course, a careful empirical approach would be to apply other relaxation strategies to the same problem to see if they produce the same effect. However, a client is not likely to have such scientific interests and may well be quite enthusiastic about his or her apparent ability to modify a specific symptom. The result is what we might term *superstitious specificity*, or the premature inference of causality between specific technique and symptom reduction.

Limitations of Specificity Hypotheses

In general terms, specificity models suffer many of the problems of the relaxation response hypothesis. Their greatest success is in differentiating techniques according to initial somatic effects. However, as we have seen, such effects are often achieved in a short period of time; once achieved, there are no differences among techniques. In addition, most symptoms, as well as relaxation treatments, are complex.

There is more to relaxation than symptom reduction. This point is often difficult to appreciate, given the pervasiveness of relaxation response and specificity hypotheses. However, the reductionistic bias of such hypotheses becomes clear if we examine other areas of human experience. For example, what are the defining criteria of, say, love or sadness? In common life, they are cognitions and behaviors. We know our love is true through our thoughts and actions. We know our sadness is deep through our thoughts and actions. Indeed, researchers use such criteria to measure "affiliation" and "depression" through self-report and observable behavior. Love and sadness may well have physiological correlates. These may be interesting. But it would be foolish to fall into the trap of reductionism and consider somatic correlates as defining criteria. Love is more than a beating heart, sadness more than a tear, and relaxation more than arousal reduction.

RELAXATION, THE BRAIN, AND INCREASED AROUSAL

It may seem counterintuitive to think that relaxation can involve *increased* physiological arousal. However, a journey into the cosmos is not over when one has left the atmosphere; there is the descent home. A bit more down to earth, what happens in a relaxation session cannot be just the reduction of stress arousal; there is also the process of return to active, wakeful life, refreshed and renewed. Much has been written about the first part of the journey into relaxation, little about the processes involved in the return trip.

Another example is a bit more direct. While listening to intensely moving music, you may be filled with great wonder and joy. During such moments you forget all of your worries and cares, or as a specificity hypothesis would say, experience reductions in cognitive arousal. Surely, this is a moment of genuine relaxation but also one associated with increased joyful arousal. Indeed, if you ask ordinary people (as I have done several thousand times) what they do for relaxation, many will genuinely report pursuits that may well represent increased arousal— nature walks, singing to oneself, hot baths, and so on. Perhaps we should not discount such reports as naive responses from the psychologically unsophisticated. Real people have something important to say about relaxation.

Brain-Wave Activity

We can further appreciate how increased arousal may be involved with relaxation if we look at the brain, specifically brain-wave activity. The brain does not generate a large amount of electrical activity, only enough to light a 25-watt light bulb. And this activity is not continuous but fluctuates in wavelike fashion many times a second. The number of waves (frequency) and their height (amplitude) define various categories of general brain wave, or electroencephalographic (EEG), activity: relatively fast gamma waves (cycling 30–50 times a second), beta waves (14–30 cps), alpha waves (8–12 cps), theta waves (4–7 cps), and delta waves (0.3–0.5 cps). Generally, the faster rhythms occur at lower amplitude and are more irregular. Finally, synchronized brain waves rhythmically rise and fall together, whereas desynchronized brain waves do not show this pattern.

Alpha activity is often associated with a state of "wakeful alertness." However, this is an oversimplification. Alpha waves can be associated with pleasant relaxation, inner-directed awareness of thoughts, feelings or thoughts about past experiences, or nonvisual thinking. Alpha ceases when one's attention is directed to a brief, possibly startling, external stimulus, but is enhanced when one *voluntarily* directs attention. Biofeedback techniques can be directed toward enhancing alpha activity and reducing beta activity in an attempt to reduce anxiety.

Theta activity emerges as we become drowsy, when alpha activity fades and the external world recedes. Theta is associated with daydreaming and fantasy. Individuals well trained in self-hypnosis show more theta activity both during hypnosis and in wakefulness (Austin, 1998). As with alpha, precise correlates of theta are difficult to identify.

Beta activity is often linked to ordinary wakefulness, in contrast to relaxation. But this, again, is an oversimplification. During beta activity, some feel tense and anxious; some feel excited, concentrated, and alert; some feel loving, warm, and even contented. Pleasurable affective states that often emerge in relaxation may be associated with increased beta activity (Austin, 1998).

Sleep

Two areas of research have found correlates between aroused brain wave activity and relaxation: sleep and meditation. All relaxers from all traditions get drowsy, nap, and sleep from time to time. Typically, sleep is arbitrarily viewed as an impediment and distraction, a sign that relaxation is not working. But sleep happens, and all levels of sleep most likely can occur for all types of relaxation. Practitioners of techniques as different as PMR and transcendental meditation (TM) may spend up to 50% of their relaxation time in sleep (Austin, 1998). Perhaps relaxers, particularly meditators, are able to generate sufficient RAS activity to hold themselves at a transitional level, neither awake nor asleep or drowsy (Stigsby, Rodenberg, & Moth, 1981). Perhaps sleep is an essential, unrecognized physiological relaxation process. Indeed, one overall goal of sleep, physiological restoration, is the same as the claimed outcome of the relaxation response.

The brain waves of an awake and alert person display high frequency and low amplitude, beta and alpha waves. As one falls asleep, changes in frequency and amplitude occur (Guevara, Lorenzo, Ramos, & Corsi-Cabrera, 1995), which, along with changes in muscle activity and eye movement, define six states of sleep (Armitage, 1995; Dement & Kleitman, 1957).

Stage 0. This is a prelude to sleep. One is relaxed, with eyes closed. Synchronized alpha activity predominates. Muscles begin to relax, heart rate and body temperature begin to decline. This stage is sometimes described as "relaxed wakefulness" and is often associated with feelings of reverie. One may drift off and experience *hypnogogic imagery*, dreamlike images experienced as if they were real and externally produced.

Stage 1. Eyes start to roll, and theta waves begin to dominate. Physiological arousal (heart rate, breathing rate, etc.) decreases.

Stage 2. Minutes later, EEG shows rapid bursts of activity (sleep spindles) as well as bundles of waves with increased amplitude (K-complexes).

Stage 3. Synchronized theta and delta waves begin to emerge, with a reduction of sleep spindles and K-complexes.

Stage 4. Delta waves are dominant (appearing more than half the time). It is difficult to be roused from Stage 4. When aroused, one typically feels groggy and confused.

REM Sleep. After 30 to 40 minutes in Stage 4 sleep, one returns to Stage 2 sleep and enters REM (rapid eye movement) sleep, or "active sleep." EEG activity becomes desynchronized, resembling that of an alert, waking person. However, unlike Stage 1 sleep, activity increases and resembles that of one who is awake and not necessarily relaxed. There is one major exception: skeletal (voluntary) muscle tone declines to a very low level, near paralysis. One may begin to twitch and display spasms in the face and hands. Finally, most dreaming occurs during REM sleep.

It is beyond the scope of this book to untangle the physiology of sleep. Instead, my point is to show just how complex sleep is. One simply does not descend into lowered activity and lose consciousness; instead, the brain cycles between complex stages of lower and higher activity, touching all stages within just 30 minutes. And because relaxation often involves sleep, it is at least as complex as this universal realm of human experience.

Meditation

Researchers have studied extensively EEG patterns in meditation, which, as in sleep, display decreases and increases in activity. Briefly, during early meditation, EEG shows increased alpha activity, followed by theta. Here theta may not be associated with increased drowsiness (Austin, 1998). Low-voltage beta and gamma waves may be superimposed on alpha and theta waves, perhaps associated with intense "deep meditation" or "transcendence" in meditation (Fenwick, 1987).

Increased alpha activity is associated with focused attention, either auditory or visual, especially on a simple monotonous task, such as re-peating a meditative mantra, walking meditation, or prayer. It tends not to occur when one "idles" mentally or simply defers attention. A variety of supplementary exercises can enhance sustained relaxed attention, in-cluding deep and more active breathing, intense stretching generating stimulation from the joints, vivid imagery, and the like.

But alpha in meditation may reflect more than simple sustained atten-tion. Austin (1998) has suggested that faster alpha frequencies may be associated with emotional arousal in relaxation. In addition, several studies on transcendental meditation appear to find increased alpha coherence in which EEG waves rise and fall in synchrony over the whole cerebral surface. Coherence can last for over 40 seconds and involve alpha, theta, and beta activity. TM researchers suggest that alpha coherence is most common in the frontal lobes and is associated with "clarity" of an ongoing experience and suspension of respiration. In contrast, one is less likely to display alpha coherence when falling asleep.

Finally, Ornstein (1972) has suggested that some relaxation techniques may cultivate a shift in how the brain processes information, from one that is primarily "linear" and associated with the left cerebral hemisphere, to one that is more "holistic" and possibly visual, associated with the right hemisphere. Although there is no doubt that these and many other dramatic experiences can occur during a relaxation session, there is little evidence that these are associated with just a shift in hemisphere dominance (Pagano & Warrenburg, 1983). Compounding the picture is the possibility that EEG activity, which is measured primarily at the surface of the cortex, may dissociate from behavior and other brain activity during deep phases of relaxation (Austin, 1998). If so, this has several implications. Surface

EEG measures may simply miss important neurological events. In addition, a relaxer may shift abruptly from theta to beta to alpha, not progressing through the usual gradual transitions.

Ecstatic and Mystical States

Dramatic things can happen in relaxation. In sleep, we can have intense dreams. And waking relaxers can report intensely pleasurable sensations. William James (1902) identified four characteristics of such experiences: ineffability, noetic quality, transiency, and passivity. Other have suggested many lists of characteristics. Deikman (1966) lists "realness, unusual percepts, experience of unity, ineffability, and cosmic insight." Together, the lists of such experiences include every intense positive state imaginable—peace, joy, love, beauty, harmony, and so on. It is far beyond the scope of this chapter to speculate on the psychophysiology and neurology of such states, except to provide three observations. Such states may occur in all of relaxation. Such states may be an important part of what makes relaxation work, at least providing positive reinforcement for sustaining practice. Finally, such states surely cannot be described through simple arousal-reduction hypotheses or be associated with any simple combination of EEG changes. A complete understanding of relaxation must include the entire brain and nervous system, including all structures and processes involved in the experience of all of emotion.

TOWARD A BROADER VIEW OF RELAXATION

Research on the physiology of relaxation is complex, perhaps more so than many trainers realize. However, if we stand back and look at what we know, it is possible to see order among the many perspectives we have considered.

The Relaxation Response and EEG Alpha Perspectives

There is indeed some value to two global perspectives that have attracted considerable criticism: the relaxation response hypothesis of global, reduced arousal and the "EEG alpha" perspective that links a state of relaxed awareness to alpha brain wave activity. Both points of view can be useful training tools, providing compelling rationales for relaxation to novice practitioners. The relaxation response hypothesis makes a persuasive case that relaxation can be healthy and useful for preventing and treating many physical disorders. A substantial body of research links chronic arousal to a wide range of physical disorders (Lehrer et al., 1994; Smith, 1993b; *see also* Table 1.1).

The EEG alpha perspective posits a physiological basis for a psychological state of restful alertness that many, if not most, clients may view as desirable. One can include both perspectives and claim that a state of relaxed awareness helps promote a healing relaxation response and that the relaxation response reduces distractions to a state of relaxed awareness.

The Physiology of the Cycle of Renewal

If we want to understand relaxation more deeply, we must go beyond the relaxation response and EEG alpha perspectives. Perhaps the next step is to consider the physiology of relaxation in terms of the cycle of renewal—withdrawal, recovery, and opening up. To withdraw in relaxation is to cease deliberate, active, and discursive involvement in the external world. At the very least, this can involve deliberately ceasing physical activity, stopping whatever one is doing and taking time out to relax. Progressive muscle relaxation (and perhaps some active yoga stretches and breathing exercises) cultivate the very act of "letting go"; one lets go with a shrugged shoulder, a stretch, or a deep breath. Mild hypercapnia and the internal focus of physical relaxation can contribute to additional reductions in awareness of the external world.

Recovery can occur at four levels, some beyond the scope of this book. Level 1 recovery involves engaging in a relaxation exercise in order to undo carryover arousal activity. A business executive client may have ceased discursive activity in order to withdraw into relaxation. She may find that she continues tensing her shoulders (as if still carrying her briefcase), breathing shallowly and rapidly (as if still confronting a difficult supervise over the phone), straining her face (to look presentably pleasant at work), sitting up straight in her sofa (as if preparing to work on the computer), and thinking rapidly (maintaining vigilance for the next challenge). However, such arousal represents a carrying over of active discursive involvement. Our client may reduce such carryover effects by stretching her shoulders, doing PMR, thinking autogenic phrases, and the like.

When deliberate and carryover activity have been reduced, a client may still experience the immediate and short-term aftereffects of stress, including the accumulation of striated muscle tension and toxic chemical by-products of stress and fatigue in the blood and skeletal muscles. Removing this through sustained relaxation is Level 2 recovery.

We have seen that the hormonal effects of stress arousal, when mediated through the HPA pathway, can linger for days or weeks. Reduction of the lingering aftereffects of stress is Level 3 recovery. A single session of relaxation is not sufficient for Level 3 recovery; one may need several days or weeks.

Finally, when stress has taken its toll and has caused bodily harm, Level 4 recovery is required to enhance the healing process. Cancer, heart disease, skin problems, and the like, when they have a strong stress component, may require a sustained change in one's relaxation lifestyle.

The physiology of opening up is beyond the scope of the book. Clearly, EEG alpha and occasionally various patterns of beta activity may be involved. Opening up may be facilitated by increased oxygenation of the blood through deep breathing exercises or through vivid kinesthetic stimulation provided through yoga breathing exercises.

The Problem of Psychological Relaxation States

All physiological models of relaxation can go only so far. At some point one must ask what relaxers are experiencing and consider the world of relaxation states. Relaxation researches have provided haphazard and impressionistic self-report criteria for the validity of identified physiological processes. If we look back, we find that, taken together, researchers have correlated various physiological aspects of relaxation with something of a grab bag of psychological states, including (to name only a few):

Concentration	Increased sense of realness	Reduced self-reported
Confusion	Ineffability	physical symptoms
Contentment	Joy	Reduced worry
Cosmic insight	Love	Relaxed awareness
Dreaming	Mental clarity	Reverie
Drowsiness	Noetic experiences	Sleep
Ecstasy	"No thought"	Trance
Excitement	Pleasurable affective states	Transcendence
Grogginess	Reduced self-reported	Warmth
Heaviness	negative emotion	Well-being

The bias of some may be that such self-reports are somehow "less real" than "objective" measures of physiological process. More often they are viewed as distractions to actual relaxation. Jacobson (1929) viewed any state of drowsiness or anything approaching a hypnogogic or trance state to be anathema. Virtually all meditative traditions view positive affects in relaxation to be transitory illusions and distractions. I have yet to see a prayer book consider the value of feeling "limp" and "loose." However, in my opinion, much of relaxation research has put the cart before the horse. Can we really understand the physiology of relaxation without a fuller understanding of the experience of relaxation? To explore the worlds of relaxation carefully, we need a psychological map.

3

R-States

Ask clients how they feel when relaxed, and they may say many things. Some may feel "calm," others "happy," and still others "distant and far away." Rarely will a client say, "I am experiencing the relaxation response," "I am experiencing reduced cognitive or somatic arousal," or "I am experiencing increased alpha brain wave activity." In every other realm of psychology, we take seriously what our clients say; it is time we do the same for relaxation. Relaxation states, or R-States, are at the heart of ABC Relaxation Theory.

ABC Relaxation Theory defines relaxation in terms of sustained passive simple focus. However achieved, such an attentional act triggers withdrawal, recovery, and opening up—a cycle of renewal that can help us organize the physiology and psychology of relaxation. For example, we have seen that through the physical act of tensing up and letting go, one lets go of active discursive involvement in the outside world. Stretching and breathing may help the body release and recover from the toxic aftereffects of stress and also contribute to heightened awareness and opening up (Table 3.1).

We have also seen that R-States can be organized according to the cycle of renewal (Table 3.2). To review, Sleepiness, Disengagement, and Physical Relaxation may primarily reflect withdrawal from active discursive involvement in the world. Physical Relaxation, Mental Quiet, and Mental Relaxation appear to be manifestations of recovery from physical, cognitive, and affective stress. Strength and Awareness, Joy, Love and Thankfulness, and Prayerfulness depict opening up.

The cycle of renewal is an abstract hypothetical construct, whereas R-States are the observable mediators of what makes relaxation work. Given this, the first task of ABC relaxation research has been to detail the world of R-States. Years ago, I began the task of developing a comprehensive

TABLE 3.1   Relaxation Techniques Organized
According to the Cycle of Renewal

Technique	Withdrawal	Recovery	Opening Up
PMR AT	Physically ceasing discursive activity through "letting go." Restricted somatic focus pulls attention from externally directed discursive activity.		
Stretching, breathing exercises	Reduced awareness of outside world through mild hypercapnia; letting go of a yoga stretch or inhaled breath.		
Stretching, breathing, AT		Release of striated muscle tension; increased skeletal muscle blood flow helps wash away toxic physical after-effects of stress.	
Stretching Breathing		Reduction in stressful posture and breathing habits.	
Stretching Breathing			Increased oxygen contributing to alertness.
Stretching Breathing			Vivid stimulation maintaining alertness.
Imagery	Can contribute to any global effect, depending on imagery theme (e.g., themes may in themselves target withdrawal, recovery, and opening up). Generally, pleasant imagery is cortically activating, fostering opening up.		
Meditation	Can contribute to all, depending on level of skill level and preexisting state of meditator. For example, a fatigued and tired meditator will experience sleep and withdrawal; one burdened with accumulated tension, tension relief; and an alert meditator with little distracting tension, opening up.		

PMR, progressive muscle relaxation; AT, autogenic training.

TABLE 3.2   R-States and the Cycle of Renewal

R-State	Withdrawal	Recovery	Opening Up
Sleepiness	Yes		
Disengagement	Yes		
Physical Relaxation	Yes	Yes	
Mental Quiet	Yes	Yes	
Mental Relaxation		Yes	
Strength and Awareness		Yes	Yes
Joy			Yes
Love and Thankfulness			Yes
Prayerfulness			Yes

relaxation questionnaire. My first job was to collect and catalog words used to describe the subjective relaxation states. Such a strategy is not new. Five-factor model personality researchers (Wiggins, 1996) have proposed that everyday "natural language" of personality terms reflects how most people conceptualize personality attributes. Similarly, I propose that the natural language of relaxation may well reflect an underlying pattern of relaxation states. The preferred empirical strategy of five-factor model personality researches has been to look for dimensions of personality by factor-analyzing (primarily principal components or principal axis analysis with varimax rotation) comprehensive catalogs of personality words. I deployed the same strategy. But the task proved to involve much more than collating words. Words had to be screened for meaningfulness and ambiguity and combined and placed into sentences to enhance clarity. Over time, I constructed no fewer than seven versions of relaxation questionnaires. Those interested in the details of this process should consult Appendix A.

THE NINE (CURRENT) R-STATES

At the time of this volume, I have found it useful to consider nine R-States. Here are their current working titles (in both noun and adjective forms).

Sleepiness (Sleepy)

Disengagement (Disengaged)

Physical Relaxation (Physically Relaxed)

Mental Quiet (Mentally Quiet)

Mental Relaxation (Mentally Relaxed)

Strength and Awareness (Strengthened and Aware)

Joy (Joyful)

Love and Thankfulness (Loving and Thankful)

Prayerfulness (Prayerful)

Sleepiness

This dimension is currently defined by the following relaxation words: "dozing off, napping, drowsy, sleepy." Whether or not sleepiness is an impediment or an intrinsic part of the process of relaxation is an empirical question. I identify two aspects of Sleepiness: dozing off and drowsiness. One reflects an actual loss of consciousness; the other does not. As a global relaxation effect, sleepiness obviously is a form of withdrawal of consciousness from the world.

Disengagement

Item content: "distant and far away from cares and concerns; indifferent and detached." This dimension has consistently appeared in all of our factor-analytic studies. Most generally, disengagement involves pulling away from and becoming less aware of the world (Smith et al., 1996), reflecting the global effect of withdrawal. Clinically, one might view this R-State as low-level, potentially adaptive dissociation.

Conceptually, Disengagement can be differentiated into five components: somatic/sensory ("loss of sensation of extremities"), cognitive-spatial (feeling "far away and distant"), cognitive-attitudinal ("detached and indifferent"), perceptual ("loss of awareness of external surroundings, including relaxation trainer"), and memory ("forgetting where one is"). The content of Disengagement has varied slightly in different factor-analytic studies. Holmes, Ritchie, and Allen (in press) found that "drowsy," "physical relaxation," and "loss of sensation" all load on a global Disengagement factor for grouped items; however, when items were presented in random order, two Disengagement factors emerged, a physical disengagement factor containing the words "drowsy," "physical relaxation," and "loss of sensation" and a cognitive Disengagement factor defined by "forgetting," "indifferent," and "distant." This suggests that our dimensions Sleepiness and Physical Relaxation may well share some of the functions of Disengagement (pulling away from and becoming less aware of the world).

In the present version of R-States, the item "drowsy" has been subsumed under the dimension of Sleepiness, and Physical Relaxation has been designated a separate R-State. I felt this differentiation was appropriate given the clear conceptual differences among Sleepiness, Disengagement, and Physical Relaxation. I retained "distant" and "detached" as core defining elements for Disengagement because they are the only Disengagement items to consistently appear together in all factor-analytic studies to date (Holmes et al., in press; Smith et al., 1996). Future research may reveal that cognitive-spatial (distancing) and cognitive-attitudinal (detached, indifferent) disengagement have different properties.

Physical Relaxation

Item content: "physical warmth and heaviness, feeling limp." The lexicon of words people use to describe physical relaxation includes: "bathed, caressed, cool, dissolving, elastic, flexible, floating, flowing, heavy, high, light, limber, limp, listless, liquid, loose, massaged, mellow, melting, motionless, sedate, sinking, slack, slow, smooth, soft, supple, throbbing, tingling, warm." All of these words seem to reflect recovery from physical stress and possibly the relaxation response. In addition, I propose that the experience of Physical Relaxation also reflects withdrawal, especially because when physically relaxed, one is not actively engaged in external discursive pursuits.

It was relatively easy to identify key words depicting Physical Relaxation. Some words were deleted from consideration because of low factor loadings ("elastic, listless, massaged, motionless, slack, supple, tingling"). Others were eliminated because of ambiguity and overlap with other factors. For example, it is difficult to explain to clients what "dissolving" means. And "sinking" has a spatial-cognitive connotation similar to "far away" in Disengagement.

"Limp" emerges as the clearest item for physical relaxation. To this we added "physical warmth and heaviness" simply because of the overwhelming preference for these terms as descriptors of physical relaxation by instructors of progressive muscle relaxation (PMR) and autogenic training. In spite of this history, we find "warmth" and "heaviness" are confounded by affective connotations. To elaborate, clients often feel "warm" while feeling "Joyful," "Loving and Thankful," and even "Prayerful." Clients may feel "heavy" when Disengaging and feeling "far away" or even when feeling depressed. To minimize confusion, I now place "warm" and "heavy" in a sentence context that clearly limits interpretation ("My hands, arms, or legs feel relaxed, *warm* and *heavy*").

Mental Quiet

Item content: "My mind is quiet and still; my mind is silent, not thinking about anything." We have struggled with this dimension for years. It first appeared in Alexander's (1991) factor analysis as "silent, speechless, quiet, wordless." Smith et al. (1996) found a similar factor consisting of "silent, simple, speechless." The meaning of this factor has been ambiguous, at times correlating with Disengagement and at times with Prayerfulness. Interviews with relaxation practitioners revealed a variety of contradictory interpretations, primarily reflected by the word *speechless*. To elaborate, "speechless" could mean: (1) "I am in a very quiet relaxation environment, one that makes me feel speechless"; (2) "I feel awestruck and speechless"; (3) "I feel very lazy and unmotivated; I just can't think of anything to say; I feel speechless"; and (4) "My mind is speechless, quiet, and without thought." Meaning 1, the assessment of a quiet environment, is perhaps not an appropriate item for a questionnaire of relaxation states. Such a variable instead reflects relaxation technique and external environment. Meaning 2, "speechless, awestruck," is perhaps fully conveyed by the dimensions Joy and Prayerfulness. Meaning 3, low motivation and inertia, is perhaps conveyed and detachment and drowsiness. My current definition of Mental Quiet reflects meaning 4: "My mind is quiet, without thought" and "I feel an inner stillness, not thinking about anything."

Mental Relaxation

Item content: "At ease, at peace." Initial item content (Smith et al., 1996) for this factor is revealing: "At ease, carefree, contented, laid back, peaceful, refreshed, relaxed, rested, restored, soothed." Dictionary definitions of these items reveal that they all connote an absence of tension ("calm, relaxed"), conflict ("peaceful"), threat ("carefree"), desire and frustration ("contented"), fatigue ("rested, refreshed, restored"), pain ("soothed"), or effort ("at ease, laid back"). The most inclusive term for this is Mental Relaxation, defined most generally as an absence of effort, conflict, and tension. The final items selected to represent Mental Relaxation were chosen carefully. Rejected items included "carefree" (denotes more of an R-Belief), "laid back" (too casual and imprecise), "calm" (too global and could also denote Mental Quiet), "relaxed" (also too general and often denotes Physical Relaxation), "refreshed" and "restored" (perhaps an R-State in its own right, correlates highly with Strength and Awareness), "rested" (too restrictive in focus, denotes aftereffect of sleep), "restored" (perhaps not so much relaxation as a consequence of relaxation), "contented" (too restricted), and "soothed" (too limited in focus, restricted to specific pain or discomfort, such as a burn or rash). "At ease" and "at peace" were chosen to depict Mental Relaxation resulting from alleviation of effort, conflict, and tension.

Effort, conflict, and tension can interfere with mastery of relaxation skills. A troubled client may be distracted by worry and negative emotion, preoccupied with conflict, or simply fatigued from dealing with the chronic distress. Each of these can limit one's ability to sustain passive simple focus and benefit from relaxation. As personal problems are resolved, perhaps through effective coping or psychotherapy, a client may experience Mental Relaxation and display a readiness for deeper relaxation. Put differently, a client's ability to experience Mental Relaxation may be an indicator of readiness to go beyond withdrawal and recovery as a targeted global relaxation effect and to attempt techniques targeted at opening up. (More on this later.)

Strength and Awareness

Item content: "aware, focused, clear; energized, confident, and strengthened." Although all six items consistently combine into a single factor, conceptually "aware, focused, clear" appear to reflect intensified deployment of attention, whereas "energized, confident, and strengthened" seem to convey the affective correlates of such increased attentiveness. One can speculate that Strength and Awareness is a consequence of successful recovery from physical and mental tension (Physical Relaxation and Mental Relaxation). Tension can distract full awareness. As tension is reduced, one can attend, strengthened and energized, for longer periods of time on a restricted stimulus. Put poetically, if tension can be thought of as dust on a window, then the R-State Strength and Awareness is analogous to a window clear of dust.

Joy

Item content: "joyful, happy." Smith et al. (1996) initially found this to be a huge factor, accounting for the largest portion of relaxation variance (15.6%). We offered this interpretation.

[Joyful] items appear to describe various types of positive appraisal and affect, including: positive appraisals of activity ("fun"), global positive appraisals of self and world ("harmonious"), positive insight ("inspired"), positive appraisals of the future ("optimistic"), appraisals of deeper understanding ("timeless"), and finally, an appraisal of thankfulness. (p. 72)

In the constellation of relaxation words, *joy* has a strong gravitational pull and is associated with many other relaxation-related experiences. Put differently, I suspect each joy-related feeling has a strong halo effect or is strongly suggestive of other joy-related states. Someone feeling "love" can, with very little suggestion, feel "beauty," "optimism," and the like. The same can be said for other joy-related states.

Pruning the initial list of 32 joy-related words (Smith et al., 1996) was a difficult task. We removed all items that on other factor analyses emerged as or loaded on separate factors. Most notable of these were "timeless and infinite" (a separate factor still under investigation), "optimistic and hopeful" (loads with Spiritual [Holmes et al., in press]); and "loving and thankful" (a conceptually distinct dimension). Most other items were removed because of consistently marginal loadings, ambiguity, or conceptual redundancy. That left us with two items that loaded highly in all factor analyses: "joyful" and "happy," both global terms that reflect active pleasurable involvement in a relaxing activity, as well as a passive appreciation ("joyful beauty, harmony, love, etc.").

Joy may be a consequence of sustained, undistracted awareness. Once the window is free of dust, one can attend clearly. In time, as one sustains attention, one opens up to a world of beauty and joy.

Love and Thankfulness

Item content: "loving, thankful." Love and Thankfulness has never emerged as a distinct factor. However, the two have consistently appeared together, as a part of either the factor Joy or the factor Prayerfulness. I chose to designate Love and Thankfulness as a distinct R-State for the following reasons: (1) their consistent pairing, (2) the frequency with which these states are mentioned in the world's relaxation literature, (3) their possible significance as intense motivational states in relaxation, (4) the possibility that Love and Thankfulness may correlate strongly with beliefs associated with relaxation (chapter 4). However conceptualized, Love and Thankfulness is another manifestation of opening up. Encountering a world of beauty and joy, one feels Love and Gratitude.

Prayerfulness

Item content: "prayerful, reverent, spiritual." Factor-analytic studies consistently reveal one or more spiritual factors, with somewhat shifting content. Alexander (1991) found a factor Prayerful ("worshipful, prayerful, spiritual, blessed, reverent, thankful, answered, reborn, cleansed, surrendering"). Smith et al. (1996) found a single factor Prayerful ("prayerful, spiritual, reverent, and selfless"); both of Holmes's factor analyses found a spiritual factor. Our current R-State definition is consistent with research (Smith, in press) showing that those who engage in prayer and meditate, and perhaps those who believe in God, are most likely to report feeling "prayerful, reverent, and spiritual."

PATHS OF R-STATES

In most general terms, R-States may emerge in linear sequence (Figure 3.1). However, earlier I have proposed (Smith et al., 1996) that such a linear sequence is highly artificial. Indeed, just about any sequence might be possible:

> For example, a client may experience (a) a static end state of tension relief ("I just want to feel relaxed and at ease"); (b) movement from tension relief to passive disengagement ("I want to relax and forget my troubles"); (c) movement from tension relief to passive engagement ("I want to relax and just enjoy being alive"); (d) movement from passive disengagement to passive engagement ("I want to forget my troubles, let go and relax, and just enjoy being live"); or . . . (e) simultaneous passive disengagement and engagement ("As my worries become more and more distant, I become increasingly aware of my meditation"). At this point it is inappropriate to designate one path as superior. The relative value of various relaxation dimensions or sequences is an important empirical question. At the very least, clinicians who select one relaxation goal, whether it be tension relief, disengagement, or engagement, should be mindful of the possibility that other goals may be appropriate later on. (p. 87)

At this time, I propose two paths of R-States, both perhaps leading to Prayerfulness (Figure 3.2). One might be described as a "path of Disengagement" and the other a "path of Joy."

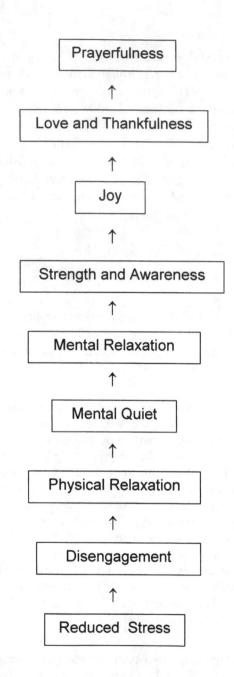

FIGURE 3.1   Paths of R-States.

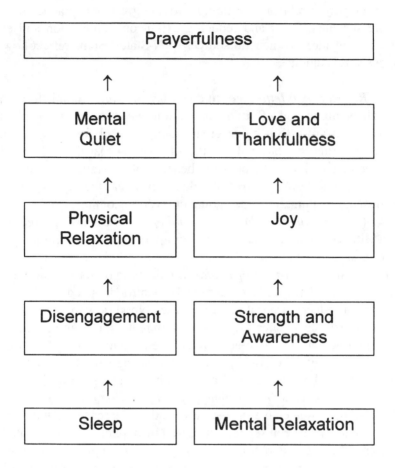

FIGURE 3.2   Dual paths of R-States.

RELAXATION-INDUCED NEGATIVE STATES (N-STATES)

During the course of a relaxation session, a practitioner may experience negative relaxation states (N-States). These can include any distracting or distressing thoughts, images, emotions, or physical sensations. Others (Smith, 1990) have given this phenomenon a variety of names, including stress release, abreactive experiences, uncovering experiences, and most frequently, relaxation-induced anxiety (Heide & Borkovec, 1984). It is quite likely that any approach to relaxation has the potential for evoking N-States. Indeed, most relaxation trainers claim that such states are an important part of relaxation training, providing valuable practice in maintaining sustained focus and reducing extraneous stimulation and effort. First we consider two general sources of N-States. Some reflect how one appraises relaxation:

1. *Resistance to letting go.* In everyday life we accomplish our tasks through planning and effort; in relaxation, we must let go of planning and effort in order to achieve greater simplicity of focus. A beginning relaxer can find this basic shift difficult, feeling that the task of letting go in order to achieve the possible benefits of relaxation is impossible.

2. *Fears of losing control.* A relaxer may fear the task of letting go and mistakenly think it means "going crazy," "becoming sick," and so on.

3. *Concerns about reduced personal efficacy.* Clients may fear relaxation will contribute to laziness, giving up, or reduced ability to work or perform at peak efficiency.

4. *Negative appraisal of R-States.* Clients may not be familiar with many of the R-States we have previously identified, including physiological signs of reduced arousal (e.g., increased blood flow to the extremities, reduced breathing and heart rate), symptom reduction, feelings of somatic and cognitive tension relief, as well as Disengagement and Mental Quiet. Not knowing such experiences are a normal part of relaxation, clients may find them threatening and fear becoming ill, going "crazy," and so on.

5. *Previous aversive experiences with relaxation.* An occasional client may have had an aversive or even traumatic experience related to relaxation. Clients have been sexually harassed by hypnotists, manipulated and threatened by yoga instructors, lied to by meditation gurus, taught ineptly by coercive PMR trainers, or simply taught that relaxation is "weird and occult." Past negative experiences with relaxation can limit a client's willingness to attempt relaxation again and create distress in the course of relaxation training.

6. *Negative associations to relaxation techniques.* A relaxation technique may remind a client of a negative experience that has nothing to do with the technique itself. For example, a client may relax with imagery that involves an ocean beach, only to remember a painful childhood sunburn. Such relaxation "booby traps" are most common when techniques are mechanically imposed on clients with little attempt to individualize.

Other forms of N-States reflect secondary processes set into motion through sustained passive simple focus:

1. *Increased sensitivity.* One consequence of all relaxation training is the reduction of potentially distracting internal and external stimuli. In the quiet of a practice session, a relaxer may simply notice subtle sources of stimuli that ordinarily go undetected. He or she may be aware of breathing, heart rate, underlying emotional state, and so on. Unprepared, a client may appraise such experiences as threats.

2. *Disengagement, disorientation, and depersonalization.* Through Disengagement the relaxer pulls away from and becomes less aware of the outside world. In relaxation this contributes to singular focus on a restricted stimulus by minimizing distraction. However, if a relaxer resumes everyday activities while remaining Disengaged, he or she may experience disruptive depersonalization or disorientation.

3. *Reduction of defensive barriers.* Relaxation can reduce defensive efforts to deny or ignore threatening thoughts and feelings. For a skilled psychotherapist, the resulting emergence of threatening material can be useful in treatment. However, such uncovered material can interfere with the course of relaxation if not properly managed.

4. *Reductions in critical thinking and reality testing.* As one relaxes, one reduces deliberate efforts at analysis and control, including critical and analytic thinking. In some contexts this can contribute to enjoyment, as when one temporarily suspends disbelief and becomes absorbed in a movie or novel. However, lessened critical thinking and reality testing may make one more susceptible to troublesome thoughts and fantasies that might arise in relaxation. For example, in the course of a day's events a client may casually wonder, "Sometimes I feel like I am floating in relaxation. Do I really float?" He or she may ordinarily appraise such a feeling reasonably, "Of course, I am not really floating; I'm just experiencing a relaxation effect." However, if such a thought were to arise in deep relaxation, our client may well "suspend disbelief," and actually believe he or she is levitating, and experience distress.

5. *Hyperventilation/hypoventilation.* We have seen that changes in breathing in relaxation can result in decreased or increased blood levels of carbon dioxide (CO_2). Such hyper- or hypoventilation can lead to aversive subjective states, including dizziness, anxiety, and so on.

6. *Presumed shifts in brain functioning.* As relaxation deepens, parts of the brain (perhaps the cerebral cortex) may become relatively less active. Other parts (perhaps those less active in everyday life) become relatively more active. This could result in increased spontaneous wakeful dreamlike activity, including vivid imagery, novel or intense emotional

states, changes in body image (sensations of floating, changing size), and even apparent paranormal phenomena.

THE ABC RELAXATION DEEPENING CYCLE

I propose that both R-States and N-States play a central and cyclical role in all of relaxation, contributing to the development of relaxation skills. To begin, the central attentional act of relaxation can evoke R-States in two ways. First, passively sustaining simple focus can itself evoke an R-State; sustained relaxed attention can be *intrinsically reinforcing*. Second, exercise components that facilitate sustained passive simple focus may be *extrinsically reinforcing* (see chapter 5). To elaborate, the process of tensing and letting go in PMR can itself alter blood flow to the extremities and generate the pleasant R-States of Physical Relaxation ("loose," "liquid," "warm," "heavy," and "sinking"). Breathing exercises can change blood CO_2 levels, contributing to rewarding feelings of Physical Relaxation, Disengagement, or Strength and Awareness (with increased oxygenation). Yoga stretching can enhance reticular activating system (RAS) arousal, evoking positive feelings of Strength and Awareness. Imagery exercises can, through the imagery topic selected, evoke a variety of R-States. A pleasant scene might evoke feelings of Joy, for example.

One begins a relaxation deepening cycle by passively letting go and focusing on a simple stimulus. This may evoke an N-State or R-State, which in turn distracts sustained, passive simple focus. At this time the relaxer has a choice: make the distraction the central focus of attention and process it or divert attention from the distraction, let it go, and resume attending to a focal stimulus. Diverting attention interrupts the relaxation session, at least temporarily; letting go of the distraction and returning attention to the focal stimulus not only sustains relaxation but provides practice in establishing and sustaining a stance of passive focusing.

To illustrate, a practitioner of imagery may first let go of daily concerns and focus on a pleasant image of a vacation beach. In time she may feel a bit "guilty for experiencing something pleasurable not earned through hard work" (an N-State). If she becomes preoccupied with guilt, the relaxation session is interrupted. By putting her guilt aside (perhaps by resolving it or just avoiding it), she can continue focusing on her relaxing image.

To consider another example, a practitioner of PMR may feel pleasantly warm and heavy, or a meditator may be filled with feelings of inner peace. He may choose to savor these pleasures and "bask" in the feelings evoked.

Doing this interrupts the course of relaxation. Or he may choose to put these R-States aside and resume attending to the singular focus of PMR or meditation.

It is easy to confuse the focal stimulus of a relaxation activity with the R-States that focused attention can evoke. Often the difference is subtle. For example, a practitioner of PMR may tense and release shoulder muscles and then attend to the ensuing tingling warmth. Here, the relaxer has the option of continuing to attend to the sensation of tingling warmth or resume the act of tensing and letting go, thereby targeting other sources of tension that may be hidden. A practitioner of yoga may complete an extensive stretch of the arms and torso and then stop to savor the resulting feelings of refreshed calm or resume stretching. The difference can be more pronounced in meditation. The focal stimulus for meditation is utterly simple—for example, a single word or visual image. Any extraneous experience, even a pleasurable R-State, is a distraction to this singular focus. One of the most difficult tasks of meditation is learning to let go of the pleasures of meditation to resume the meditative act of simply focusing.

Thus, all of relaxation involves a cyclical movement from focus to distraction to focus again. The actual value of periods of distraction and sustained focus depends on the circumstances. There may be times in which dwelling on an N- or R-State is useful. A psychotherapist may wish to pursue hidden traumatic memories that emerge in relaxation. A cardiac patient may discover that interrupting PMR and basking in pleasant feelings of warmth and heaviness lowers blood pressure. However, once again, if skills at sustaining passive simple focus are to develop, the relaxer must eventually cease attending to a distracting R- or N-State and resume attending to the relaxation task.

The Function of R-States

Traditionally, stress and relaxation researchers have tended to overlook and even discount R-States. We have seen that R-States may have an important value as positive reinforcement or as a source of motivation. Potentially, every R-State we have identified could conceivably be a reinforcement; one may seek to practice a relaxation technique in order to feel Sleepy, Disengaged, Physically Relaxed, Mentally Quiet, Mentally Relaxed, Strengthened and Aware, Joyful, Loving and Thankful, or Prayerful.

However, a thoughtful analysis of the process of relaxation suggests a more complex function. To begin, when one has achieved a reinforcement, an R-State, what more is there to gain? Why continue practicing? An R-State can be either an end in itself or a transition to some other relaxation objective. One may practice PMR in order to go to sleep. Sleep may be the primary goal or preparation for a particularly demanding day ahead. Joyful imagery may be an entertaining end or a means to facilitate generation of ideas for a creative project. Mental Quiet may be a goal of meditation, or it may point to some other potential goal, for example, seeing the world more clearly, working more effectively.

I suggest that simple reinforcement can be augmented by the following other R-State process or outcome functions.

Process Functions

- R-states may enhance *focusing*. Feelings of Strength, Joy, Love and Thankfulness, and Prayerfulness may help one sustain focus. I think this directive function is separate from the reinforcing or energizing function of an R-State. One may not feel particularly energized yet still continue focusing. Perhaps less obvious, one might continue work in a particular direction, even when a goal or reinforcement is not apparent.
- R-States may enhance one's ability to become *passive* or reduce unnecessary deliberate planful effort. Feeling Joyful, a relaxer may be more willing to put aside the urge to use relaxation time for other activities.
- R-States may *mediate* other R-States. One may sleep in order to feel Strengthened and Aware, foster Strength and Awareness in order to feel Prayerful, feel Disengaged in order to induce Physical Relaxation, use Physical Relaxation as a tool for enhancing Mental Relaxation, and so on. The mediating potential of R-States is one way of interpreting the failure of some relaxation words to consistently load on a single relaxation factor. For example, the word *refreshed* has, in different studies, loaded on Mental Relaxation and Strength and Awareness. For this reason, "refreshed" does not appear as a descriptor of any single R-State. However, one can speculate that "refreshed" is a mediating state, one that defines a transition between Mental Relaxation and Strength and Awareness. Put simply, after a relaxation exercise a client may initially feel refreshed. In time, this feeling may evolve into feeling Strengthened and Aware. (Of course, the causal sequence may be in the opposite direction: one may first feel Strength and Awareness and then, in time, refreshed, and eventually Mentally Relaxed. For purposes of simplicity, we will describe only one causal direction, recognizing that others are possible).

- Other transitional mediating relaxation words can be identified: "optimism" may mediate Strength and Awareness, Joy, Love and Thankfulness, and Prayerfulness. That is, when a client feels optimistic in a relaxation, he may soon experience feelings of joy. "Harmony" and "beauty" may mediate Joy with Love and Thankfulness and Prayerfulness. "Sinking" and "heavy" may mediate Disengagement and Physical Relaxation. "Drowsy" may mediate Sleep and Disengagement. "Timeless" and "infinite," as well as "love" and "thankfulness" may mediate Joy and Prayerfulness. See Table 3.3.
- R-States merge and differentiate for different individuals and situations. I propose that factor analyses will show that some R-States combine into a single factor for some groups and activities, and differentiate in other contexts. For example, Love and Thankfulness and Prayerfulness may differentiate for groups that value these states, perhaps religious prayer groups. These same states may combine into one factor for nonreligious individuals. Furthermore, the R-State Strength and Awareness may well separate into distinct factors of Strength and Awareness for Zen Buddhist meditators who value these states highly.
- An R-State may *potentiate* a desired ability or process. One may cultivate an R-State in order to enhance dreaming, creativity, hypno-

TABLE 3.3 Possible Mediating R-States

First R-State	Mediating R-State	End R-State
Mental Relaxation	Refreshed	Strength and Awareness
Strength and Awareness	Optimism	Joy, Love and Thankfulness, Prayerfulness
Strength and Awareness	Hope	Joy, Love and Thankfulness, Prayerfulness
Joy	Harmony	Joy, Love and Thankfulness, Prayerfulness
Joy	Beauty	Joy, Love and Thankfulness, Prayerfulness
Disengagement	Sinking	Sleep
Disengagement	Heavy	Sleep
Disengagement	Drowsy	Sleep
Joy	Timeless	Prayerfulness
Joy	Infinite	Prayerfulness
Joy	Love	Prayerfulness
Joy	Thankfulness	Prayerfulness

tizability, immune system functioning, reduce blood pressure reduction, and the like.

* R-States may serve as sources of *insight*, providing a meaningful context for practice. R-States may cultivate, support, and provide a means of expression for *R-Beliefs* conducive to deepened and generalized relaxation (more on this in a later chapter).

Outcome Functions

* Relaxation trainers try to help clients live more relaxed lives; this is one outcome of relaxation training. More precisely, an *R-Disposition* is the propensity to consistently experience an R-State outside the relaxation practice session. For example, a client suffering from interpersonal anxiety (when going on a date, talking to supervisors, etc.) may discover that a combination of breathing exercises and yoga evoke Mental Relaxation and Strength and Awareness. By consistently practicing brief breathing and yoga exercises before stressful interpersonal encounters, he may find that feelings of Mental Relaxation and Strength and Awareness generalize. In clinical terminology, interpersonal anxiety desensitizes. The R-States Mental Relaxation and Strength and Awareness have generalized as R-Dispositions in interpersonal stress situations.

* I define an *R-Motivation* as the desire to experience an R-State more often or more intensely. Acquisition of such a desire is in itself one successful outcome of relaxation training. A tense and driven client may simply not know what Mental Relaxation feels like; encountering such an experience in a relaxation session for the first time can provide a profound motivation to learn to relax. One can conceptualize R-States, R-Motivations, and R-Dispositions as a sequence of outcomes in relaxation training. When learning to relax, a client may first learn to experience a brief R-State in the session. He may meditate and feel a moment of Mental Quiet. The client may then decide that Mental Quiet is a state he would like to experience more often. An R-Motivation has emerged. Through consistent practice of meditation, he may indeed experience increased levels of Mental Quiet through life. He has acquired an R-Disposition.

I hope the above hypotheses stimulate research on relaxation. Broadly speaking, the question is, what are the subjective, behavioral, and physiological correlates of R-States? In the presence of specific R-States, what do people do? What can they do?

4

How Are Relaxation Techniques Different?

Are all approaches to relaxation the same, interchangeable because they evoke the same global relaxation response? Can we meaningfully divide approaches into those that are cognitive and those that are somatic? ABC Relaxation Theory proposes that higher levels of differentiation may be possible.

In a previous book (Smith, 1985), I proposed three basic relaxation skills—focusing, passivity, and receptivity (openness to unfamiliar relaxation experiences)—that permit us to organize popular approaches to relaxation along a single hierarchy. Progressive muscle relaxation (PMR) is the easiest approach on this hierarchy, requiring the least focusing, passivity, and receptivity, and meditation is the most difficult. All other techniques—contemplation, imagery, autogenic training, breathing exercises, yoga stretching—reside somewhere in between.

Recently, I changed my mind. I now think that this linear ordering of techniques breaks down. Put simply, for any approach, there is no one standard exercise. Some versions of PMR, particularly covert PMR, can be particularly challenging. Some forms of imagery and meditation can be extremely easy. Indeed, there are easy and difficult versions of every type of relaxation. It is perhaps more meaningful to think of many relaxation hierarchies, one for each approach, rather than a global all-inclusive hierarchy. I also believe that the core dimension of receptivity is perhaps best viewed not as a skill but as a characteristic of beliefs that may support relaxation. (More on this in a later chapter.)

THE SEVEN FAMILIES OF RELAXATION

I propose that all approaches to relaxation, both casual and professional, can be sorted into seven *families* defined in terms of the target focal stimulus. These families in turn fall into three groups: *internal physical*, in which the target stimulus is an internal physical sensation; *internal cognitive*, in which one focuses on a thought or image; and *external sensory*, in which one attends to an outside stimulus (Table 4.1).

1. *Somatic/emotional*. The first family of relaxation activities is in the internal physical group and involves focusing on somatic sensations or simple emotions. For example, when sunbathing, one might savor pleasant feelings of warmth. A professional massage may generate vivid sensations of muscle relaxation. Everyday positive emotions often have a somatic component. One might feel limp and warm after a good laugh, tingling and warm when filled with joy, and so on. A variety of professional approaches to relaxation target internal somatic sensations, for example, PMR ("tense—let go") and autogenic training ("warm and heavy"). Kundalini meditation involves attending to internal physical "energy centers," or chakras—for example, feelings of warmth in the abdomen (solar plexus), feelings of warmth in the heart, and so on. Zen hara meditation exercises involve focusing on abdominal warmth.

2. *Breath*. A second internal physical family involves focusing on sensations related to breathing. Casually, one might breathe by singing, chanting, sniffing relaxing fragrances, yawning, even blowing bubbles. Formal breathing exercises range from those that involve vigorously bowing and stretching while breathing in and out, to simply closing one nostril with a thumb and breathing slowly and evenly. One might attend to the flow of breath into the nostrils, through the breathing passages, and into the lungs. Or one might attend to the refreshing sensations resulting from breathing deeply. Breathing meditation involves simply attending to the flow of breath itself.

3. *Movement/posture*. The third family is also internal physical and involves movement and posture. Everyday manifestations include slow dance, rocking in a rocking chair or hammock, floating, stroking children or pets, and simply resting still in bed. More formal movement/posture exercises involve virtually all forms of hatha yoga, tai chi, the Alexander technique, walking Zen meditation (in which one slowly walks and attends to each foot movement), and even the slow and graceful Zen tea ceremony, in which a careful sequence of hundreds of tea-making motions is precisely completed.

4. *Cognitive vocal/auditory*. The fourth family belongs to the internal cognitive group and involves attending to some form of mental activity, usually vocal/auditory. Quietly, in one's mind, one can sing, chant, hum,

talk to oneself, and repeat verbal suggestions and affirmations. One may repeat poems or stories or simply recall the pleasant sounds of an evening in the forest. More formal techniques involve hypnotic self-suggestion, in which a client is trained to repeat suggestions silently to oneself. Mantra meditation is the most popular form of verbal meditation.

5.　*Cognitive visual.* The fifth family, cognitive visual, is also internal cognitive and involves most forms of imagery and visualization. Passive relaxing daydreaming and fantasy are casual examples. Although visualization can involve all sense modalities, for most people the sense of vision plays a key role. Visual meditation involves attending to a simple image, such as a point of light.

6.　*External sensory vocal/auditory.* The final two families involve attending to external stimuli. External vocal/auditory stimuli can involve listening to music, the sound of the wind, chants from others, and so on. External sensory vocal/auditory meditations can involve listening to another person repeat a mantra or ring a meditation bell.

7.　*External sensory visual.* External stimuli can be visual. One might enjoy a sunset, a nature walk, or a meditative candle flame or religious symbol.

RELAXATION HIERARCHIES

Within each family, both everyday casual relaxation activities and formal professional relaxation techniques can be ranked on a hierarchy of sustained passive simple focus. Consider somatic/emotional approaches of PMR and autogenic training. Overt PMR involves actively and somewhat effortfully tensing up and releasing muscle tension. The focus is complex, on many muscle groups. And the technique is not particularly passive. One actively tenses up. Sustaining attention and passivity are made easy by vivid target stimuli and continuous guiding instructions. Minimal PMR involves tensing a single muscle group very slightly and letting go. Greater focus is required because the stimulus is less complex and changing (one muscle group rather than a sequence of many). The approach is obviously more passive; one does not effortfully tense up. Greater skill at sustaining focus and passivity is required because the instructor is more likely to remain silent as the relaxer simply attends to the faint sensations of tensing slightly and letting go.

Passivity and simple focus are even more emphasized in autogenic training. Beginning autogenic exercises involve attending to feelings of warmth and heaviness associated with relaxation in the skeletal muscles.

TABLE 4.1 Families of Relaxation

	Physical			Internal Cognitive		External Sensory	
	Somatic/Emotion	Breathing	Movement/Posture	Vocal/Auditory	Visual	Vocal/Auditory	Visual
Low Passivity/Focusing — Casual and formal nonprofessional activities	Massage	Singing	Dance (slow)	Singing	Stories	Music	Art
	Hot tubs	Chanting	Rocking	Chanting	Poetry	Music appreciation	Nature walks
	Showers	Sighing	Floating	Humming	Daydream		Art appreciation
	Steam baths	Yawning	Stroking pets	Saying "Ahh"	Fantasy		
	Sunbathing	Sniffing fragrances	Resting still in bed	Soothing "baby talk"			
	Hugging						
	"Warm" feelings after laughter	Blowing bubbles					
	"Warm" feelings associated with positive emotions						
Formal professional techniques	Progressive muscle relaxation (PMR; overt)	Active yoga breathing	Active stretching exercises; Hatha yoga				

(continued)

TABLE 4.1 (continued)

	Physical			Internal Cognitive		External Sensory	
	Somatic/Emotion	Breathing	Movement/Posture	Vocal/Auditory	Visual	Vocal/Auditory	Visual
High Passivity/Focusing	PMR (Minimal) PMR (Covert) Beginning AT exercises (standard; organ-specific). Postexercise "cooling off": Attending to physical relaxation sensations (without autogenic suggestions).	Passive yoga breathing	Passive stretching exercises Sustained yoga postures	Autogenic organ-specific exercises (when organs are not available to detection) Self-suggestion	AT imagery preparation AT beginning exercises (with imagery) Narrative imagery Sense imagery Insight imagery	Hypnotic suggestion (external or "hetero" hypnosis) Some music therapy	Some art therapy
	Prayer	Prayer	Prayer	Prayer	Prayer	Prayer	Prayer
	Somatic M Kundalini M Zen Hara M	Breath M	Walking M Rocking M	Mantra M	M on an image	M on an external sound	M on a visual stimulus
	Mindfulness	Mindfulness	Mindfulness	Mindfulness	Mindfulness	Mindfulness	Mindfulness

PMR, progressive muscle relaxation; AT, autogenic training; M, meditation.

This requires little focusing skill; most people can generate such sensations simply by squeezing and releasing muscles. More advanced autogenic exercises direct attention to subtle sensations associated with the heart or solar plexus, for example. These require considerably more ability to detect a restricted stimulus, attend to it, and remain passive. In beginning autogenic exercises, passivity and focus are sustained by repeating mental formulas; advanced exercises, which may not require such mental repetition, require greater sustaining skill.

In the family of breathing, beginning exercises involve taking a vigorous deep breath (easy to focus on, not particularly passive), whereas advanced exercises involve a highly focused and passive act of attending to and tracing the delicate flow of breath through the nasal and bronchial passages. In the movement/posture family, active yoga stretches can involve vigorously bowing over and then stretching the entire body to the sky; more focused, simple, and passive exercises might involve calmly and delicately balancing, maintaining an unmoving erect posture while standing on one foot. Finally, in the cognitive visual family, imagery exercises can range from complex, active, and changing vacation activities, to a focused, simple, and passive sunset. Table 4.2 (at the end of this chapter) more fully reviews relaxation hierarchies for the major approaches to relaxation.

To continue, everyday relaxing activities can readily be ranked along a hierarchy of sustained passive simple focus. Taking a walk, strolling through an art museum, listening to vigorous music are all relatively complex and changing activities, requiring little focus. Listening to an extended stretch of very quiet music, fishing in a quiet pond, and watching a sunset are more passive and simple.

MEDITATION, PRAYER, AND ABC
RELAXATION THEORY

Secular health professionals and consultants are often uncomfortable when considering prayer and meditation. Such activities are often seen as not the purview of relaxation science but of religion and even cult. But surely more of our clients pray and meditate than practice any other relaxation technique. And prayer and meditation are not the exclusive property of any one religion or cult. I firmly believe that secular psychologists can have something important to say about such spiritual matters.

Prayer

Prayer is a diverse internal activity. One does not pray just for relaxation but for thanksgiving, petition, surrender, commitment, worship, and so on. The objectives of prayer are perhaps as complex as those for any human encounter. However, in all prayer, the practitioner in one way or another relates to that which is greater than himself or herself.

The typical lot of television preachers often appear to display examples of prayer that are anything that relaxing—desperate pleas for forgiveness or cure, demands that God punish certain groups of sinners, defiant proclamations of self-righteousness or religious superiority, and so on. It beyond the scope of this book to consider the impact of such utterances on any presumed supreme being. However, as students of relaxation, we can restrict our attention to a certain type of prayer, one in which personal concerns, worries, and negative emotion become secondary to God, Allah, or one's ultimate singular concern. In this global sense, such acts of prayer meet our attentional definition of relaxation. One sustains passive simple focus.

One can pray, that is relate to a greater or deeper reality, in many ways—physical, cognitive, or sensory. One might feel inner loving warmth toward a religious figure (somatic/emotional family), sing praises or attend to the very breath of life (breath), kneel in temple (movement/posture), give thanks in the quiet of one's mind (cognitive vocal/auditory), visualize a religious story (cognitive visual), appreciate the stained glass windows of a temple (sensory visual) or the sound of the choir (sensory auditory). Each of these can be prayer. Each of these involves putting aside the discursive efforts of the day and sustaining passive simple focus on a stimulus or task that transcends oneself.

Meditation

As a technique, meditation involves sustaining attention on an utterly simple and unchanging stimulus; for example, one focuses on a burning candle flame or the mental repetition of the word *one*. The slightest thought or effort disrupts this highly focused activity. Clearly, meditation is the simplest manifestation of our definition of relaxation; one does nothing but focus simply and passively.

Each of our seven families of relaxation has a meditative variation. The meditative version of PMR can be seen as the quiet and passive "cooling off time" at the end of a practice session: the relaxer does and thinks nothing while calmly attending to and enjoying the sensations associated with deep self-relaxation. In meditative autogenic training one simply attends to a single inner sensation of relaxation (feelings of warmth in the abdomen; also in Zen hara) without quietly repeating autogenic phrases. Breathing meditation involves simply attending to the flow of breath without trying to regulate or control breathing in any way. A meditative yoga stretch might involve silently sitting in a yoga cross-legged position. Meditative imagery involves nothing more than attending to an utterly simple and unchanging mental image (say, a point of light). Even everyday relaxation activities can be meditative; one might continuously attend to a sunset or the sound of wind at night.

Meditation has a unique place in our ordering of approaches to relaxation. Each form of meditation is the most sustained, passive, simple, and focused version of all approaches in a family. One attends to the target stimulus and nothing else. Indeed, to "sustain passive simple focus" can be seen as a working definition of meditation. Other approaches to relaxation add to this core meditative act. In PMR, one attends while tensing and letting go; a breathing exercise might add a vigorous inhalation; yoga, a deliberate stretch. As tasks are added, relaxation becomes more and active, less singularly sustained, and more discursive. Such additions serve an important function. Some augment the target stimulus, making it more identifiable and an easier focus of sustained attention. Tensing and letting go, stretching, deep breathing, and vivid imagery serve this function. Some exercises facilitate the act of maintaining passivity by detecting and reducing extraneous effort.

Mindfulness is a special type of meditation in which (at least in pure form) there is no formal target stimulus. Instead, one meditates on the moment-to-moment flow of all stimuli, attending to each stimulus as it comes and goes. The task of mindfulness is often poetically described as "being like a mirror, neutrally reflecting the world without bias or comment." As such, mindfulness meditation belongs to no stimulus family; it has no specific target stimulus. All stimuli may be objects of attention. Mindfulness is also the most passive of all approaches to relaxation. One does not even exert the minimal effort of identifying a target meditative stimulus or returning attention to it after every distraction. These features place mindfulness at the end point of all our relaxation hierarchies.

AFFECT, ABSTRACTION, AND TENSION

R-States differ according to degree of affective energy and abstractness. For Joy, Love and Thankfulness, and Prayerfulness, the affective component is obvious. Mental Relaxation, which I have described as an absence of effort and conflict, is strongly defined by such descriptors "peaceful," "at ease," and "contented." What distinguishes these descriptors from Mental Quiet (the simple absence of thought) is a certain amount of affect.

Similarly, three of the defining of descriptors for Strengthened and Aware have distinct affective content ("confident," "energized," and "strengthened"). The remaining descriptors ("focused," "aware," and "clear") may not be associated with affect but rather may reflect attentive energy. However, our research suggests that "focused," "aware," and "clear" are usually linked with some type of affect. I hypothesize that "focused/aware/clear," divorced from its affective component, could in some circumstances characterize a low affective energy state; i.e., one might be clearly aware of being physically relaxed and limp; or mentally quiet, without thought, and clearly focused. Finally, Sleepiness, Disengagement, Physical Relaxation, and Mental Quiet appear to reflect low levels of affective energy.

In addition, R-States may be concrete or abstract. To elaborate, the source of meaning for a concrete R-State is a specific, potentially identifiable, defining context. On experiences Sleep in bed, at the end of the day, or when napping. One Disengages (feels "far away, indifferent") from a source of tension. One identifies the signs of Physical Relaxation in a concrete setting. Similarly, one feels Strengthened and Aware at sports, with friends, during and effective session of relaxation. One Loves and is Thankful to another. In contrast, abstract R-States are experienced as having meaning even in the absence of any specific, identifiable, defining context. One may feel Mental Quiet, a state of mind characterized by a complete absence of thought, and Prayerfulness and Timelessness anywhere, without any defining context.

Taken together, we have two interacting organizing continua: level of experienced affective energy and level of abstractness. This permits the organization of R-States shown in Table 4.3.

Relaxation techniques may differ to the extent to which they are concrete or abstract or may involve low or high affective energy. Purely physical

TABLE 4.3 R-States Organized According to Affective Energy and Level of Abstraction

	Low Affective Energy	High Affective Energy
Concrete	Sleepiness	Mental Relaxation
	Disengagement	Strength and Awareness
	Physical Relaxation	Joy
		Love and Thankfulness
Abstract	Mental Quiet	Prayerfulness
	Timelessness	

exercises, such as PMR and AT are in themselves concrete and perhaps conducive to concrete and low affective energy R-States: Sleepiness, Disengagement, and Physical Relaxation. Put differently, the predefined concrete physical target stimulus of such exercises may preclude focusing on an abstract stimulus. Stretching and breathing may well have a stimulating component (increasing oxygen content in the blood, stimulating muscles and joints), making them more conducive to concrete higher energy R-States. Meditation, prayer, and some types of imagery are less bound to a specific, predefined target stimulus and perhaps may be more conducive to abstract experiences.

This conceptualization may have practical implications. For a client burdened by internal demands, including personal conflict, pain, and discomfort, the task of relaxation becomes one of moving away from these demands and recovering from their impact. Energy is directed toward withdrawal and recovery. Little energy is available for experiencing strong affective states in relaxation. Given the concrete nature of their distress, such individuals may be more likely to experience concrete R-States. Such clients may benefit most from the R-States Sleepiness, Disengagement, and Physical Relaxation evoked through PMR and autogenic training, techniques actually used most frequently by clinical psychologists.

The dimensions of concreteness/abstractness and affective energy may be a function of a variable we have yet to consider, underlying beliefs. Such cognitive structures can clearly be concrete or abstract and often have an strong affective component. It is to this topic we turn in the following chapter.

TABLE 4.2 Relaxation Hierarchies for Specific Approaches

Technique	Level of Focusing	Level of Passivity	Level of Sustaining Effort
Progressive muscle relaxation (PMR)			
PMR: Overt	One attends to vigorously tensing up and releasing tension in a targeted muscle group. Sensations are vivid and easily detected; hence, little focusing is required.	One does not attend to sounds of the room, thoughts about the day, muscle groups not targeted. One tenses up only a targeted muscle group; when letting go, one lets go completely.	Vivid target stimuli, variety of target stimuli, plus continuous instructor "patter" helps sustain attention, reducing need for focusing skill.
PMR: Minimal	One attends to minimally tensing up and releasing tension in a targeting group.	In the tense-up phase, one generates the least noticeable degree of tension. One does not vigorously tense up (as in overt PMR).	Instructor patter is less, requiring more skill at sustaining passive focus. Target stimuli may still be varied, easing the task of sustaining attention.
PMR: Covert	Tensing up is omitted from the target stimulus; one attends to only letting go.	One does not initially tense up (as in overt and minimal PMR).	Difficult to sustain focus and passivity because of target stimulus simplicity and subtlety.
Meditative cooling off	Tensing up and letting go are omitted from the target stimulus. One simply attends to the somatic sensations of relaxation, typically those associated with the skin and skeletal muscles.	One does not tense up or let go but simply attends to the somatic sensations of relaxation.	Difficult to sustain focus and passivity because of target stimulus simplicity and subtlety.

(*continued*)

TABLE 4.2 *(continued)*

Technique	Level of Focusing	Level of Passivity	Level of Sustaining Effort
Autogenic training			
Initial standard exercises: mentally repeating suggestions of "warmth heaviness" in hands and arms	Little focusing required because feelings of "warmth and heaviness" are easily detected sensations in skeletal muscles, often the aftereffect of tensing up and letting go.	Outside instructor can repeat suggestive phrases, increasing complexity of stimulus environment. One passively repeats relaxation phrases, without deliberately trying to achieve result.	Complexity and accessibility of stimuli, plus external suggestion, facilitate sustaining focus and passivity.
Later standard exercises: mentally repeating suggestions of "calmly beating heart," "warmth in solar plexus," and other internal sensations.	Sensations associated with internal organs and processes are less readily detected than skeletal muscle sensation, hence, more focusing required.	Externally presented suggestion is reduced.	Subtlety of internal focal stimuli and reduction of instructor patter increase difficulty of sustaining focus and passivity.
Meditative attending to inner physical sensations (heartbeat, abdominal warmth, etc.)	Subtle sensations, with no assistance from mental repetition of suggestion; requires considerable focusing.	Any outside suggestive instruction would be distracting. No repetition of relaxation phrases, no effort to achieve result.	No supportive instructor patter.
Breathing exercises			
Active yoga breathing	Vivid target stimulus; active stretching (e.g., bowing over, reaching up) while inhaling and exhaling.	Breathing that is too strained represents excessive effort.	Complexity of typical exercise (combining several exercises) makes sustaining focus and passivity easy.

66

TABLE 4.2 (*continued*)

Technique	Level of Focusing	Level of Passivity	Level of Sustaining Effort
Diaphragmatic breathing	Active manipulation of diaphragm (pulling stomach in while exhaling, etc.) during breathing.	Any attempts to stretch while breathing are extraneous. One must minimize any attempts to try to force or regulate the breathing process more than necessary.	It can be challenging to sustain attention on manipulating the diaphragm.
Passive breathing	Target stimulus is more subtle: the simple act of breathing itself as well as the flow of breath.	Trying not to exert any effort whatsoever beyond that needed to inhale and exhale.	Level of passivity and focusing required make sustaining exercise difficult.
Breath meditation	The simple flow of breath as one passively or "automatically" inhales and exhales.	Even efforts at inhaling and exhaling should be avoided.	Difficult to sustain focus and passivity because of target stimulus simplicity and subtlety.
Stretching exercises			
Active yoga stretching	One attends to a readily identified stimulus; physical pleasures of completely stretching.	One lets go of unnecessary thoughts, physical tension; one stretches slowly, smoothly, and gently. Attempts to rush or force a stretch are extraneous effort.	Easy to sustain exercise because of complexity.

(*continued*)

TABLE 4.2 *(continued)*

Technique	Level of Focusing	Level of Passivity	Level of Sustaining Effort
Passive yoga stretching	One attends to sensations associated with minimal stretch.	One stretches as little as possible.	Exercise still complex.
Postures	One attends to sensations associated with maintaining posture and balance for a sustained period of time.	One does not move at all, simply assumes a posture; straining to sustain posture is extraneous effort.	Difficult to sustain focus and passivity because of simplicity of target stimulus.
Rocking, walking meditation	One meditates on a simple repetitive movement.	Any effort is extraneous; movement should be automatic.	Difficult to sustain focus and passivity because of target stimulus simplicity and subtlety.
Imagery			
Autogenic preparatory imagery	One attends to spontaneous and often interesting spontaneous retinal activity.	Irrelevant thoughts, sensations; attempts to control or modify images are to be avoided.	Relatively easy to sustain attention on spontaneous retinal phenomena that occur without effort.
Narrative imagery	One attends to images of sense impressions of a relaxing setting and activity.	One can move in the imagined activity or attempt to directly control or modify images.	Activity and complexity of image make sustaining focus and passivity easy.
Sense imagery	One attends to images of sense impressions of a relaxing setting.	Execution of any narrative plot is unnecessary activity.	Sustaining focus and passivity is more difficult because of lack of activity in image.

TABLE 4.2 *(continued)*

Technique	Level of Focusing	Level of Passivity	Level of Sustaining Effort
Insight imagery	One attends to a singular image, waiting for "insight."	Activity or extraneous sense images can be distracting; any attempts to define or direct insight are to be avoided.	Avoiding extraneous activity and sense stimulation make sustaining focus and passivity difficult.
Meditative imagery	Attending to a singular image, waiting for nothing (just attending, nothing else).	Any expectation of change or insight would be distracting effort. Any effort to direct image would be distracting.	Singular focus makes sustaining exercise difficult.
Sense relaxation			
Vigorous activities: dance, hiking, listening to vivid, engaging music, etc.	Stimulus is complex, changing, and intense—easy to focus on.	Often much extraneous stimulation.	Easy; wide range of permitted focal stimuli and activities.
More passive, simple and focused activities; appreciating quiet music, art, nature, etc.	Stimulus is less complex, changing, and intense—more difficult to attend to unless one is already calm.	Less extraneous stimulation.	Somewhat more difficult to sustain passive focus; tense individuals may wish to "get active."
External stimulus meditation	Attending to a candle flame, the sound of a waterfall, etc.	Any extraneous effort is potentially distracting.	Singular simplicity of exercise makes it most difficult to sustain attention.

5

What Makes Relaxation Work?

What makes relaxation work? What enables a relaxer to withdraw, recover, and open up? What generates the rainbow of R-States and the relaxation deepening cycle we have previously described? First, it is important to recognize that such questions are a bit like asking what is love or beauty. The answer is complex and perhaps ultimately unfathomable. Nonetheless, I find it useful to identify three groups of basic psychological processes. *Primary attentional reinforcement processes* describe how sustained passive simple focus evolves over the course of relaxation. The *assimilative processes* of articulation, working through, and cognitive restructuring consolidate and enhance the effects of primary processes. Through *crossover processes*, practice of a technique in one family affects a technique in another family.

PRIMARY ATTENTIONAL REINFORCEMENT PROCESSES

In chapter 3 we saw how the emergence of R-States can be useful distractions, providing opportunities to strengthen relaxation skills. Through the relaxation deepening cycle, one moves from distraction to focus and cultivates the ability to sustain passive simple focus. In this chapter we consider how such focusing skill evolves through the course of relaxation. One first learns to withdraw, reduce stimulus input and output, and experience the rewards of tension relief. Next, one learns to direct attention to the specifics of a relaxation technique and experience its unique extrinsic positive reinforcements. Eventually, one develops the skill of establishing a sustained internal environment of passive simple focus and enjoy the rewards of opening up.

Withdrawal and the Extrinsic Rewards of Relaxation

Arousal and symptoms are, in part, triggered and aggravated by stimulus input and response output. Listening to an outside barking dog or climbing stairs raises heart rate, breathing rate, and so on; closing the window or taking a break from climbing stairs contributes to reduced arousal. By sustaining passive simple focus on a relaxation task, the relaxer deliberately reduces stimulus input and response output and thereby deprives arousal and symptoms of support. Subjectively, one is increasingly likely to experience symptom reduction and tension relief as well as the R-States Sleepiness, Disengagement, and Physical Relaxation. These effects may be supplemented by technique-specific physiological processes (breathing deeply to induce mild hypercapnia, tensing up and letting go to release muscle tension and increase blood flow). In sum, initial attempts to sustain passive simple focus are sustained through negative and positive reinforcement (arousal symptom reduction and R-States).

With less distraction from symptoms, the relaxer is free to become more engaged in relaxation and more fully enjoy exercise-specific or extrinsic rewards. Sustained passive simple focus is maintained through positively reinforcing R-States, especially Physical Relaxation, Mental Quiet, Mental Relaxation, Strength and Awareness, and Joy.

Specificity

A variation of the above process may contribute to the somatic specificity of progressive muscle relaxation (PMR) and autogenic training (AT) exercises. How can attending to reduced shoulder muscle tension, increased blood flow to the hands, even heart rate and the like actually contribute to these effects? Generally, the task in such exercises is to direct attention to the specific process or organ in question. Once that occurs, a client is simply more likely to discover internal strategies for changing that somatic activity.

Specifically, a client may practice an activity such as PMR or AT that evokes generalized reduced arousal, reducing internal noise. This technique also facilitates directing attention to one component of arousal reduction. For example, by tensing up and letting go of hand muscles or thinking the phrase "hands warm and heavy" one restricts attention to reduced arousal in the hands. Once a client has reduced potentially distracting stimuli and effort and directed attention to a physical organ or process, he or she is more likely to recognize change in this attentional target, noticing when the hands actually begin to relax. The relaxer can then readily detect any explicit instrumental act—that is, when he or she does something that helps reduce hand muscle tension even more. The relaxer may note, "Ah, when I relaxed my shoulders, it was easier to let go of tension in my hands."

The processes so far have been identified before (Schwartz, 1995). Let me hypothesize an extension, which might be termed *implicit behavioral shaping*. Passive instrumental acts contributing to relaxation may well be implicit, that is, not identified by the relaxer. A client may report, "I don't know how I got my hands warmer and relaxed. I simply stopped trying and sort of attended with indifference. Whatever I did, it worked. I feel relaxed." At this moment she is doing absolutely nothing deliberate to maintain relaxation; in fact, any thought or action could well disrupt relaxation. Let us assume that some unidentified process is sustaining her relaxation and that this specific process is beyond her awareness at the moment. Perhaps she has slowed her breathing without knowing it. If we assume that the resulting R-States are reinforcing and that some implicit process (undetected reductions in breathing rate) is maintaining these reinforcements, then we have identified a reinforcement contingency that should enhance the implicit relaxation processes. All the relaxer must do to maintain and deepen relaxation is keep out of the way, remain passive, and continue focusing on the target stimulus (warm hands).

Opening Up

Through practice, sustained passive simple focusing skills develop, permitting greater freedom from distraction and ability to attend to the focal task of relaxation. The relaxer is increasingly capable of reducing stimulus input and response output and of sustaining attention on a simple stimulus. He or she experiences the rewards of an exercise with greater intensity, breadth, and depth. Such rewards include the R-States Mental Relaxation, Strength and Awareness, Joy, Love and Thankfulness, and Prayerfulness.

Four processes—habituation, desensitization, extinction, and the *ganzfeld* effect—contribute to maintain an internal environment of sustained passive simple focus. The brain tends to tune out or cease reacting to stimulus and response constancies. This process of *habituation* partly explains why we cease responding to such constancies as the drone of an air conditioner, outside traffic, and the like. In relaxation, one deliberately establishes broad classes of continuous and unchanging internal and external stimuli. One picks a quiet room, sits or reclines in a stationary position, attends to a relatively simple stimulus, and so on. Even distractions are treated as neutral and monotonous repetitions to be put aside again and again. In sum, such stimuli cease to evoke a response.

Desensitization (Wolpe, 1958) is a popular psychotherapy for phobias. Graduated versions of an anxiety-arousing stimulus, say snakes, are repeatedly presented while a client is deeply relaxed. Eventually, the stimulus is desensitized and is more likely to evoke relaxation than anxiety. An analogous process may contribute to focusing. Instead of an anxiety-arousal stimulus, any stimulus or N-State with the potential for disrupting passivity or reduced stimulus input that consistently emerges in the context of relaxation loses its disruptive quality through desensitization and becomes a cue for deeper relaxation.

A similar process might contribute to self-augmentation of passivity. Responses that go unrewarded tend to cease or *extinguish*. The family dog will eventually stop rolling over if the supply of dog treats cease. In a relaxation session, urges to interrupt passive simple focus and to engage in some form of activity frequently emerge. The relaxer may want to eat a hamburger, phone a friend, or plan the day's activities. However, in relaxation one does not respond to such impulses. Deprived of reinforcement, they eventually extinguish, contributing to further reductions in response output.

Ornstein (1972) has proposed a global meditation effect that can apply to other forms of relaxation. For decades, North Pole aviators have encountered an intriguing threat. When the snow-covered earth and snow-filled sky blend into one unchanging white world, an aviator can experience "blankout," a type of temporary blindness that can lead to disastrous consequences. Theoretically, here is what appears to happen. A homogeneous and unchanging experiential field is called a *ganzfeld*. Whenever a *ganzfeld* is established, parts of the brain that process associated stimuli display reduced activity, perhaps associated with prolonged bursts of sometimes synchronized alpha activity. When such a *ganzfeld effect* occurs, one ceases to be aware of all stimuli associated with the field.

Highly focused forms of relaxation, especially meditation, involve establishing a sustained passive simple experiential field, augmented by habituation, desensitization, and extinction. One attends only to feelings of warmth and heaviness, a continuous posture, the flow of breath, a mantra, an image. If something like a *ganzfeld* is established, one might postulate a *ganzfeld* effect, a diminished responsivity displayed by a reduced propensity to engage in discursive and distracting thought. One becomes increasingly capable of apprehending oneself and the world in a nondiscursive, nonanalytic, and nonverbal manner. Such "opening up" and eventually "going beyond oneself" can be intrinsically reinforcing.

ASSIMILATIVE PROCESSES

All of the processes we have considered have the paradoxical potential for creating their opposites—N-States of increased response output and stimulus input, reduced focus on a rewarding stimulus, and increased awareness of aversive stimuli. Regardless of their source, N-States are essential for the development of attentional skills in relaxation. Each distracting N-State is an opportunity to redeploy relaxation skills, to reduce extraneous response effort and extraneous stimulation, and sustain passive simple focus. Through such challenges, relaxation skills strengthen. Furthermore, it is often through the emergence of such divergent processes that one's beliefs and attitudes concerning relaxation are challenged. This brings us to our consideration of *assimilative processes* in relaxation.

The relaxer, through sustained passive simple focus, may discover new worlds of unexpected effects, including N- and R-States. One identifies and makes sense of such experiences by means of three assimilative processes: articulation, working through, and cognitive restructuring. These processes prepare for and consolidate growth in relaxation and contribute to the deepening and generalization of relaxation to life at large.

Articulation

Through articulation one identifies and finds words or images for a relaxation experience. This occurs at all levels of training. The beginning practitioner of PMR or AT may learn to discriminate subtle sources of striated muscle tension. The practitioner of yoga stretching may discover sensations from tendons, joints, and muscles associated with a successful posture or stretch. A student of breathing yoga may learn to detect minute sensations associated with the flow of breath through nasal passages, throat, bronchial passages, and lungs. In imagery and meditation one may find words or images for new and unexpected feelings associated with energy and joy.

The articulation of a relaxation experience is an important event in relaxation training, one that provides something of a base for further movement and exploration. This process is analogous to what Gendlin (1981) has called *focusing* in psychotherapy. To paraphrase Gendlin, a therapy client may initially report, or articulate, a somewhat vague or undifferentiated feeling ("I feel blue," "I'm nervous"). In "Gendlin's focusing" (not to be confused with "Smith's focusing"), the client does not attempt to deliberately figure out or analytically process such feelings; instead, he or she passively attends to the feeling and waits for words or images to emerge that clearly convey its gist, or affective meaning. A variety of words and images may emerge, most of which may not fit particularly well. In time, the client may discover a word or image that successfully conveys the "felt meaning." When such articulation occurs, the feeling may well shift, revealing an underlying feeling. We can see the process of Gendlin's focusing in the following sequence of covert statements:

Client:	"I feel blue."
Therapist:	"What is the gist, the most important thing about this feeling?"
Client:	"Let me try to analyze or figure out this feeling blue. Oops, I stopped focusing. Let's put aside the thinking cap and calmly attend to this blue feeling inside. What's its gist?"
Client:	"I got a C in my French class? . . . No, that doesn't get at the gist of my feeling. . . . I miss my pet cat. . . . No, that's not really it. . . . I want a raise . . . doesn't feel like it. . . . I feel down in the dumps . . . I feel lonely. . . . Aha, that's exactly it . . . I'm really lonely!"

In Gendlin's focusing, a client uncovers underlying feelings. A key step is passively articulating—identifying and symbolizing—what he or she feels. Once this is achieved, a client can move deeper and explore associated feelings further. I propose that the same process is central to relaxation: a relaxer identifies and symbolizes both R- and N-States. The process may not be as formal as in Gendlin's focusing, but the effect is the same. Once a client can articulate the gist, or felt meaning, of a relaxation experience, change can occur. Underlying, associated, or contributing relaxation feelings can emerge. We see this process in the following example (Smith, 1985)

"What is relaxing to me at the moment?"
"Hmmm . . . I feel kind of good . . . warm and mellow"
"I now quietly attend to the 'warm and mellow' feeling, without trying to figure it out, keep it, or push it away. I wait for pictures or words to come up that feel right in conveying the most important thing about this feeling."

"Warm and mellow . . . powerful?"

"The word 'powerful' just came to mind. I ask myself, 'does it fit how I feel?' It doesn't, so I return to attending to the warm and mellow feeling deep inside."

"Warm and mellow . . . warm and mellow . . . "

" 'Secure' . . . does this word fit? Yes, that's it, that's just how I feel . . . nice and secure."

"Now I attend to this somewhat new good feeling, the feeling 'nice and secure,' without trying to figure the feeling out, or keep it, or push it away. I continue to wait for pictures or words to come up that feel right and get at what is most important about the feeling." (pp. 176–177)

Working Through

The process of working through involves exploring the applications and implications of a relaxation effect. A practitioner of yoga breathing may feel peacefully refreshed after a session. Later, he or she may discover that such feelings enhance work performance (application) but are apparently incompatible with beliefs that tension and anxiety contribute to success (implication).

Cognitive Restructuring

The course of relaxation can be profoundly influenced by what one thinks about relaxation. *Relaxation Beliefs* (*R-Beliefs*) are cognitive structures conducive to enhanced, deeper and more generalized relaxation, and *Relaxation Attitudes* (*R-Attitudes*) are structures that interfere with relaxation. Cognitive restructuring involves rethinking R-Beliefs and R-Attitudes in light of relaxation. A practitioner of PMR might feel "heavy and limp" after a session and fearfully appraise such feelings as "signs of losing control." Such an R-Attitude could well lead a relaxer to practice with less enthusiasm, or even quit. However, after some thought (cognitive restructuring), the relaxer may conclude that feeling "heavy and limp" is a good sign, possibly an indication of somatic relaxation, one that may indicate that PMR is working and is worth continuing. This relaxer has changed his or her thinking about PMR, and may well continue practicing with increased commitment.

In another example, a relaxer may discover a conflict between specific R-Beliefs and R-Attitudes. For example, he or she may hold the R-Attitude "be in control of everything in life," yet when relaxing recognize the wisdom of the R-Belief that "deeply satisfying feelings of peace come when I accept that some things cannot be controlled." Through cognitive restructuring, he or she may then discover that letting go of control in relaxation can actually enhance performance at work, and that living a life of sensible acceptance does not mean relinquishing control.

The challenges and issues involved in cognitive restructuring often differ for beginning and advanced practitioners of relaxation. Beginners must often consider their motivation for learning relaxation, their commitment to practice, and willingness to put up with frustrations and unexpected effects. Advanced practitioners of relaxation often face a more encompassing task, that of developing a personal philosophy of life conducive to deeper and more generalized relaxation.

CROSSOVER PROCESSES

Techniques often fit in more than one relaxation family. A yoga stretch is both a movement/posture exercise and an exercise that can affect breathing. Practice of a technique in one family can facilitate growth in another family. Similarly, attentional and assimilative processes can affect each other. Such cross-activity reflects what we can term *crossover processes*. To elaborate, learning to breathe deeply and calmly, a breathing family activity, can facilitate the practice of yoga stretches. Slowly bowing and stretching can contribute to deep breathing. Mastery of PMR and acquisition of the ability to attend quickly to body sensations related to relaxation may facilitate sense imagery.

Suggestion is an important crossover process. When a relaxer sustains passive simple focus on an internally or externally repeated phrase, he or she is engaging in a form of relaxation that can be placed in the cognitive or sensory verbal/auditory families. This has a potential for evoking relaxation in and of itself, as the client becomes passive and limits attention to repeated phrases. But if the phrase is also suggestive of an effect in another family, say "warmth and heaviness" in the extremities or visual imagery, then the exercise has the potential for evoking the crossover process of suggestion. Through suggestion, the noted effect may appear in the targeted family.

The conditions for suggestion are less likely when instructions primarily call for directing and sustaining attention to a simple stimulus and ceasing unnecessary activity, without mention of possible effect (attend to "stretching," "the flow of breath," "an internal mental image," and the like).

However, in most forms of relaxation, some degree of suggestion supplements processes we have outlined earlier.

A variety of external factors can contribute to suggestion. For example, voice quality can suggest a variety of relaxation effects. A suggestive PMR voice is loud and forceful in the "tense up" phase and slow and drawn out in the "tension release" phase; a breathing relaxation voice has a "breathy" quality, with instructions to inhale and exhale paced with instructor breathing; a yoga voice is slow and smooth with elongated vowels; imagery can be effectively presented with a somewhat colorful, lively, "storytelling" voice; and meditation requires a voice that is simple and quiet, with short phrases.

Finally, the context of relaxation training can contribute to expectations suggestive of relaxation effects. Training that proceeds in a sterile and technologically sophisticated hospital environment, with trainers wearing hospital uniforms, may evoke expectations of scientifically proven physiological effect; training done in an outdoor monastic setting rich with spiritual symbols may evoke a quiet and different expectational set, perhaps one promoting feelings of opening up. Such contextual elements are numerous and include promotional materials, rationales, trainer appearance, and environmental setting.

Suggestion plays an unavoidable part in all of relaxation and can be a valuable tool. However, it is important to consider why a client wants to learn relaxation. Is the goal to produce an immediate R-State, whether it be Physical Relaxation, Mental Relaxation, or Strength and Awareness? If such goals are targeted, then a trainer can consider trying whatever techniques work, including suggestion. If a client has a more philosophical objective, perhaps to explore what one considers to be personal or objective reality, suggestion may be a distraction, an unnecessary stimulus or form of effort to be avoided or identified as of minimal importance.

RELAXATION COMPETENCE AND GENERALIZATION: MARKERS ALONG THE PATH

How do we know when relaxation works? Most clinicians would state that symptom reduction is the criterion for success. Indeed, reductions in somatic and emotional distress are what clients pay for when they seek relaxation training. Such outcomes can be assessed through self-report/ interview, behavioral observation, or biofeedback. But knowing that a client can reduce a headache is not enough. Such outcomes fail to answer the following questions:

- What is the likelihood the client will continue practicing once the external support of therapy is gone? Put differently, what practice-sustaining rewards has a client discovered?
- Does the client have "room to grow" with his or her relaxation technique? Once the initial goal of learning relaxation has been met, can the client entertain and progress to other goals? Once the headache client has learned to treat the headache, is she prepared to consider the meaning of life if that, years from now, becomes a relaxation goal?
- Does the client understand how his or her specific relaxation achievements fit into the broader context of beliefs?

We have already suggested that achievement of any relaxation effect, or desired R-State, can be considered an indicator of mastery of relaxation. As relaxers progress, they experience a broader range of R-States. However, the development of full relaxation competence is a broader objective, with movement indicated by changes in manifest processes, relaxation effects, progression across and within families of relaxation activities, and generalization to life at large.

Technique-specific Processes

To some extent, all the relaxation processes we have considered work at all levels of relaxation. However, different processes dominate at different levels of training. At the onset of training, technique-specific processes are perhaps most important. For example, deliberate tense-release cycles of PMR may initiate a "relaxation rebound" effect, yoga stretches may contribute to increased peripheral blood flow, deep breathing may increase blood carbon dioxide (CO_2) level, and so on.

Attentional and Reinforcement Processes

We have seen that, from the onset of training, relaxers restrict attention to a simple stimulus and reduce physical and cognitive activity. Early on, sustained passive simple focus is more likely to be overt and involve reducing stimulus input (e.g., turning off the lights, taking the phone off the hook) and response output (ceasing the tasks of the day and sitting in a comfortable chair). As training progresses, the attentional task of relaxation becomes more cognitive, with the relaxer putting aside distracting thoughts and ideas.

At first, relaxation skills are used concretely; one simply attends to and lets go. However, as one becomes more proficient at relaxation, skills are deployed in increasing degrees of abstraction or generality. Focusing can become a small act of dedication, of deciding to deploy one's attention in relaxation in spite of the impulse to do otherwise. Passivity can be viewed as an act of letting be, of relinquishing unnecessary control. For this to happen, a degree of assimilation must occur.

Finally, the nature of reinforcement changes as relaxation progresses. At first, practitioners are likely to enjoy concrete, physical relief from tension. The rewarding focal stimulus may in time become more cognitive and include pleasing thought or imagery. Eventually, understanding and insight become salient rewards; one practices an exercise not only because it "feels good" but because it "is interesting" or "meaningful."

Advanced meditative techniques, in which one calmly attends to a singular stimulus, or to nothing at all, call for high levels of skill deployment. At this point the nature of reinforcement changes profoundly. The advanced meditator may already experience a state of calm, free of distracting symptoms. So the potential for symptom relief is absent. The meditator may attend to very little, perhaps a meaningless syllable or nothing at all. So, unlike exercises such as yoga stretching, breathing, or imagery, there is no potentially rewarding focal target. Because the most conspicuous experiential fact of meditation is that one attends, any reinforcing R-States must be associated with the very act of attention. Sustained passive simple focus can be profoundly reinforcing in and of itself.

Assimilative Processes

As training progresses, the nature of assimilation changes, resulting in R-Beliefs that are increasingly abstract and differentiated. This is perhaps one of the most important processes in relaxation, one we consider in the following chapter.

Generalization of Effects

Relaxation generalizes when a client can experience sustained, passive simple focus outside the practice session. The beginner may experience a relaxation effect within the confines of a practice session and experience tension for the rest of the day. An important sign of growth of relaxation is generalization of relaxation effects to life at large. To some extent generalization may be spontaneous, particularly for immediate aftereffects lasting for the remainder of the day. Deeper generalization may require additional effort outside the practice session. These are the greater tasks of relaxation; they include anything done to enhance a calm and rewarding life. Examples include the following:

- Restructuring attitudes and philosophies that contribute to tension and interfere with relaxation.
- Mastering new coping skills for everyday problems to reduce tension that interferes with relaxation.
- Processing issues in psychotherapy.
- Changing one's work or home environment.

Such lifestyle changes become increasingly salient as relaxation progresses and the relaxer develops increasingly profound personal philosophies conducive to relaxation.

6

R-Attitudes, R-Beliefs, and Relaxation Philosophies

One's beliefs and attitudes about relaxation can have a profound impact on the course of relaxation training. A hostile and negative client may not even give relaxation a chance to work. Among those willing to try, positive beliefs can transform what could be a mechanical health chore to an activity that is a source of meaning and strength for all of life.

NEGATIVE THINKING AND R-ATTITUDES

Negative thinking makes a problem needlessly severe or difficult to solve. In the context of relaxation, negative thinking consists of R-Attitudes that discount the possible benefit of relaxation, or one's ability to practice and achieve a benefit. Albert Ellis's ABC model (not to be confused with Smith's ABC Theory) outlines the impact of negative thinking on stress and coping. *A* refers to *A*ctivating stress event; *B*, one's *B*eliefs about the event; *C*, the *C*onsequences, usually distressing emotions or symptoms. For example:

> My boss rejected my report (A). I think I should always be compli-
> mented for my efforts even when I make a few mistakes (B). I got
> depressed when my expectations were not met (C).

> My children won't follow my suggestions (A). I think children should
> always obey their parents (B). I got very angry (C).

> I was stuck in a traffic jam (A). I think everyone else on the highway
> should be considerate, recognize that I'm in a hurry, and let me pass
> (B). I wish I could just ram my car into them (C).

For relaxation, Ellis's *A* might refer to the actual relaxation activity, perhaps a yoga stretching exercise, *B* refers to one's R-Attitudes and R-Beliefs about this activity ("Yoga stretching is voodoo, a waste of time, something lazy people do"), and *C* refers to the consequences of successful practice of relaxation ("I refuse to practice this worthless silly voodoo exercise"). Please note that a "belief" for Ellis would include both R-Attitudes and R-Beliefs.

Texts of cognitive modification list types of negative irrational and maladaptive thinking. Most include the following (Smith, 1993a):

Types of Irrational/Maladaptive Negative Thinking

Distortions in Making Inferences

All-or-none thinking: viewing the world in rigid black and white, either/or categories, and not leaving room for alternatives.

Fortune-telling: acting as if one knows the precise outcome (usually negative) of some event, precluding the possibility of the unexpected.

Mind-reading: acting as if we know what others want, think, or feel without asking.

Selective abstraction: Making up one's mind too early on the basis of little evidence; forming conclusions based on one isolated negative detail of an event, discounting the positive.

Overgeneralization: Taking conclusions one has already formed and inappropriately applying them to other situations.

Arbitrary inference: Leaping to conclusions in the absence of relevant evidence, wrong evidence, or simple emotions.

Distortions in Evaluating Importance

Thinking with "shoulds, ought to's, musts": turning simple wishes and desires into dire necessities.

Awfulizing: exaggerating the importance of negative events; taking too seriously the consequences of unmet "musts; turning honest frustration and disappointment into disasters.

Egocentrism (a type of awfulizing): thinking of oneself as the center of the universe; assuming one has some special status, rights, and privileges others do not have.

Childhood fantasy (a type of awfulizing): assuming (like children) that everything should go our way, everyone is loving, the world should be perfect, and all stories should have happy endings.

Minimizing: understating the true significance of events in such a way that problems eventually become worse through inaction.

Distortions in Attributing Responsibility or Control

Blaming: inappropriately assuming that other people or circumstances are responsible for one's stress; finger-pointing, scapegoating, or idle complaining.

Personalizing: needlessly pointing the finger of blame at oneself.

Helpless thinking: Giving up; forgetting that stress situations are problems to be solved. (pp. 61–63)

Any R-Attitude from this somewhat dismal dictionary can interfere with growth in relaxation, as illustrated below:

Distortions in Making Inferences

All-or-none thinking: "My relaxation technique will either work perfectly or not at all."

Fortune-telling: "Relaxation won't work for me. I'm not that type of person."

Mind reading: "My boss will think I'm a nut if I join a meditation class."

Selective abstraction: "I had a bad experience with TM. It taught me that relaxation won't work for me."

Overgeneralization: "I tried hypnosis and found it boring. I would probably find meditation equally boring."

Arbitrary inference: "I'm an 'in control, take charge' type of person. Relaxation is clearly wrong for me."

Distortions in Evaluating Importance

Thinking with "shoulds, ought to's, musts": "I must relax."

Awfulizing: "I joined a relaxation class and wasted a week trying to practice. It was a complete disaster. I won't try that again!"

Egocentrism: "My problems are so special and unique that no simple relaxation technique will ever make a difference."

Childhood fantasy: "I want to have a deep religious experience (see God, get enlightened, cure all my problems get high, etc.) in relaxation."

Minimizing: "When I learned progressive muscle relaxation, I just felt a little distant and far away. That was nothing."

Distortions in attributing responsibility or control: "No one really knows how to teach relaxation."

Distortions in Attributing Responsibility or Control

Blaming: "My yoga instructor was so bad that I don't trust any relaxation guru."

Personalizing: "I'm too lazy to relax."

Helpless thinking: "I just can't do it."

FROM NEGATIVE THOUGHTS TO GUIDING PERSONAL PHILOSOPHIES: HIERARCHIES OF ABSTRACTION

All concepts differ according to level of abstraction. A single abstract concept covers or encompasses a variety of more concrete concepts. For example, "pear, apple, orange, and peach" are all concrete terms. All are covered by a more abstract concept, "fruit." To continue, "fruit, bread, meat, and eggs" are all covered by an even more abstract concept, "food." Similarly, it is useful to consider negative beliefs at various levels of abstraction. The most concrete are negative thoughts, what people say to themselves throughout the day. Thoughts can reflect more enduring and abstract attitudes and beliefs, which in turn are encompassed by even more abstract guiding personal philosophies (see Figure 6.1).

Ellis suggests ten beliefs that often create stress for people. These beliefs are typically not overt and proclaimed but implicit, revealed through actions rather than words. It is easy to see how each might act as an R-Attitude that interferes with relaxation (I've suggested R-Attitudes in parentheses):

1. You must have the love and approval of everyone important in your life. (Don't think about learning your relaxation technique well but focus on impressing your instructor.)
2. You must prove yourself competent and adequate all the time. (You must be perfect at your relaxation technique, right away.)
3. You must view life as awful, terrible, or catastrophic when things do not go your way. (Not experiencing immediate symptom relief while practicing your relaxation technique is terrible.)
4. People who harm you or commit misdeeds are wicked, bad, or villainous people, and deserve severe blame, damnation, and punishment. (It's OK to ruminate about all the bad people in your life while you do your relaxation exercise.)
5. If something seems dangerous or fearsome, you must become terribly preoccupied and upset about it. (During your relaxation exercise, maybe you should continue obsessing about the threats in your life.)

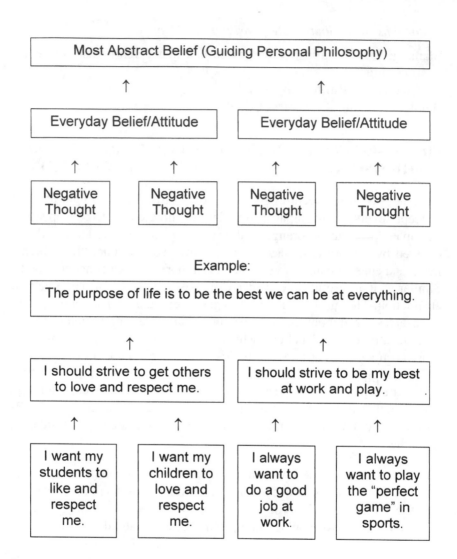

FIGURE 6.1   Levels of abstraction.

6. People and things should turn out better than they do. You have to view it as terrible if you do not quickly find good solutions to life's problems. (You must find the right relaxation technique immediately.)
7. Emotional misery comes from external pressures, and you have little ability to control your negative feelings. (You can't find time to relax because of all the external pressures and interruptions.)
8. You will find it easier to avoid facing life's difficulties than to undertake more rewarding forms of self-discipline. (You can put off learning relaxation until some other day.)
9. Your past remains all-important, and because something once strongly influenced your life, it has to keep determining your feelings and behavior. (You were just born a tense person, and that's why you can't relax.)
10. You can achieve happiness by inertia and inaction, by passively enjoying yourself. (Sitting and doing a relaxation technique is no fun.)

CATALOGING RELAXATION ATTITUDES (R-ATTITUDES)

For the past five years I have been collecting negative R-Attitudes expressed by clients. My initial catalog included 115 items. Recently I surveyed 115 college students who either started a relaxation technique and quit, or considered learning relaxation and never started. Participants rated the extent to which each R-Attitude applied to them. Most frequent R-Attitudes concern practical constraints (not having the time or money), distractibility, desire for quick answers, lack of understanding of relaxation's uses, and fear of losing control (see Table 6.1).

My plan is to eventually subject this list to factor analysis, and investigate personal and situational variables associated with resulting dimensions of resistance. Hopefully, once we discover why clients do not comply with their preferred relaxation techniques, we can offer targeted assistance.

RELAXATION BELIEFS AND PHILOSOPHIES

Relaxation beliefs, or R-Beliefs, are thoughts that enhance, deepen, and foster the generalization of relaxation. Specifically, R-Beliefs not only provide a rationale for practicing a relaxation technique but also facilitate every component of our four-word definition of relaxation: sustained, passive, simple focus. We can see this in the following examples:

"I believe that I have to give my yoga technique sufficient time before I can expect any benefits" (a belief that may facilitate sustaining relaxation)

"I believe I have to put aside my urgent desire to be an accomplished meditator before meditation will start working" (a belief that may facilitate passivity)

"I believe that trying to do too many things in my imagery distracts from its value" (another belief facilitating passivity)

"I believe it is best to focus my attention on my muscle groups in PMR, not on pleasing the instructor" (a belief that may facilitate focusing)

More generally, R-Beliefs provide a meaningful context for R-States and N-States that may emerge in relaxation practice. Both can be seen as indicators that relaxation is working. A client who experiences the R-State Physical Relaxation ("I feel warm and heavy") is less likely to be concerned if he or she recognizes that this state can be a normal by-product of relaxation and not the sign that something is going wrong. Finally, R-Beliefs enable generalization of the effects of relaxation to life at large. More on this later.

R-Beliefs exist at several levels of abstraction. A relaxer may initially develop concrete and simple supportive beliefs ("Stretching will help my back tension," "I can find time to practice deep breathing once a day"). In time, more abstract and differentiated personal philosophies may evolve ("Live one day at a time," "God's will be done"). The more abstract and differentiated an R-Belief, the more likely it will contribute to generalization of the effects of relaxation to life at large. We can see this organization in Figure 6.2.

Elsewhere (Smith, 1990), I have proposed a cyclical process whereby R-Beliefs evolve in relaxation. A practitioner's R-Beliefs may at first be relatively simple and concrete, with limited application. For example, a meditator may believe that "it is counterproductive to try too hard to make meditation work." Eventually, N-States and R-States may emerge that challenge this belief. The meditator may be distracted by the thought "I must not forget to clean the car." At this time, she has a choice: expand existing R-Beliefs to apply to the newly encountered experiences or stop the relaxation session. Specifically, the belief "It is counterproductive to try too hard at meditation" may be expanded to "It is counterproductive to try too hard at meditation . . . and to cope with outside activities in the meditation session."

As additional N-States and R-States challenge relaxation, the restructuring task is repeated. One's R-Beliefs become increasingly abstract and

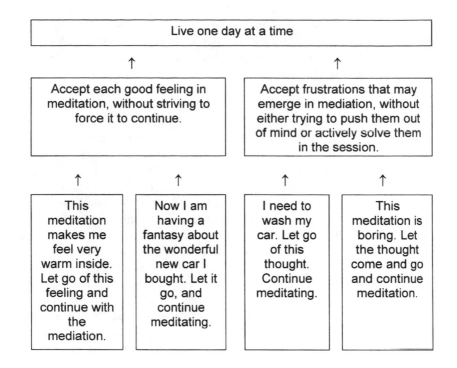

FIGURE 6.2   Abstract and concrete R-Beliefs.

differentiated, applying to a greater variety of potential relaxation experiences. Eventually, personal philosophies may evolve with universal applicability, extending both to specific events in a relaxation session and to life at large. In our example, "It is counterproductive to try too hard at mediation" may evolve into "Live one day at a time," an abstract and differentiated structure that applies to the relaxation session as well as work, relating to others, sports, and so on.

Elsewhere I have suggested that highly abstract and differentiated R-Beliefs reflect a certain paradox of passivity. I first introduced this idea in 1996 (Smith et al., 1996) when discussing the preliminary set of relaxation states that were eventually revised in our current listing. Although this passage includes some concepts that I no longer use (such as "passive engagement"), it still makes a point:

In many of life's endeavors, success results from goal-directed and analytic striving; yet in relaxation, growth and movement paradoxically occur when such activity ceases. The less one tries to control or direct a relaxation exercise, whether it be a yoga stretch, passive breathing, or meditation, the better it works. Similarly, the less one tries to deliberately evoke relaxation states (and deliberately conjure up feelings of "strength," "joy," "reverence," and so on), the more likely these states will emerge. A personal philosophy of passive engagement must somehow acknowledge this central paradox of passivity and identify an outside locus of change. Individual efforts and plans are important for removing impediments (such as distracting tension) or laying the groundwork for change to occur.

To continue, goal-directed and analytic striving is self-conscious when one attempts to monitor and control one's own thoughts, feelings, and behaviors. Our catalog of relaxation states (particularly those related to passive engagement) may display a pattern of decreasing self-conscious effort. In tension-relief, self-conscious attempts to monitor and moderate strain, fatigue, pain, frustration, conflict, and threat lessen, and one feels "restored" and "refreshed," ready to face the world. In the factor state Aware, one can attend to the world with "clear" "focus." With fewer self-conscious concerns about personal weaknesses and doubts about the ability to grow in relaxation, one feels "strengthened," "energized," and "confident," ready for enhanced awareness. In the factor state Prayerful, the relaxer experiences the world with diminished distraction from personal concerns and enhanced "selfless" and "reverent" attention to external stimuli. He or she is more likely to report feeling "blessed," "loved," and "thankful." Such joyful states are seen as implying a source, resource, or strength outside of or beyond oneself that further reduces the need for self-conscious effort. In sum, as one becomes passively engaged, distracting self-conscious preoccupation lessens, and one becomes increasingly aware of a greater world. A personal philosophy of passive engagement must somehow make sense of this transcendent shift.

Clients often share deeply felt words about their experience of relaxation, words that go beyond tension reduction. They may describe a rainbow of personal philosophies about the source of joyful feelings and speak of "God," "the Void," "the flow of the present," "the creative unconscious," "the inner spirit," "the remarkable fact of being alive," or perhaps "the wonderful mystery of it all." I propose that for some, perhaps all, such philosophies can contribute substantially to growth and generalization of relaxation. (pp. 87–88)

The paradox of passivity has two elements: (1) the less one engages in deliberate, planful, and discursive effort, the better a relaxation technique works; and (2) the deeper rewards of relaxation, the most pleasurable and meaningful R-States often imply a source, resource, or strength outside of or beyond oneself that works best when one reduces self-conscious effort.

IDENTIFYING BASIC R-BELIEFS

What beliefs are associated with relaxation? First, it is useful to make a distinction. Many researchers have cataloged beliefs that may facilitate coping with external stressors and challenges (Smith, 1990). These include:

Active coping. Actively attempting to remove or circumvent a stressful situation, or ameliorate its effects. Techniques include taking direct action, increasing effort, and executing a coping plan in reasonable steps.

Planning. Thinking through how one will cope. This involves generating strategies and selecting and deciding how to implement steps.

Confrontational coping. Standing one's ground, assertively seeking to meet one's needs and wishes, and actively attempting to change the behavior of others.

Suppression of competing activities. Putting other projects aside, trying to avoid becoming distracted by other events, even letting other things slide, if necessary, in order to deal with the stressor.

Self-control. Trying to keep one's feelings to oneself.

Restraint coping. Waiting until an appropriate opportunity to act presents itself, holding oneself back, and not acting prematurely.

Search for social support for instrumental reasons. Seeking advice, assistance, or information for help in coping with a stressor.

It is important to recognize that R-Beliefs reflect ways of coping with the *task of relaxation*, not with external stressors. The R-Belief "forget your problems for now" may well facilitate the process of sustained, passive, simple focus in a relaxation session but prove disastrous when applied to external stressors (and, for example, prompt one not to get out of the way of an approaching train).

EIGHT R-BELIEFS

What is the universe of R-Beliefs, as distinct from that of coping beliefs? Various religions and schools of philosophy and psychology tend to approach this question dogmatically by referring to the unchallenged wisdom of an established expert and guide. As with R-States, my approach is to look at the evidence. What are the actual beliefs practitioners display when they relax successfully?

I began exploring this question about 15 years ago by simply asking relaxation trainees to describe any personal beliefs and philosophies they have that help them relax. I also asked student relaxation trainers to ask their trainees the same question, and report to me. Eventually, I accumulated something of a master list of R-Beliefs, gathered from over 1,000 trainees of progressive muscle relaxation (PMR), autogenic training, breathing relaxation, yoga stretching, imagery, and meditation. The initial list of 34 beliefs is presented in Table 6.2. I then followed a strategy similar to that used in identifying R-States and, with the assistance of students and colleagues, performed several factor analyses on various tentative item lists. After each analysis, items were deleted or added (see Appendix B). This effort culminated in two studies (Mui, in press) on a combined and diverse sample of 1,663 participants. We found and replicated a clear and meaningful pattern of eight R-Beliefs:

OPTIMISM: Viewing the world with optimism
> I'm optimistic about how well I will deal with my current hassles.
> I believe in being optimistic.

ACCEPTANCE: Accepting things the way they are
> I can accept things as they are.
> There's no need to try to change what can't be changed.

HONESTY: Being honest with oneself and others
> I believe in being direct and clear in what I say, think, and do.
> I believe in being honest and open with my feelings.

TAKING IT EASY: Knowing when to let go and take it easy
> Sometimes it is important to simply take it easy.
> It is important to know when to stop trying, let go, and relax.

LOVE: Relating to others with love and compassion
> It is important to love and respect others.
> It is important to treat people with compassion and understanding.

INNER WISDOM: Trusting the healing wisdom of the body
> I trust the body's wisdom and healing powers.
> There are sources of strength and healing deep within me.

GOD: Trusting God's love and guidance
> God guides, loves, and comforts me.
> I put myself in God's hands.

DEEPER PERSPECTIVE: Putting one's concerns in deeper perspective
Life has a purpose greater than my personal wants and desires.
There's more to life than my personal concerns and worries.

R-Beliefs have a number of characteristics. First, they are *integrative* and provide a rationale for their connection to each other and to R-States ("I believe in being loving and compassionate. This requires that I be

TABLE 6.2   Initial Catalog of Reported Relaxation Beliefs

At the deepest level "I feel at peace with myself—I am an OK person."
Let go of that which cannot be changed.
My concerns seem less urgent when seen in true perspective.
There is more to life than my worries and problems.
God loves me and has a plan for my life.
I trust that things will work out OK.
Inside, I am a beautiful person.
My desires are not as urgent as I sometimes feel.
Not everything is my responsibility.
I am just an actor in the larger game of life.
I accept myself as I am.
It is good for me to let go and relax.
I am on earth to enjoy the gift of life.
Live with things as they are, even if they are not exactly as I desire.
Life's meaning becomes more apparent to me in the quiet of relaxation.
I need not strive so much for perfection.
Enjoy deeply every moment.
Live simply.
Selfish worries distract from a deeper reality.
Do not worry about things that cannot be changed.
Let the healing forces of life within do their work.
Live one day at a time.
God's will be done.
I need not dwell on the past.
There are more important things than my everyday hassles.
Let answers come from deep within.
If it is meant to be, it will happen.
In time, my troubles will pass.
Be open to my feelings.
It is OK if I do not get exactly what I want.
Love is what really matters.
Be not too concerned with things that do not matter.
I can accept that I am not in control of some things in my life.
It is good to be alive.

honest with myself and others. These beliefs give me peace and joy"). R-Beliefs are *modular*; any number can be combined in any way. Both R-Beliefs and R-States are *interpotentiating*. To elaborate, a client may well evoke feelings of Mental Relaxation ("at ease, at peace") and Mental Quiet ("mental stillness") by practicing a specific relaxation technique. In this state of mind, he or she may find it easier to contemplate and possibly decide to accept a philosophy of acceptance. Conversely, a client may be strongly committed to a philosophy of love. This may increase the probability of actually experiencing the R-State Love and Thankfulness in relaxation. R-Beliefs *enhance generalization*, enabling the practitioner to extend the benefits of the relaxation session to life at large. R-Beliefs are *motivating*, facilitating regular practice. R-Beliefs may provide a rationale for putting aside potentially disruptive distraction and continuing practice and may offer insight as to the overall direction in which relaxation may proceed. Finally, we have seen that R-Attitudes and R-Beliefs form *"umbrellas of abstraction,"* with more abstract notions covering or encompassing those that are more concrete. This umbrella-like quality has important implications for relaxation training. One could identify, challenge, or encourage specific thoughts. However, it would be much more efficient to consider the abstract attitudes and beliefs such thoughts reflect. Once an abstract attitude or belief is changed, then subordinate thoughts are more likely to follow suit.

We can see how R-Beliefs can function in the following hypothetical internal dialogues of relaxers.

Internal dialogue (a practitioner of yoga stretching): "I want my yoga to produce immediate effects. I am impatient with how slow it seems to be working. However, I realize it takes time. Everyone grows at their own pace. I'll just have to accept things as they are and continue practicing."

Discussion (R-Belief: Accept things as they are): Articulation of this belief enabled the practitioner to put his frustration aside and continue.

Internal dialogue (a practitioner of imagery): "I chose as my relaxation image a peaceful vacation with my two small children. I forget my everyday hassles and pains and attend, filled with feelings of love."

Discussion (R-Belief: Love and respect others): This belief provides the motivation to continue attending to the object of attention. The R-State Love facilitates sustained attention.

Internal dialogue (a skin cancer patient practitioner of autogenic training): "I think the phrase 'warmth and healing' flowing to my tumor, I feel warm and healing blood flowing to my tumor. Let the healing powers do their work."

Discussion (R-Belief: Trust the healing powers of the body): Provides rationale for proceeding with relaxation exercise.

Internal dialogue (a client receiving a massage): "It makes no sense to think about work during my massage session. Sometimes it is important just to take time for relaxation and enjoy myself."

Discussion (R-Belief: Know when to let go and take it easy): Enables client to put aside distracting thoughts and let go of muscle tension.

Internal dialogue (a client practicing a series of breathing exercises before an interview): "I can't keep my mind on breathing slowly and deeply. I keep thinking about my upcoming interview. I have prepared for this interview and will do the best I can. I'm optimistic about how I will deal with this challenge. I can now put this thought aside and relax."

Discussion (View the world with optimism): Optimistic appraisal of distracting concern about a future challenge facilitates putting distracting thought aside and focusing on the relaxation exercise.

Internal dialogue (same client above, not so sure about readiness for upcoming interview): "I keep thinking about my interview and can't relax. I need to relax for the next 20 minutes. This time is for relaxation; there is nothing I can do about my interview for the next 20 minutes. So I can put this thought aside temporarily."

Discussion (Accept the world as it is): Even though client is unsure of how well she will do on her interview, she successfully compartmentalizes concern about the interview so that she can relax for the duration of the relaxation session.

Internal dialogue (a client engaged in prayer): "Very worried about my life situation, I do my nightly prayer. At first I find myself hoping for an instant solution to my problems. When I decide to put myself in God's hands and trust His wisdom, I relax."

Discussion (Trust God's love and guidance): Belief in God enables client to put distracting concern aside.

Internal dialogue (a student of meditation): "My daily routine is ultimately less important when seen in deeper perspective. I feel deeply at peace when I attend to the night sky above and realize that I am part of a larger universe."

Discussion (Put your concerns in deeper perspective): Provides a rationale for putting distraction aside (distractions are less important) and meditating on the night sky; cultivates an R-State (timeless) that supports sustained focus.

A CLOSING WORD:
RELAXATION PROFESSIONALS AND
RELAXATION PREACHERS

Doubtless many relaxation trainers politely ignore the thoughtful abstract ruminations of their clients. Others may be tempted to subtly challenge philosophical ideas that emerge in treatment. But clients have important thoughts about the implications of relaxation. We serve our clients best when we listen to what they have to say.

I would like to close with a personal thought. The proper goal of a relaxation professional is to help clients rethink attitudes that may interfere with relaxation and articulate beliefs that may support relaxation. Once trainers promote their own personal philosophies, they abandon the role of relaxation professional and take on the role of a relaxation preacher. Unfortunately, there are many such preachers cloaked as professionals. Perhaps a true test of professionalism occurs when a trainer helps a client develop R-Beliefs that may be contrary to his or her own. Put very simply, an appropriately professional Christian relaxation trainer helps an atheist client become a better and more relaxed atheist. An atheist relaxation professional helps a Christian be a better and more relaxed Christian. Buddhists help Moslems become better Moslems, Moslems help Buddhists become better Buddhists, Jungians help Jews, Jews help Jungians, New Agers help fundamentalists, and fundamentalists help New Agers. You serve a useful and helpful role as relaxation professional by helping clients discover their own beliefs. You become a relaxation preacher when you promote your own beliefs.

TABLE 6.1 Initial Listing of Relaxation Attitudes (R-Attitudes)

N	Item
59	"I do not have time."
43	"There are so many techniques; I wouldn't know where to start."
40	"I don't have the money."
36	"I might be distracted by other things to do."
34	"It takes effort, not relaxation, to solve my problems."
33	"I'll try relaxation later."
32	"I have other more important things to do."
31	"I have an active lifestyle; relaxation doesn't fit."
30	"I'm the type of person who wants quick answers."
30	"I might not take it seriously enough."
30	"I'll practice relaxation only when I need to (whenever I'm stressed)."
30	"I forget to practice."
27	"I am too lazy to practice these techniques."
26	"I'm too impatient for relaxation techniques; I want quick results."
25	"I can't concentrate enough for relaxation techniques to work."
25	"I find it hard to put relaxation to use in everyday life."
24	"I'm an 'in control, take charge' type of person."
22	"I am concerned I would not be particularly good at relaxation."
21	"I don't like others controlling my mind."
20	"Some stress is good and actually helps me be my best."
19	"I already know how to relax."
19	"I might feel less energetic the rest of the day."
19	"I am concerned relaxation just won't work for me."
18	"I can't find a private or quiet place to relax."
17	"I might get too lazy or passive."
17	"I might feel anxious."
16	"Relaxation will just make me drowsy the rest of the day."
16	"I might experience things I don't understand."
16	"I can't slow down enough for these techniques to work."
16	"Relaxation is useful only when you are nervous or tense."
16	"I don't have the discipline to practice."
14	"I might become too sensitive to my problems."
13	"I might slow down too much."
13	"Relaxation might distract me from more important things."
13	"Relaxation techniques might be boring."
13	"I might start sleeping too much."
12	"Relaxation effects are too slow, and I need something quick."
11	"I don't really trust those who teach relaxation."
10	"I might lose touch with reality."
10	"The effects of relaxation are superficial or temporary."
10	"I might get lost in my fantasies."
10	"I might become more aware of my problems."

(continued)

TABLE 6.1 *(continued)*

N	Item
9	"I might withdraw."
9	"My relaxation trainer may not tailor relaxation techniques to me."
9	"If I relax too much, I might leave my problems unsolved."
9	"My relaxation trainer may not be qualified."
8	"Relaxation techniques are just a fad."
8	"I might have strange (or uncomfortable) experiences."
8	"I might become somewhat addicted to relaxation."
8	"I might become too self-conscious."
8	"Other successful people I know don't need to practice these techniques."
7	"I might become indifferent and not care about things."
7	"I might become less effective at work or school."
7	"Relaxation is too much like daydreaming."
7	"I get uncomfortable when I practice a relaxation technique."
7	"Relaxation technique(s) do not work for me."
6	"It might interfere with my religion."
6	"I might have excessive sexual thoughts."
6	"I might lose some self-control."
6	"I might discover things I don't want to know."
6	"I am concerned about what others might think."
6	"My problems are too serious or complicated for relaxation techniques to have any value."
6	"My relaxation trainer may not pay enough attention to my concerns."
6	"I don't need to relax."
6	"I might spend less time at things that are important."
6	"Relaxation techniques take too much time."
6	"Relaxation is self-indulgence."
6	"The techniques are too difficult."
6	"I might find relaxation too pleasurable."
6	"Relaxation is a state that occurs naturally; there's nothing I can do to make it happen."
5	"No one really knows how to teach relaxation."
5	"My relaxation trainer may not teach me what is best for me."
5	"You have to be a little 'different' to do relaxation techniques."
5	"I might get depressed."
5	"I would be troubled by worries."
5	"I might spend too much time by myself."
5	"Relaxation instructions are too complicated."
5	"I might feel 'out of it.' "
5	"Relaxation techniques are only for those who have real problems."
5	"These are not appropriate Christian activities."
4	"Relaxation techniques require awkward postures or positions."

TABLE 6.1   *(continued)*

N	Item
4	"I am concerned about what people might think of me."
4	"Relaxation techniques might make my problem worse."
4	"I might have strange feelings."
4	"I'm not spiritually ready for relaxation."
4	"Practicing relaxation requires changes in diet or exercise habits."
4	"I might feel guilty if I practice relaxation."
4	"Relaxation is just knowing how to sleep, and I can do that."
3	"I might go into some sort of hypnotic state or trance."
3	"Relaxation techniques are mostly for religious or spiritual people."
3	"I might start taking drugs."
3	"It might weaken my religious faith."
3	"These techniques involve hypnosis or self-hypnosis."
3	"My relaxation trainer may not know when a technique isn't working."
3	"I might become forgetful."
3	"I might get 'high.' "
3	"I might have sinful thoughts."
2	"This is not how God wants me to spend my time."
2	"I might become too detached."
2	"I might lose touch with my feelings."
2	"I associate relaxation with astrology and the occult."
2	"I might start eating more."
2	"Relaxation is associated with religions I do not believe in."
2	"All relaxation techniques are alike—if you tried one, you've tried them all."
1	"I might start drinking alcohol."
1	"Relaxation might interfere with my sleep."
1	"I might start smoking cigarettes."
1	"It is not a men's thing; it is more for women."
1	"My relaxation trainer may talk to me about his/her beliefs."
1	"I do not feel comfortable with people who do relaxation techniques."
0	"I might become more religious."
0	"I might uncover problems if I do relaxation techniques."
0	"I will practice relaxation once my other problems aren't interfering."
0	"I'm too old to practice these techniques."
0	"If you want to relax, it is better to go to a doctor or a psychologist."

Total N = 115
(39 males, 65 females, 11 not indicated; average age = 23.39, *sd* = 6.96)

7

The Wisdom of a Thousand Voices: Research Evidence

Years ago I began my studies with a simple question. "How do you feel when relaxed?" Quickly I discovered that the answer depended on whom you ask. Psychologists, for example, typically respond: "I feel an absence of tension and anxiety" or "My muscles are relaxed." In contrast, ordinary, everyday people give answers like this: "When I am truly relaxed I feel deeply at peace," "happy," "far, far away." At first this pattern amused me. Have those of us in the healing professions been jaded (perhaps stunted) by decades of school? However, the implications are serious; what health professionals are taught does not always correspond to what people experience.

"How do you feel when relaxed?" This, of course, is a question calling for evidence, not dogma. But there have been more than enough dogmatic answers: "You should feel the relaxation response," "You should feel the grace of God," "You should feel enlightened." Why not simply ask our clients for the answer, rather than tell them what we think the answer should be? To me, this is the first question of relaxation science.[1]

SHOULD WE BELIEVE OUR CLIENTS?

No writer likes to have his or her work rejected. However, rejection letters can be informative (as well as good lessons in humility). I recall the comments of one anonymous rejection letter from a noted relaxation journal. It went something like this: "So what? The author's relaxation participants are simply spouting back the cultural biases they have accumulated over the years." This brings into focus a philosophical question that may underlie the persistence of the reductionist relaxation response hypothesis. Which is more real: Polygraph measures of a client's physiological state or client self-report? And what is a self-report anyway—a mechanical regurgitation of a cultural bias?

First, all self-reports are real. Otherwise, we should tell our clients to remain silent. Therapists and counselors do not ignore client descriptions of love and sadness (waiting for a confirmative physiological printout). Love is more than a heartbeat, and sadness more than a tear.

I doubt if self-reports of relaxation are merely mechanical repetitions of cultural milieu. Most likely, clients assimilate a rich mix of ideas about relaxation from a variety of sources. Such ideas shape and color the experience of relaxation, indeed in ways that may differ from the single-theme perspectives of various relaxation texts and holy books. I suspect many priests, gurus, and relaxation experts would be surprised at what their followers actually believe. A client may say she believes in "accepting things that cannot be changed" and report feeling "at peace" in relaxation. Who knows where she got these ideas—perhaps a bit from Christianity, a bit from a wise Jewish uncle's advice, a bit from a TV special on Buddhism, and a bit from a favorite pop song. What is important is that the client has served as something of an ultimate processor of diverse information concerning relaxation. She has found what ideas work and how to put them to use. Her reports of R-States, Dispositions, Motivations, and Beliefs are the products of processes that are both exquisitely sophisticated and, above all, eminently practical.

It may seem that I am dwelling on the obvious. But it is important to remember that the vast majority of relaxation practitioners and researchers have been oblivious to the richness of relaxation self-report. Of the over 2,000 studies on relaxation, less than 1% have ever asked clients to report if and how they were actually relaxed. Those few studies that ask such questions have typically restricted their focus to a raised finger ("raise your finger if you are now relaxed"). Of the half million or so psychologists, social workers, counselors, and nurses who teach relaxation, few have been taught to listen with a refined ear. At best, relaxation textbooks advise us to ask if a client is successfully relaxed or is having any of a variety of practice-related difficulties (cramps, sleepiness, dizziness, etc.).

The perspective of this book puts self-report in a new light. By assessing the reports of actual relaxers, we are essentially examining the practical assimilations of diverse sources of information by many ultimate processors. This is the wisdom of a thousand voices.

ABC RELAXATION RESEARCH

This book represents the first comprehensive effort to assess the experience of relaxation. To date, 30 studies have been completed, involving at total of 6,000 participants and reflecting most major approaches to relaxation. Here are some highlights.

Assessing Relaxation

ABC Relaxation Theory suggests that the assessment of relaxation go beyond measurement of arousal during the training session, or symptom reduction when the session is over. Relaxation is a rich and complex task; we serve our clients best when we attempt to understand all facets of their journeys.

A client brings to a relaxation session a history of beliefs and experiences. For ABC relaxation, part of the task of training involves cognitive restructuring, that is, identifying, reinforcing, and reducing beliefs and attitudes when appropriate. To this end, I have developed two inventories, modestly named the Smith Relaxation Beliefs Inventory (SRBI), which taps beliefs supportive of relaxation, and the Smith Relaxation Attitudes Inventory (SRAI), which taps attitudes that interfere with relaxation.

Furthermore, most clients already know something about relaxation and have discovered R-States and casual activities they prefer. A skilled relaxation trainer can capitalize on this history by introducing formal techniques similar to what the client already knows, in terms of family of activity, level of sustained passive simple focus required, and R-States evoked. For example, a client may prefer the casual activities of dance and walking (movement/posture family activities), have little capacity to sustain passive simple focus, and report feelings of Strength and Awareness. Using behavioral shaping (beginning with easy, familiar versions of techniques), a trainer might begin with simple yoga stretching, an approach from the movement/posture family that appears to foster Strength and Awareness and (at simple levels) calls for little sustained passive simple focusing. Assessment of relaxation history can be assisted through my Smith Recalled Relaxation Activities Inventory (SRRAI), a test that asks clients to describe how they already relax, and what R-States they already experience.

It is also useful to know what R-States a client generally experiences and desires, and what outcomes he or she desires from relaxation. The Smith Relaxation Dispositions/Motivations Inventory (SRDMI) taps R-

States clients report experiencing at a dispositional (or "trait") level, in other words, how generally relaxed (on each R-State) a client is throughout the course of a two-week period. The same inventory measures a client's desire to experience more of any particular R-State, his or her R-Motivations. Finally, the Smith Relaxation Concerns Inventory (SRCI) taps problems and goals clients most often identify as reasons for learning relaxation (managing pain, improving performance, etc.). Such reports of relaxation disposition and motivation can help a trainer tailor relaxation training.

Relaxation training has immediate and delayed reinforcements—short-term and long-term outcomes. A client during a session may experience rewarding reductions in stress and increments in specific R-States. These reinforcements can be assessed through the Smith Relaxation States Inventory (SRSI). In time, he or she may experience intermediate and long-term changes in all aspects of relaxation, including desired R-States (SRDMI), R-Dispositions (SRDMI), targeted problem concerns and goals (SRCI), attitudes resistant to relaxation (SRAI), beliefs supportive of relaxation (SRBI), and casual everyday activities that reinforce relaxation outside the practice session (SRRAI).

In sum, comprehensive understanding of relaxation must examine a variety of dimensions. As we shall see, relaxation research is beginning to provide insights as to how these variables are interrelated. (*See* Table 7.1 for a summary of all Smith Relaxation Inventories.)

TABLE 7.1 Smith Relaxation Inventory Series

Inventory	Target Behavior
SRRAI: Smith Recalled Relaxation Activity Inventory	Recalled description of one's "most rewarding and Effective" relaxation activity, and associated R-States
SRSI: Smith Relaxation States Inventory	Immediate, current R-States and stress
SRDMI: Smith Relaxation Dispositions/ Motivations Inventory	Long-term R-Dispositions and stress (R-States one generally displays over time); R-Motivations (R-States one desires)
SRBI: Smith Relaxation Beliefs Inventory	R-Beliefs: Beliefs associated with deeper and more generalized relaxation.
SRAI: Smith Relaxation Attitudes Inventory	R-Attitudes: attitudes that potentially interfere with or prevent the practice of relaxation.
SRCI: Smith Relaxation Concerns Inventory	R-Concerns, or problems and goals people generally treat with relaxation

Reported Prevalence of Relaxation Activities, Benefits, States, and Beliefs

How do people relax? Holmes, Ritchie, and Allen (in press) surveyed a total of 742 students from Chicago universities and junior colleges. People relax most often by listening to music, daydreaming, and taking showers. Somewhat less popular are walking, prayer, petting pets and children (see Table 7.2 at end of chapter).

People relax for many reasons. Smith (in press-b) asked 434 individuals to indicate all the benefits they experience when practicing their "most rewarding and effective form of relaxation and renewal." Most people (nearly 75%) relax to manage stress, particularly frustration, worry, anxiety, and depression (see Table 7.3 at end of chapter). Nearly half the sample relax to enhance sleep and health. Spiritual and psychological growth are the third most popular objectives, claimed by over a third. Principal components factor analysis with orthogonal varimax rotation revealed nine distinct benefit factors (see Table 7.4 at end of chapter). Five involved coping or dealing with various problems: Medical Benefits (preparing for and recovering from surgery and dental procedures, coping with medications), Substance Abuse, Psychological Distress, Sleep and Pain, Interpersonal Stress; four involved developing or enhancing various desired attributes: General Health, Creativity, Spirituality, and Athletics.

Examining our archival data base, I pulled tests from 2,237 individuals (college students) who indicated their R-States in relaxation, R-Dispositions, R-Motivations, and R-Beliefs. The most desired R-States are Joy, Strength and Awareness, and Mental Relaxation (which people generally would like to feel "somewhat more often"); next most popular are Physical Relaxation and Mental Quiet (which people would like to feel "a little more often"); least popular are Disengagement, Prayerfulness, and Sleepiness. What R-Dispositions, States, and Beliefs do people claim to already possess? Love and Thankfulness, Joy, and Strength and Awareness, Sleepiness, and Mental Relaxation are the most prevalent R-Dispositions. Less so are Physical Relaxation, Prayerfulness, Mental Quiet, and Disengagement. In their "most rewarding and effective" relaxation activity, people are generally most likely to report the R-States Mental Relaxation, Joy, and Strength and Awareness; somewhat less likely to report Love and Thankfulness and Prayerfulness; and least likely to report Sleepiness, Disengagement, and Physical Relaxation.

Finally, people are most likely to hold the R-Beliefs Love, Taking It Easy, and Honesty, less likely to believe in Deeper Perspective and Optimism, and least likely to believe in Inner Wisdom, God, and Acceptance. Interestingly, the R-Beliefs people report most often (Love, Taking It Easy, Honesty) are (as we shall see below) least associated with the R-States most desired (particularly Mental Relaxation and Strength and Awareness).

R-States, Dispositions, and Beliefs Associated with Relaxation Techniques and Activities

What R-States and R-Dispositions are associated with different relaxation activities? Smith, Amutio, Anderson, and Aria (1996) assessed 663 practitioners of massage, PMR, yoga stretching, breathing, imagery, meditation, and various combinations of these techniques. In all, 11 technique groups were examined, each with at least 20 participants (see Table 7.5 at end of chapter). Participants were asked to check R-States they experienced while practicing. (The R-State Mental Quiet was not assessed). Practitioners of PMR report low levels of Joy and high levels of Disengagement and Physical Relaxation. This suggests the appropriateness of PMR for targeting physical tension and for emotionally disturbed individuals prone to relaxation-induced anxiety (a topic we shall consider below). However, given the absence of strong intrinsic reinforcement, clients practicing PMR may have to be highly motivated, or the technique should be presented with considerable external support and encouragement.

Yoga stretching, breathing exercises, and meditation score high on the R-State Strength and Awareness. Such techniques may be most appropriate for individuals wanting to enhance work or school performance. All combinations of meditation score high on Prayerfulness, suggesting the appropriateness of such techniques for spiritual exploration and growth.

Ritchie, Holmes, and Ailen (in press) conducted a similar study that examined everyday passive relaxation pursuits. One hundred sixty-five participants were asked to describe the "most rewarding and effective" activity they had participated in for relaxation and renewal over the previous 2 weeks and then rate R-States they experienced during this activity. The R-State Mental Quiet was not assessed. (See Table 7.6 at end of chapter for listed activities.)

First, all activities appear to be equally effective in reducing stress. This is consistent with Benson's (1975) relaxation response hypothesis, that all techniques have the same impact in reducing arousal. However, dramatic technique differences emerge when we examine R-States. Consistent with what Smith, Amutio, Anderson, and Aria (1996) found, yoga is associated with the R-State Strength and Awareness. Numerous other patterns emerge (see Table 7.7 at end of chapter), providing clinicians with a rich set of simple, inexpensive suggestions for supplementing relaxation.

Finally, Smith (in press-a) examined practitioners of prayer ($N = 572$), yoga ($N = 33$), meditation (all forms, $N = 168$), some combination of prayer with meditation and/or yoga ($N = 23$), and those practicing no technique ($N = 839$). Those practicing a combination of yoga and meditation are physically relaxed, those who practice meditation are mentally relaxed, and practitioners of prayer report higher levels of Love and Thankfulness as well as Prayerfulness.

Beliefs can be organized according to whether they characterize practitioners of prayer, yoga/meditation, or both yoga/meditation and prayer. As previously noted, belief in God is most exclusively associated with Prayer. Belief in Taking It Easy is most associated with yoga/meditation. And belief in Deeper Perspective, Inner Wisdom, and Optimism is most likely to characterize practitioners of both Eastern and Western techniques.

Practice Variables and the Effects of Yoga, Meditation, and Prayer

Smith (in press-a) also found that those who believe in God ("God loves, guides, and comforts me," "I put myself in God's hands") and experience prayerfulness are more likely to regularly practice yoga, meditation, or prayer. In addition, those who believe in being honest with themselves and others ("I believe in being direct and clear in what I say, think, and do"; "I believe in being honest and open with my feelings") are more likely to practice yoga/meditation regularly. ABC Relaxation Theory predicts such an association between belief and pratice. This study suggests that belief in God may well enhance regularity of practice for a wide range of Western and Eastern techniques. An alternative motivating belief is personal honesty.

Smith, Rice, Cucci, and Williams (in press) assessed R-Dispositions of 119 practitioners of various combinations of yoga and meditation. Again, regularity of practice was the best predictor of relaxation, including lower levels of anxiety, depression, and muscle tension and higher scores on Disengagement, Mental Relaxation, Strength and Awareness, Joy, Love and Thankfulness, and Prayerfulness.

Smith et al. (in press) also found that the number of years in which one has practiced is associated with higher levels of relaxation (Mental

Relaxation, Strength and Awareness, Joy, Love and Thankfulness); however, these correlations disappear when adjusted for number of days practiced.

Finally, those who practice group yoga/meditation regularly in a group are less likely to report a desire for increased Strength and Awareness (Smith, in press-a). One might speculate that the motivations for those practicing individual and group variations of Eastern techniques differ; individual practice may be associated with personal goals of self-improvement, whereas group practice may be maintained by other reinforcements, perhaps affiliation. In addition, overall inspection of the results suggests that solitary practice of yoga/meditation, more than group practice, is associated with relaxation (dispositions and beliefs). In contrast, both solitary and group practice of prayer are associated with relaxation. Again, perhaps people practice yoga/meditation in groups for purposes other than relaxation.

R-Beliefs and Their Association with R-States, R-Dispositions, and R-Motivations

Using an archival sample of 981 individuals, Ghoncheh, Sparks, and Wasik (in press) examined the relationship between R-Beliefs, R States, R-Dispositions, and R-Motivations (See Tables 7.8–7.10 at end of chapter). Generally, all R-Beliefs predict higher affective-energy R-States in one's preferred relaxation activity. That is, if one's goal is to evoke Sleepiness, Disengagement, or Physical Relaxation, it appears not to matter much what one believes. Beliefs become increasingly important as the level of abstraction of R-States increases from Mental Relaxation to Strength and Awareness and from Joy to Love and Thankfulness and Prayerfulness.

Belief in Taking It Easy and Honesty

R-Beliefs Taking It Easy and Honesty correlate negatively with R-Dispositions Mental Quiet and Disengagement. Those who believe in the importance of Taking It Easy score higher in R-Motivations Mental Relaxation, Disengagement, and Mental Quiet; in contrast, those who believe in Honesty show no such pattern. This suggests that those believing in Honesty are content with their low levels of Mental Quiet and Disengagement; in contrast, those who believe in Taking It Easy, although they may also display low levels of Disengagement and Mental Quiet, also want more (including more Mental Relaxation).

Those who believe in Honesty, Taking It Easy, and Acceptance express no particular desire for more Prayerfulness; in contrast, those who believe in Deeper Perspective, God, Inner Wisdom, and Love want more Prayerfulness in life. Individuals with such beliefs may benefit from relaxation taught in a religious or spiritual context (prayer groups at temple, synagogue, or church; yoga or meditation retreats that have a spiritual focus). However, as we shall see, possession of some spiritual beliefs in itself may be no guarantee of deeper relaxation.

Belief in Love, Acceptance, and Understanding

Those who believe in Love are neither particularly relaxed nor emotionally disturbed; yet they desire more of just about every R-State (except Sleepiness and Disengagement). One might speculate that continued dedication to others can have its personal costs. Such self-sacrificing individuals may yearn to relax but resist doing so because of a perception that relaxation might be incompatible with such efforts.

Acceptance, Optimism, Inner Wisdom, and Belief in God

Belief in God (specifically belief that God guides, loves, and comforts one, and putting oneself in God's hands) appears to enhance the immediate state effects that occur while one is practicing a specific relaxation technique. Specifically, Belief in God appears to enable one to feel, at least temporarily, Strength and Awareness, Joy, Love and Thankfulness, and Prayerfulness. However, just about any other relaxation belief will have the same effect. Put differently, deeply positive relaxation states can be experienced by atheists who hold such diverse beliefs as (1) seeing one's problems in deeper perspective; (2) trusting in inner wisdom; (3) knowing when to take it easy; (4) being honest, direct, and clear in one's words, feelings, thoughts, and actions; (5) relating to others with understanding, love, respect, and compassion; (6) accepting that the world is as it is and cannot change; and (7) being optimistic in general and about specific current hassles.

The immediate R-State effects of relaxation can be viewed as intense short-term reinforcements to practice, which may have positive and negative implications. For a relaxation trainer who wishes to maintain regularity of practice by introducing strong immediate reinforcement, cultivation of some, indeed just about any, relaxation belief (preferably the client's own) is a reasonable option. Unfortunately, less than scrupulous leaders of relaxation-based cults, pseudotherapies, or religious groups can also cultivate regularity of practice and by implication, commitment to their approach, through manipulation of R-Beliefs. However, if one's objective is to go beyond short-term state effects, and enhance a generalized life of relaxation, our research has something else to say.

This may pose a challenge for the devout: belief in God is not correlated with one's propensity to experience the three relaxation dispositions people want most: Mental Relaxation, Strength and Awareness, and Joy. This is worth repeating and spelling out in detail: belief in God, in and of itself, has no relationship to one's general propensity to feel

- at peace, at ease, and mentally relaxed
- energized, strengthened, and confident
- focused, clear, aware
- happy and joyful

Belief in God, along with trust in the body's wisdom and healing powers and belief in sources of strength and healing deep within, do, however, have one general dispositional effect: they are associated with increased feelings of prayerfulness, spirituality, and reverence throughout the week.

What may be particularly challenging to much of conventional wisdom is that three secular personal beliefs do correlate with the R-Dispositions people want most: (1) accepting things as they are, not trying to change what cannot be changed; (2) maintaining optimism, both in general and about one's ability to deal with current hassles; and (3) believing in and trusting sources of wisdom, strength, and healing deep within onself.

Another way of looking at R-Beliefs is to examine which predict the most desired R-States—high affective anergy, low abstractness states of Mental Relaxation, Strength and Awareness, and Joy. Ghoncheh, Sparks, and Wasik (in press) found that combination scores of these three preferred R-States were predicted by a combination of belief in Optimism, Inner Wisdom, and Acceptance (Adjusted $R^2 = .208$).

Some might think that belief in God, specifically "putting oneself in God's hands" or "trusting God's love, guidance, and comfort" might automatically confer "acceptance of things that cannot change" or "optimism concerning how well one can deal with current hassles," and perhaps even trust in inner wisdom and strength. This may not be the case. Many devout believers are tense individuals, and many tense individuals use their beliefs maladaptively. And perhaps some religious teachings increase tension and anxiety or negate acceptance, optimism, and trust in inner wisdom. Whatever the case, counselors, both pastoral and otherwise, working with a devout client should consider whether their clients' religious beliefs support acceptance, optimism, and trust in inner wisdom, perhaps reinforced by feelings of prayerfulness associated with the practice of relaxation. Conversely, if a client does not believe in God, then conversion to a religious belief system is no guarantee of increased relaxation. A more appropriate goal would be to accept a client's lack of belief and focus on cultivating a sense of acceptance and optimism consistent with this lack of belief.

Finally, there may well be some religious beliefs we have not explored that are associated with dispositional Mental Relaxation, Strength and Awareness, and Joy. However, the theistic belief statements we have identified correlate very highly (in the high .80's) with every other theistic statement we have investigated. Indeed, factor analyses consistently show our theistic statements to have the highest loading. See Appendix B. Or possibly simple verbal claims of God-related beliefs are not enough to maintain long-term relaxation; perhaps such claims must expressed in some sort of action. See Tables 7.8–7.10 for R-Belief correlations.

MetaModels of R-States

ABC Relaxation Theory offers two ways of organizing R-States. The cycle of renewal proposes that relaxation states reflect withdawal (Sleepiness, Disengagement, Mental Quiet), recovery (Physical Relaxation, Mental Relaxation), and opening up (Strength and Awareness, Joy, Love and Thankfulness, and Prayerfulness). The 2 × 2-factor model specificies affective energy and abstractness as the primary differentiating dimensions. Low-affective-energy R- States include Sleepiness, Disengagement, Physical Relaxation, and Mental Quiet; and states characterized by high affective energy include Mental Relaxation, Strength and Awareness, Joy, Love and Thankfulness, and Prayerfulness. Superimposed on affective energy is a dimension of concreteness/abstractness; concrete states include Sleepiness, Disengagement, Physical Relaxation, Mental Relaxation, and Strength and Awareness; abstract R-States include Mental Quiet, Love and Thankfulness, and Prayerfulness.

I examined data from 1,309 participants, drawn from seven separate studies in Smith (in press) and subjected R-States, rather than individual idems, to factor analysis. Results yielded 2 factors, one defined by Sleepiness, Disengagement, and Physical Relaxation, and the other by Mental Relaxation, Strength and Awareness, Joy, Love and Thankfulness, and Prayerfulness (Mental Quiet was not included). This is strongly consistent with the 2 × 2 factor model. When R-States are forced into three factors, results are consistent with the 2 × 2 model rather than the withdrawal–recovery–opening up model, with Love and Thankfulness and Prayerfulness merging as high-abstractness, high-affective-energy states, and Mental Relaxation, Strength and Awareness, and Joy merging as low abstractness, high-affective-energy states. In conclusion, the withdrawal–recovery–opening up model may well prove to be useful for understanding the physiological effects of relaxation. It may provide a loose understanding of the overlapping effects of R-States. However, the 2 × 2 Abstractness × Affective Energy model appears to reflect more precisely the actual content of R-States. See Tables 7.11–7.24.

TABLE 7.11   Two R-State Factors: Smith et al.[a] Data

	1	2
Joy	.889	.005
Love and Thankfulness	.801	.002
Mental Relaxation	.764	.317
Prayerfulness	.620	−.001
Strength and Awareness	.677	.148
Physical Relaxation	.002	.867
Disengagement	.159	.836

Eigenvalues and total % of variance accounted for: Factor 1 = 2.969, 42.277; Factor 2 = 1.072, 57.588.
37 males, 71 females, mean age = 41.52, SD = 15.658.
[a]In press.

TABLE 7.12   Two R-State Factors: Leslie and Clavin[a] Data

	1	2
Joy	.896	.158
Love and Thankfulness	.871	.161
Strength and Awareness	.822	−.005
Mental Relaxation	.810	.138
Prayerfulness	.765	.169
Physical Relaxation	.147	.837
Disengagement	.007	.822

Factor 1 = 3.369, 48.130; Factor 2 = 1.279, 66.398.
43 males, 63 females, mean age = 37.38, SD = 12.06.
[a]In press.

TABLE 7.13   Two R-State Factors: Sohnle[a] Data

	1	2
Love and Thankfulness	.787	.001
Strength and Awareness	.675	−.288
Prayerfulness	.689	.001
Joy	.670	−.212
Mental Relaxation	.590	.108
Physical Relaxation	.136	.781
Sleepiness	−.128	.769
Disengagement	−.010	.731

Factor 1 = 2.497, 31.207; Factor 2 = 1.744, 53.003.
72 males, 149 females, mean age = 26.347, *SD* = 9.013.
[a]In press.

TABLE 7.14   Two R-State Factors: Anderson[a] Data

	1	2
Love and Thankfulness	.884	.009
Joy	.814	−.003
Prayerfulness	.806	.118
Strength and Awareness	.753	−.258
Mental Relaxation	.494	.193
Physical Relaxation	.009	.792
Sleepiness	−.002	.750
Disengagement	.004	.750

Factor 1 = 2.820, 36.497; Factor 2 = 1.735, 58.179.
60 males, 94 females, mean age = 23.801, *SD* = 8.754.
[a]In press.

Gender Differences

Gender differences are rarely discovered in relaxation research. However, Smith, Rice, Cucci, and Williams (in press), in a previously mentioned study of yoga and meditation, found that males practice more regularly than females do and more times a day. Males also display lower levels of dispositional anxiety, depression, and muscle tension and higher levels of dispositional Disengagement, Physical Relaxation, Mental Relaxation, and Strength and Awareness. Several interpretations come to mind. For whatever reason, it may take a greater level of motivation for males to attend a yoga and meditation training program than is necessary for

TABLE 7.15   Two R-State Factors: Holmes et al.[a] Grouped Data

	1	2
Love and Thankfulness	.824	.005
Prayerfulness	.758	.174
Strength and Awareness	.756	−.175
Joy	.752	−.006
Mental Relaxation	.634	.146
Physical Relaxation	.003	.805
Disengagement	.115	.800
Sleepiness	−.009	.754

Factor 1 = 2.907, 36.342; Factor 2 = 1.911, 60.288.
125 males, 288 females, 1 no response; mean age = 30.298, *SD* = 12.580.
[a]In press.
[b]Questionnaire items were listed in groups reflecting this sequence of R-States: Disengagement, Physical Relaxation, Mental Relaxation, Strength and Awareness, Joy, Love and Thankfulness, and Prayerfulness.

TABLE 7.16   Two R-State Factors: Holmes et al.[a] Randomized Data

	1	2
Love and Thankfulness	.794	.009
Strength and Awareness	.755	−.183
Joy	.734	−.163
Prayerfulness	.695	.004
Mental Relaxation	.486	.158
Physical Relaxation	.115	.791
Disengagement	−.002	.756
Sleepiness	−.159	.741

Factor 1 = 2.539, 31.736; Factor 2 = 1.790, 54.11.
95 males, 195 females, 11 no response; mean age = 28.576, *SD* = 11.345.
[a]In press.
[b]Six versions of the test questionnaire were distributed, each using a different random order of items.

females. Males may lack the time for extramural training. Perhaps there is a social stigma associated with males learning yoga and meditation. Select, highly motivated males may be predisposed to experience reinforcements associated with yoga and meditation, specifically feeling reduced stress and greater levels of Physical and Mental Relaxation.

Bowers, Darner, and Goldner (in press) also examined gender differences in relaxation and R-Dispositions, as well as in R-Motivations and

TABLE 7.17   Two R-State Factors: Mui[a] Combined Data

	1	2
Strength and Awareness	.848	−.130
Mental Relaxation	.784	.002
Joy	.782	.008
Love and Thankfulness	.704	.202
Physical Relaxation	.559	.292
Prayerfulness	.401	.343
Sleepiness	−.205	.832
Disengagement	.333	.493

Factor 1 = 3.155, 39.434; Factor 2 = 1.115, 53.369.
197 males, 279 females, 5 no response; mean age = 22.773, SD = 7.939.
[a]In press.

TABLE 7.18   Three R-State Factors: Leslie and Clavin[a] Data

	1	2	3
Joy	.897	.132	−.005
Love and Thankfulness	.869	.299	−.008
Strength and Awareness	.826	−.310	.251
Mental Relaxation	.811	.001	.177
Prayerfulness	.764	.276	−.005
Physical Relaxation	.146	.870	.302
Disengagement	.008	.251	.924

Eigenvalues and cumulative % variance accounted for: Factor 1 = 3.708, 52.970; Factor 2 = 1.276,
71.203; Factor 3 = 683, 80.957.
[a]In press.

R-Beliefs. Again, males appear to be more relaxed and score higher on Mental Relaxation, Strength and Awareness, Mental Quiet, Physical Relaxation, and Disengagement; females score slightly higher on Love and Thankfulness. When considering R-Motivations, females desire more of all R-States except Sleepiness. Interestingly, females score higher on such R-Beliefs as Deeper Perspective, Belief in God, Belief in Love, and Honesty but not higher on R-Beliefs associated with Mental Relaxation, Strength and Awareness, and Joy (R-Beliefs Acceptance, Optimism, Inner Wisdom). In sum, males are more relaxed but do not appear more likely to desire or hold beliefs conducive to increased relaxation. Females are less relaxed and appear to hold beliefs conducive to some R-States (Love

TABLE 7.19   Three R-State Factors: Smith et al.[a] Data

	1	2	3
Mental Relaxation	.822	.250	.180
Joy	.814	.008	.392
Strength and Awareness	.796	.007	.005
Physical Relaxation	.010	.880	.005
Disengagement	.212	.827	.003
Prayerfulness	.110	.006	.910
Love and Thankfulness	.501	.003	.675

Eigenvalues and cumulative % variance accounted for: Factor 1 = 3.082, 44.034; Factor 2 = 1.337, 63.713; Factor 3 = .826, 75.509.
[a]In press.

TABLE 7.20   Three R-State Factors: Sohnle[a] Data

	1	2	3
Physical Relaxation	.800	.301	−.113
Sleepiness	.755	−.164	−.001
Disengagement	.719	−.218	.009
Mental Relaxation	.137	.757	.008
Joy	−.192	.710	.231
Strength and Awareness	−.279	.597	.007
Prayerfulness	.002	.009	.890
Love and Thankfulness	−.008	.323	.796

Eigenvalues and cumulative % variance accounted for: Factor 1 = 2.512, 31.395; Factor 2 = 1.744, 53.199; Factor 3 = .956, 65.148.
[a]In press.

and Thankfulness and Prayerfulness) but not others (Mental Relaxation, Strength and Awareness, and Joy).

The fact that Bowers, Darner, and Goldner (in press) found higher levels of R-Dispositions among males, including those not practicing yoga or meditation, appears to be inconsistent with the motivated self-selection hypothesis previously offered. Indeed, if anything, females appear to be more motivated to learn relaxation. Perhaps females, because of their positive beliefs and motivations about relaxation, are sensitized to possible deficiencies in R-Dispositions. Males, not valuing relaxation as much, may simply not recognize the R-Dispositions they may lack. Hopefully future research will help illuminate this puzzling and complex pattern of gender differences.

TABLE 7.21   Three R-State Factors: Anderson[a] Data

	1	2	3
Love and Thankfulness	.902	.108	.003
Prayerfulness	.851	.128	−.008
Joy	.791	−.001	.195
Strength and Awareness	.717	−.235	.263
Physical Relaxation	.003	.800	.148
Sleepiness	−.007	.755	.009
Disengagement	.152	.626	−.490
Mental Relaxation	.282	.237	.845

Eigenvalues and cumulative % variance accounted for: Factor 1 = 2.930, 36.623; Factor 2 = 1.719, 58.111; Factor 3 = .975, 70.294.
[a]In press.

TABLE 7.22   Three R-State Factors: Holmes et al.[a] Grouped Data

	1	2	3
Physical Relaxation	.812	−.109	.165
Disengagement	.798	.132	.003
Sleepiness	.749	.006	−.177
Prayerfulness	.007	.892	.156
Love and Thankfulness	.005	.848	.300
Mental Relaxation	.164	.008	.841
Strength and Awareness	−.166	.353	.729
Joy	−.005	.473	.595

Eigenvalues and cumulative % variance accounted for: Factor 1 = 2.824, 35.303; Factor 2 = 1.914, 59.230; Factor 3 = .852, 69.882.
[a]In press.

Cultural, Educational, and Religious Differences

Smith, McDuffie, Ritchie, Holmes, and Anderson (in press) examined R-Dispositions and R-Beliefs reported by African Americans (N = 71), Whites (136), Hispanics (24), and Asian Americans (12). Blacks and Hispanics score higher than Whites in the R-Disposition Love and Thankfulness. Blacks and Hispanics score higher than Whites and Asians in dispositional Prayerfulness as well as Belief in God.

    Level of education is not particularly associated with relaxation. Smith, McDuffie, Ritchie, Holmes, and Anderson (in press) examined individuals who finished high school ($N = 20$), completed some undergraduate college

TABLE 7.23   Three R-State Factors: Holmes et al.[a] Randomized Data

	1	2	3
Love and Thankfulness	.862	.004	.005
Prayerfulness	.779	.008	−.102
Strength and Awareness	.697	−.180	.009
Joy	.610	−.127	.371
Physical Relaxation	.008	.753	.006
Disengagement	−.003	.753	.006
Sleepiness	−.125	.747	−.104
Mental Relaxation	.123	.009	.931

Eigenvalues and cumulative % variance accounted for: Factor 1 = 2.478, 30.970; Factor 2 = 1.791, 53.358; Factor 3 = .91,; 64.753.
[a]In press.

TABLE 7.24   Three R-State Factors: Mui[a] Combined Data

	1	2	3
Love and Thankfulness	.849	.006	.008
Joy	.730	.294	−.130
Strength and Awareness	.675	.355	−.393
Prayerfulness	.611	−.001	.311
Mental Relaxation	.574	.483	−.269
Disengagement	.001	.828	.162
Physical Relaxation	.274	.695	−.003
Sleepiness	.003	.102	.872

Factor 1 = 3.155, 39.434; Factor 2 = 1.115, 53.369; Factor 3 = .985, 65.678.
[a]In press.

($N = 131$), received an undergraduate diploma ($N = 39$), or completed at least some graduate school ($N = 58$). The more education one has, the less likely one is to believe in God. Finally, after high school, increased education is associated with reduced belief in loving others. Different degrees of education are not associated with different levels of R-Dispositions.

Finally, these same researchers had enough data to compare Catholics (83), Protestants (20), Jews (11), and those who designated their religion as "None" (42). Catholics are more likely to feel Prayerful than are Jews and the Nonreligious. Catholics and Protestants are more likely to believe in God than Jews and the Nonreligious. Catholics and Protestants are more likely to believe in inner wisdom than are Jews. And Catholics are more likely to believe in taking it easy than are the nonreligious. Consistent with the findings of Ghoncheh, Sparks, and Wasik (in press), adherence to any particular religion or lack of religion is not associated with differences in R-Dispositions. Religious people are neither more nor less relaxed than the nonreligious.

Relaxation, Personality, and Psychopathology

Data from four independent samples, with a combined *N* of 981, clearly reveal that three R-States and Dispositions are consistently and strongly associated with reduced levels of somatic, cognitive, and emotional stress: Mental Relaxation (feeling "at peace," "at ease," "contented"), Strength and Awareness, and Joy (Smith, in press c). These are also the three R-States individuals most desire. We have already seen that these same three R-States are associated with R-Beliefs Optimism, Inner Wisdom, and Acceptance. I propose that a combination of R-States/Dispositions Mental Relaxation, Strength and Awareness, and Joy plus belief in Optimism, Inner Wisdom, and Acceptance define a pattern of *adaptive relaxation* associated with positive health.

Anderson (in press) offers evidence concerning the relationship between psychopathology and relaxation. She examined 157 individuals and found that those who display a wide range of psychological distress on the SCL-90-R report Disengaging during their "most rewarding and effective activity for relaxation and renewal." Specifically, those who report symptoms of Somatization, Obsessive-Compulsive disorder, Interpersonal Sensitivity, Depression, Anxiety, Hostility, Phobic Anxiety, and Paranoid Ideation claim they relax most effectively by pulling away from and becoming less aware of the world, that is, feeling "distant," "detached," and "indifferent."

Distressed individuals also report higher levels of worry and negative emotion during their preferred relaxation activity. Perhaps their Disengagement is a coping strategy for dealing with relaxation-induced anxiety (Heide & Borkovec, 1983). Consistent with this interpretation, Holmes, Ritchie, and Allen (in press) also found a correlation between Disengagement, Sleepiness, and stress symptoms during one's most rewarding and effective relaxation activity.

Leslie and Clavin (in press) examined 16 Personality Factor Questionnaire (16PF), relaxation session stress, and R-States for 124 college students. Those who are Emotionally Stable on the 16PF report fewer physical, cognitive, and emotional stress symptoms during relaxation, whereas those scoring high on Vigilance and Anxiety report more symptoms, suggesting that personality may well predict a propensity toward relaxation-induced anxiety.

Leslie and Clavin (in press) then divided Disengagement into self-reported feelings of distancing (feeling "far away," "distant") and indifference. Distancing is associated with both increased relaxation session stress and increased Physical Relaxation, Mental Relaxation, Strength and Awareness, and Joy. Consistently, Sohnle (in press), on a sample of 189, also found distancing to correlate with Preserving and Hesitating on the Millon Index of Personality Styles (MIPS). Perhaps distancing is an aspect of Disengagement that both reduces relaxation-induced anxiety and contributes to increased positive high affective energy relaxation states.

In contrast, individuals who report indifference in relaxation are not likely to report relaxation session stress or positive R-States; they, like distancing individuals, do appear to experience higher levels of Physical Relaxation. However, indifferent individuals also score higher on 16PF Abstractedness and lower on Emotional Stability. Sohnle (in press) found that those scoring high in indifference also score high on MIPS Dissenting. Indifference may be a dispositional variable, a global cognitive coping strategy deployed by abstracted individuals who display high levels of dispositional anxiety and lack the coping skills that define emotional stability. Such individuals may experience little relaxation-induced anxiety or little deep relaxation. ABC Relaxation Theory proposes that the emergence of N-States (relaxation-induced anxiety) and strong R-States are among the indicators that relaxation is working. If so, these findings may suggest that relaxation does not work well for indifferent, abstracted individuals who lack emotional stability and coping skills.

These studies bring into focus an important clinical question. Disturbed individuals appear to know how to disengage during relaxation. Disengagement is most associated with the relaxation technique preferred by psychologists, PMR (Smith et al., 1996). One could argue that psychologists are teaching troubled clients a relaxation skill they do not need and missing skills they lack. Perhaps troubled clients would benefit more by learning to augment their capacity to disengage with skill at evoking Physical Relaxation, Mental Relaxation, Strength and Awareness, and Joy. If so, we should be teaching clients yoga, breathing exercises, imagery, prayer, and meditation (just about anything but PMR). Conversely, a case can be made that exclusive reliance on PMR is a good idea, enhancing strengths (such as Disengagement) disturbed individuals already have.

Disengagement may be an appropriate skill for those likely to experience relaxation-induced anxiety. This is a question for future research.

The Instruction of Relaxation

Khasky (1999) divided 114 participants into four groups and taught each a different technique: 25 minutes of PMR, yoga stretching, imagery, or a control task of reading popular magazines. A single session of imagery, a cognitive technique, appears to be more effective than yoga stretching, a somatic technique, in reducing self-reported negative affect, a cognitive dimension. PMR is more effective in reducing somatic symptoms. Both findings are consistent with Davidson and Schwartz's (1976) cognitive/somatic specificity hypothesis. However, imagery and yoga practitioners scored higher than control practitioners on self-reported Physical Relaxation, a finding not consistent with the specificity hypothesis. One might speculate that self-reports of Physical Relaxation (feeling "limp, loose, liquid," etc.) may have both a cognitive and somatic component, whereas negative affect may be more purely cognitive and self-reported somatic symptoms more purely somatic.

Consistent with what Anderson (in press) and Leslie and Clavin (in press) found, individuals who report feeling Disengagement displayed higher levels of negative affect (and to some extent, worry and somatic stress) as well as higher levels of self-reported Physical Relaxation (feeling "limp, loose" etc). Also, pre-posttest scores reveal that as individuals continue to Disengage in their practice session, stress decreases and relaxation increases. This is the pattern we would expect if Disengagement is a coping mechanism.

Bang (in press) examined the effects of ABC Relaxation Training on elderly Korean residents of a nursing home in Chicago. Twenty-two Korean nursing home residents were assigned to either a 2-week relaxation group or a no-treatment group. Relaxation training utilized the ABC approach of initially teaching PMR, autogenic training, breathing exercises, yoga stretching, imagery, and meditation. A composite 20-minute relaxation sequence was developed based on those exercises preferred by residents and practiced daily for 2 weeks. Compared with controls, relaxation participants displayed a significantly greater reduction in Beck Depression Inventory scores and greater increments in the R-States Sleepiness, Disengagement, Physical Relaxation, Joy, and Love and Thankfulness. In addition, posttest depression correlated negatively with Disengagement, Mental Relaxation, Joy, and Speechless. Contrary to what has been found in previous research, Disengagement correlated positively with Joy, suggesting that the relationships among R-States may be influenced by culture.

In a Korean study, Bang and Kim (1998) randomly assigned 60 college students with high trait anxiety on the Spielberger Anxiety Scale to a guided imagery, control, and no treatment group. The imagery group received five consecutive days of imagery, a 15 minute tape including seaside, forest, and stream imagery (following the suggestions of Smith, 1999). The control group also met in 15 minute sessions for five consecutive days, and did nothing. The imagery group displayed significant decreases in State anxiety. Multiple regression analysis revealed that increased Mental Relaxation, Joy, and Love and Thankfulness predict reduced anxiety.

NEW QUESTIONS

Clearly research on R-States, Dispositions, Motivations, and Beliefs has just begun. A number of questions come to mind.

- Do preexisting or changes in variables during relaxation predict clinical outcomes of relaxation therapy?
- Do relaxation variables emerge in any predictable order during the course of relaxation training? Are some prerequisite to others? For example, must one first feel Sleepiness before feeling Strengthened and Aware? Does Disengagement come before Mental Relaxation?
- What are the physiological correlates of various R-States, Dispositions, Motivations, and Beliefs? In considering this question, one must avoid the trap of reductionism and assume that, if a physiological variable does not correlate with a relaxation variable, then the physiological variable is somehow "less real."
- What are the comparative effects of the ABC approach to relaxation when compared with traditional single-modality training for PMR, yoga, meditation, and the like?
- To what extent can modifying R-Motivations, R-Beliefs, and R-Attitudes increase the success of relaxation training?
- What is the relationship between R-Beliefs and strategies for coping in everyday life? By definition, R-Beliefs apply to events that occur within a relaxation session. They can be seen as "relaxation coping strategies." Does effective coping in everyday life contribute to effective coping in relaxation?

- What beliefs contribute to or interfere with beginning relaxation? We have seen that the current array of R-Beliefs may well be most applicable to higher energy and abstract R-States. We need to compile and factor-analyze a comprehensive catalog of statements that reflect resistance to relaxation ("It's a waste of time, laziness; it contributes to passivity in life").

CONCLUSIONS

At the very least, the theoretical perspective introduced in this book has heuristic value. ABC Theory has prompted us to ask new questions, and we have made a few discoveries. Contrary to the prevailing relaxation response worldview, different approaches to relaxation indeed have quite different effects. Most conspicuously, PMR enhances Disengagement and Physical Relaxation, while yoga and breathing exercises enhance feelings of Strength and Awareness. Techniques appear to be the same only when one restricts attention to reduced stress. Furthermore, different people have different responses to relaxation; relaxation is not the same for males and females or for those belonging to different racial, ethnic, and religious groups. Psychopathology and personality sometimes makes a difference in one's capacity to relax. Psychologically disturbed individuals Disengage when they relax. Perhaps the two most important factors that can help people relax more effectively and with greater benefit are frequency of practice and belief. Regular daily practice enhances relaxation considerably; often partial practice, even 2 or 3 days a week, has much less effect. Beliefs also make an important difference—but not necessarily all the beliefs promoted in the world's authoritarian relaxation literature. Belief in God is not as important or perhaps not as automatically effective as some claim. And key to much of relaxation are acceptance of things that cannot be changed, optimism, and trust in inner wisdom.

Most important, I believe this book demonstrates the need to go beyond the relaxation response and indeed beyond cognitive and somatic specificity hypotheses. I believe we can no longer assess the medical benefits of a relaxation treatment without also examining the mediating role of R-States, R-Dispositions, R-Motivations, R-Attitudes, and R-Beliefs. We can no longer simply ask whether yoga, PMR, or breathing works without also looking at the mediating impact of R-States, Dispositions, Motivations, Attitudes, and Beliefs. And I believe clinicians can no longer present variations of the same technique to everyone. As Lehrer, Carr, Sargunaraj, and Woolfolk (1994) warn in their classic review of relaxation, we are now obliged to learn all approaches.

In conclusion, I do not offer the ideas and findings of this volume as proven facts or expert pronouncements. They are worthy hypotheses waiting further evidence. Relaxation is indeed an unexplored world of many riches.

NOTE

1. How do you feel when relaxed? The answer depends in part on how you ask the question. First, it is likely that the content of R-States depend on whether items are phrased as states ("How do you feel right now?" "How did you feel during your most effective relaxation activity?"), dispositions ("How relaxed do you generally feel?"), or motivations ("How relaxed would you like to feel?"). In factor-analytic studies, the greatest differentiation appears when one examines R-States (Alexander, 1991; Smith et al., 1996). Fewer factors emerge when we look at R-Dispositions and R-Motivations. The number of initial items may also make a difference; Alexander and Smith et al. used questionnaires containing 230 and 82 items; subsequent studies have used from 18 to 72 items.

It is not surprising that items phrased as states display a more differentiated factor structure than dispositional/motivational items. A client describing an immediate relaxation state is providing a report less subject to the errors and distortions of recall and the passage of time. In contrast, clients describing R-Dispositions and R-Motivations are providing reports (in our studies) of how they have felt over the previous 2 weeks (a period frequently deployed in questionnaires of affect). A lot can happen over 2 weeks. Many R-States can appear together. One may feel Disengaged on Monday, Strengthened and Aware on Tuesday, Sleepy on Wednesday, and Joyful on Thursday.

Considering a different issue, my current preference is to assess R-States, Dispositions, Motivations, and Beliefs with two-item scales. Longer relaxation scales are simply too cumbersome to be usable, especially when assessing relaxation repeatedly over the course of a relaxation session. Recall that the tradition in relaxation research has been to assess relaxation with a single item ("Are you relaxed?" or "Are you tense?"). Although the factor structure of two-item scales may not be as differentiated as that for longer inventories, scales retain their distinctiveness when we examine other indices of validity.

TABLE 7.2   Passive Relaxation Activities Engaged in over a 2-Week Period

Activity	% of People Claiming Activity ($N = 742$)
Listening to music	70.802
Resting in bed	68.599
Daydreaming	63.611
Showers	60.646
Walking	40.707
Prayer	35.444
Petting pets/children	35.040
Hot tubs	33.965
Art	28.571
Reading fiction	27.763
Imagery	27.348
Nature walks	27.223
Breathing exercises	26.684
Massage	25.741
Playing music	23.854
Reading nonfiction	21.021
Inspirational reading	16.981
Meditation	15.633
Yoga	13.342
Relaxation tapes	12.129
Whistling	8.700
Steam baths	8.490
Rocking	8.355
Progressive muscle relaxation	6.738
Sunbathing	5.391
Hypnosis	2.156
Autogenic training	1.482
Transcendental meditation	8.000
Mindfulness meditation	.900
Mantra meditation	.900
Breathing meditation	.400

Adapted from Holmes, Ritchie, and Allen (in press).

TABLE 7.3   Prevalence of Claimed Relaxation Benefits

Claimed Benefit	% Claiming Benefit ($N = 436$)
Stress management	72.035
Frustration management	62.155
Dealing with worry	55.550
Anxiety management	48.624
Depression management	48.623
Enhancing sleep	47.248
Enhancing health	41.512
Spiritual growth	38.073
Psychological insight/growth	37.615
Creativity	37.385
Dealing with aggressive tendencies	35.550
Increasing productivity	34.633
Increasing strength and stamina	34.174
Dealing with interpersonal conflict	32.339
Recovery from work	30.046
Exercise workouts	29.128
Enhancing interpersonal effectiveness	28.440
Enhancing prayer	26.606
Combating insomnia	25.917
Dealing with compulsive thoughts	25.229
Pain management	24.541
Enhancing sex	22.936
Enhancing artistic expression	22.706
Enhancing mediation	22.018
Enhancing recovery from illness	19.266
Controlling overeating	16.284
Controlling physical symptoms	15.826
Enhancing resistance to disease	14.908
Tobacco use	13.761
Enhancing sports	13.532
Dealing with shyness	13.073
Recovery from surgery	7.569
Dealing with dental anxiety	6.651
Dealing with surgery	5.963
Alcohol abuse	5.733
Dealing with medication side effects	4.358
Drug abuse	2.522

TABLE 7.4   Factor Structure of Claimed Relaxation Benefits (Summary)

Factor 1: Medical Benefits
  Recovery from surgery
  Preparing for surgery
  Dental anxiety
  Medication side effects
  Recovery from illness
Factor 2: Substance Abuse
  Illegal drug use
  Tobacco use
  Alcohol consumption
  Overeating
Factor 3: Psychological Distress
  Anxiety/fear
  Depression
  Worry
  Frustration
Factor 4: Sleep/Pain
  Insomnia
  Sleep
  Pain
Factor 5: Health
  Physical health
  Strength and stamina
  Resistance to disease
  Recovery from work
Factor 6: Creativity
  Creativity
  Artistic expression
  Psychological insight/growth
Factor 7: Spirituality
  Meditation
  Prayer
  Spiritual growth
Factor 8: Athletics
  Exercise workouts
  Sports
  Sex
Factor 9: Interpersonal Stress
  Interpersonal effectiveness
  Interpersonal conflict
  Stress

TABLE 7.5   Treatment Groups Assessed in Smith, Amutio, Anderson, and Aria (1996) Study

Single Treatments
  Massage
  Progressive muscle relaxation
  Yoga stretching
  Breathing exercises
  Imagery
  Meditation
Combination Treatments
  Yoga, stretching, and breathing
  Yoga, stretching, breathing, and meditation
  Yoga, stretching, and meditation
  Breathing and imagery
  Breathing and meditation

TABLE 7.6   Frequency of Reported Relaxation Activities

	% Practicing Activity ($N - 165$)
Informal Casual Activities	
Shower, bathing, sauna, hot tubs	10.909
Listening to music, radio	10.303
Daydreaming	6.667
Sleeping	6.667
Resting (in bed, sitting, reclining)	6.061
Praying	6.061
Playing	5.455
Talking, chatting	5.455
Reading	4.848
Watching TV, movies, films	3.030
Writing (in journal, diary)	2.424
Formal Professional Activities	
Yoga (stretching, breathing, imagery)	12.121
Meditation (mindfulness; mantra; imagery)	8.484
Massage (back rubs, full body)	5.455
Breathing exercises	2.424

From Ritchie, Holmes, and Allen (in press).

TABLE 7.7   Tukey's LSD Post Hoc Comparisons for R-States
Reported for Different Relaxation Activities

Love and Thankfulness ($F = 4.283$, $p < .0005$)

  Praying > sleep,***** resting/napping,***** breathing exercises,***** bathing/show-ering,**** TV/movies,***** yoga,***** listening to music,*** reading,** massage,* daydreaming,* playing* walking*

  Meditating > sleep, ***** resting/napping***** TV/movies,**** bathing/showering,** breathing exercises,* yoga*

  Taking/chatting > sleep,***** resting/napping,***** TV/movies,**** breathing exercises,** bathing/showering*

  Playing > sleep,**** resting/napping,**** TV/movies,* breathing exercises*

  Daydreaming > sleep,**** resting/napping,*** TV/movies,* breathing exercises*

  Writing > sleep,**** resting/napping,*** TV/movies,* breathing exercises*

  Massage > sleep,*** resting/napping,** TV/movies,* breathing exercises*

  Yoga > sleep,*** resting/napping*

  Reading > sleep,* resting/napping*

  Bathing/showering > sleep*

  Walking > sleep*

Joy ($F = 3.971$, $p < .0005$)

  Play > sleep,***** resting/napping,***** breathing exercises,***** bathing/show-ering,***** yoga,*** prayer*

  Talking/chatting > sleep,***** resting/napping,***** breathing exercises,**** bathing/showering,*** yoga**

  Listening to music > sleep,***** resting/napping,***** breathing exercises,*** bathing/showering***

  Massage > sleep,***** resting/napping,*** breathing exercises,***   Daydreaming > sleep,**** resting/napping,*** breathing exercises,** bathing/showering,* yoga*

  Daydreaming > sleep,**** resting/napping,*** breathing exercises,** bathing/show-ering,* yoga*

  Writing > sleep,*** resting/napping,*** breathing exercises,*** bathing/showering,* yoga*

  TV/movies > sleep,*** resting/napping,** breathing exercises,** bathing/showering*

  Meditating > sleep,*** resting/napping,** breathing exercises,* bathing/showering*

  Reading > sleep,*** resting/napping,** breathing exercises,* bathing/showering*

  Prayer > sleep*

  Yoga > sleep*

TABLE 7.7   *(continued)*

Strength and Awareness ($F = 3.239$, $p < .0005$)

    Prayer > sleep,***** resting/napping,***** breathing exercises,**** massage,**** listening to music,*** bathing/showering*** daydreaming,** walking,* TV/movies,* yoga*

    Talking/chatting > sleep,***** resting/napping,** breathing exercises

    Yoga > sleep,***** resting/napping,** breathing exercises*

    Reading > sleep,**** resting/napping,** breathing exercises,* massage*

    Playing > sleep,*** resting/napping,* breathing exercises*

    Writing > sleep,** breathing exercises,* resting/napping*

    Bathing/showering > sleep**

    Daydreaming > sleep*

    Listening to music > sleep *

Prayerfulness ($F = 2.439$, $p < .005$)

    Prayer > TV/movies,***** sleep,***** bathing/showering,***** resting/napping,**** daydreaming,*** talking/chatting,*** massage,** yoga,* reading,* listening to music,* playing*

    Meditating > TV/movies,*** sleep,* bathing/showering*

    Listening to music > TV/movies,** sleep,* bathing/showering*

    Yoga > TV/movies,** sleep,* bathing/showering*

    Walking > TV/movies,* sleep*

    Playing > TV/movies*

    Reading > TV/movies*

    Writing > TV/movies*

Sleepiness ($F = 2.036$, $p = .01$)

    Resting/napping > walking,***** meditating,***** reading,***** playing,*** yoga,*** listening to music,*** prayer,*** writing,** talking/chatting,** breathing exercises,* sleep,* TV/movies*

    Bathing/showering > walking,*** reading,* meditating*

    Daydreaming > walking*

    Sleep > walking *

    Massage > walking,** reading,* meditating*

(continued)

TABLE 7.7 *(continued)*

Physical Relaxation ($F = 1.931$, $p < .05$)

Yoga > walking,**** listening to music,*** praying,*** TV/movies,** writing,** playing,* reading,* talking/chatting*

Bathing/showering > walking,*** listening to music,* praying,* TV/movies,* writing*

Massage > walking*

Meditating > walking*

Resting/napping >walking*

Sleeping > walking*

*$p \leq .05$, **$p \leq .01$, ***$p \leq .005$, ****$p \leq .001$, *****$p \leq .0005$.
$N = 165$
Key: "Praying > sleep" means that clients who select "prayer" as their preferred relaxation activity, when compared with those who report "sleep," experience higher levels of the R-State Love and Thankfulness during relaxation.

TABLE 7.8 Correlations Among Relaxation Beliefs and Relaxation States

	Deeper Perspective	God	Inner Wisdom
Sleepiness	−.033	−.045	.027
Disengagement	.045	.031	.097
Physical Relaxation	.016	−.071	.042
Mental Relaxation	.266*****	.137**	.203*****
Strength and Awareness	.399*****	.267*****	.269*****
Joy	.376*****	.253*****	.260*****
Love and Thankfulness	.459*****	.460*****	.420*****
Prayerfulness	.435*****	.553*****	.454*****

	Taking It Easy	Honesty	Love	Acceptance
Sleepiness	.059	.062	−.036	.023
Disengagement	.035	.055	−.012	.131**
Physical Relaxation	.095	.041	−.005	.079
Mental Relaxation	.210***	.142***	.125*	.161****
Strength and Awareness	.140***	.253*****	.226*****	.304*****
Joy	.252*****	.273*****	.218*****	.277*****
Love and Thankfulness	.274*****	.380*****	.404*****	.365*****
Prayerfulness	.251*****	.368*****	.353*****	.384*****

*$p \leq .05$, **$p \leq .01$, ***$p \leq .005$, ****$p \leq .001$, *****$p \leq .0005$.
$N = 495$ (130 males, 365 females), average age = 28.569, $SD = 12.021$.

From Ghoncheh, Sparks, and Wasik (in press).

TABLE 7.9   Correlations Among Relaxation Beliefs
and Relaxation Dispositions

Factor	Deeper Perspective	God	Inner Wisdom	Taking It Easy
Sleepiness	−.034	−.023	.003	−.108
Disengagement	−.171**	.009	.044	−.259*****
Physical Relaxation	−.108	.036	.068	−.194**
Mental Quiet	−.145*	.040	.075	−.307*****
Mental Relaxation	.140*	.045	.144*	−.019
Strength and Aware	.131*	.081	.223*****	.110
Joy	.059	.070	.148*	.020
Love and Thankfulness	.236*****	.274*****	.242*****	.317*****
Prayerfulness	.085	.408*****	.326*****	.085

Factor	Honesty	Love	Acceptance	Optimism
Sleepiness	−.117	−.039	.010	−.090
Disengagement	−.191***	−.169**	.108	−.057
Physical Relaxation	−.087	−.127*	.107	−.022
Mental Quiet	−.205****	−.123	.132*	−.070
Mental Relaxation	.012	.002	.259*****	.190***
Strength and Awareness	.110	.053	.190***	.224*****
Joy	.074	.045	.218****	.195***
Love and Thankfulness	.205****	.155*	.103	.224*****
Prayerfulness	.001	.028	.131*	.209***

M = 197, F = 289, ave. age − 22.773, SD = 7.939
*p ≤ .05, **p ≤ .01, ***p ≤ .005, ****p ≤ .001, *****p ≤ .0005.

From Ghoncheh, Sparks, and Wasik (in press).

TABLE 7.10   Correlations Among Relaxation Beliefs and Relaxation Motivations

	Deeper Perspective	God	Inner Wisdom	Love
Sleepiness	−.159**	−.033	.015	−.104*
Disengagement	.034	.075	.077	.115*
Physical Relaxation	.082	.098*	.154**	.191*****
Mental Quiet	.134**	.035	.093	.224*****
Mental Relaxation	.181*****	.048	.118*	.258*****
Strength and Awareness	.115*	−.015	.101	.189*****
Joy	.105*	.011	.037	.173*****
Love and Thankfulness	.199*****	.212*****	.197*****	.330*****
Prayerfulness	.251*****	.521*****	.191*****	.368*****

Factor	Honesty	Taking It Easy	Acceptance	Optimism
Sleepiness	−.082	.009	.072	.004
Disengagement	−.027	.167**	.130**	.093
Physical Relaxation	.013	.085	.065	.033
Mental Quiet	.043	.178*****	.040	.043
Mental Relaxation	.087	.160****	.035	.077
Strength and Awareness	.013	.109	−.014	.059
Joy	.072	.117	−.047	.075
Love and Thankfulness	.130***	.177*****	.046	.093
Prayerfulness	.103*	.046	.025	.118***

M = 197, F = 289, ave. age = 22.773, SD = 7.939.
*$p \leq .05$, **$p \leq .01$, ***$p \leq .005$, ****$p \leq .001$, *****$p \leq .0005$.

From Ghoncheh, Sparks, and Wasik (in press).

References

Alexander, L. (1991). *A factor analysis of 230 relaxation words.* Unpublished master's thesis, Roosevelt University, Chicago.

Anderson, K. P. (in press). *Relaxation states and the SCL-90-R.* In J. C. Smith (Ed.), *ABC relaxation research.* New York: Springer.

Armitage, R. (1995). The distribution of EEG frequencies in REM and NREM sleep stages in healthy young adults. *Sleep, 18(5),* 334–341.

Austin, J. H. (1998). *Zen and the brain.* Cambridge, MA: MIT Press.

Bang, S. C. (in press). ABC relaxation training as a treatment for depression for the Korean elderly. In J. C. Smith (Ed.), *ABC relaxation research.* New York: Springer Publishing Company.

Bang, S. C., & Kim, K. H. (1998). The Effects of Guided Imagery on State and Trait Anxiety. *Korean Journal of Health Psychology, 3,* 156–168.

Benson, H. (1975). *The relaxation response.* New York: Morrow.

Benson, H., & Friedman, R. (1985). A rebuttal to the conclusions of Davis S. Holmes's article: Meditation and somatic arousal reduction. *American Psychologist, 40,* 725–728.

Borkovec, T. D., & Sides, K. (1979). Critical procedural variables related to the physiological effects of progressive relaxation: A review. *Behavior Research and Therapy, 17,* 1199–1260.

Bowers, R. E., Darner, R. E., & Goldner, C. L. (in press). Gender differences for relaxation dispositions, motivations, and beliefs. In J. C. Smith (Ed.), *ABC relaxation research.* New York: Springer.

Clark, A. C. (1997). *3001: The final odyssey.* New York: Ballantine.

Conze, E. (1959). *Buddhism: Its essence and development.* New York: Harper & Row.

Davidson, R. J., & Schwartz, G. E. (1976). Psychobiology of relaxation and related states: A multiprocess theory. In D. I. Mostofsky (Ed.), *Behavior control and the modification of physiological activity* (pp. 399–442). Englewood Cliffs, NJ: Prentice-Hall.

Deikman, A. (1966). Deautomatization and the mystic experience. *Psychiatry, 29,* 324–338.

Dement, W., & Kleitman, N. (1957). Cyclic variations in EEG during sleep and their relation to eye movements, body motility and dreaming. *Electroencephalography and Clinical Neurophysiology, 9*, 673–690.

Edmonston, W. E. (1986). *The induction of hypnosis.* New York: Wiley.

Eliade, M. (1969). *Patanjali and yoga.* New York: Funk & Wagnalls.

Fenwick, P. (1987). Meditation and the EEG. In M. West (Ed.), *The psychology of meditation* (pp. 104–112). London: Oxford Press.

Gellhorn, E. (1970). The emotions and the ergotropic and trophotropic systems. *Psychologische Forschung, 34*, 48–94.

Gendlin, E. (1981). *Focusing.* New York: Bantam.

Ghoncheh, S., Sparks, P. E., & Wasik, M. A. (in press). The relationship between relaxation beliefs and global philosophies, and relaxation dispositions, motivations, and states. In J. C. Smith (Ed.), *ABC relaxation research.* New York: Springer.

Guevara, M. A., Lorenzo, I., Ramos, J., & Corsi-Cabrera, M. (1995). Inter- and intra-hemispheric EEG correlation during sleep and wakefulness. *Sleep, 18*(4), 257–265.

Heide, F. J., & Borkovec, T. D. (1983). Relaxation-induced anxiety: Mechanisms and theoretical implications. *Behaviour Research and Therapy, 22*, 1–12.

Hess, W. R. (1957). *The functional organization of the diencephalon.* New York: Grune & Stratton.

Hillenberg, J. B., & Collins, F. L., Jr. (1982). A procedural analysis and review of relaxation training research. *Behaviour Therapy and Research, 22*, 1–12.

Hirai. (1975). *Zen meditation therapy.* Tokyo: Japan Publications.

Holmes, D. S. (1984). Meditation and somatic arousal reduction: A review of the experimental evidence. *American Psychologist, 39*, 1–10.

Holmes, R. C., III, Ritchie, T., & Allen, D. (in press). The factor structure of relaxation-related experiences, stress, and the effects of grouped versus random presentation of questionnaire items. In J. C. Smith (Ed.), *ABC relaxation research.* New York: Springer.

Jacobson, E. (1929). *Progressive relaxation.* Chicago. University of Chicago Press.

James, W. (1902). *The varieties of religious experience.* New York: Modern Library.

Khasky, A. D., & Smith, J. C. (1999). Stress, Relaxation States, and Creativity. *Perceptual and Motor Skills, 88*, 409–416.

Layman, E. M. (1976). *Buddhism in America.* Chicago: Nelson-Hall.

Lazarus, A. A. (1976). *Multimodal Behavior Therapy.* New York: Springer.

Lazarus, A. A. (1997). *Brief but Comprehensive Psychotherapy: The Multimodal Way.* New York: Springer.

Lehrer, P. M., Carr, R., Sargunaraj, D., & Woolfolk, R. L. (1994). Stress management techniques: Are they all equivalent, or do they have specific effects? *Biofeedback and Self-Regulation, 19*, 353–401.

Lehrer, P. M., & Woolfolk, R. L. (1993). Specific effects of stress management techniques. In P. M. Lehrer & R. L. Woolfolk (Eds.), *Principles and practice of stress management* (pp. 481–520). New York: Guilford.

Leslie, K. A., & Clavin, S. L. (in press). Relaxation states, stress, and the Sixteen Personality Factor Questionnaire. In J. C. Smith (Ed.), *ABC relaxation research*. New York: Springer.

Lichstein, K. (1988). *Clinical relaxation strategies*. New York: Wiley.

Linden, W. (1990). Autogenic training: A clinical guide. New York: Guilford Press.

Loewenfeld, L. (1901). Der Hypnotismus, Handbuch der Lehre von der Hypnose und der Suggestion. Wiesbaden: J. F. Bergmann.

Luthe, W. (1965). Autogenic training in North America. In W. Luthe (Ed.) *Autogenic training: International edition* (pp. 71–78). New York: Grune & Stratton.

Luthe, W. (Ed.). (1969–1973). *Autogenic therapy* (Vols. 1–6). New York: Grune & Stratton.

Mui, P. (in press). *The factor structure of relaxation beliefs*. In J. C. Smith (Ed.), *ABC relaxation research*. New York: Springer.

Ornstein, R. (1972). *The psychology of consciousness*. San Francisco: W. F. Freeman.

Pagano, R., & Warrenburg, S. (1983). Meditation: In search of a unique effect. In R. Davidson, G. Schwarz, & D. Shapiro (Eds.), *Consciousness and Self Regulation* (Vol. 3, pp. 153–205). New York: Plenum Press.

Paul, G. L. (1966, September). The specific control of anxiety: "Hypnosis" and "conditioning." Paper presented at the annual meeting of the American Psychological Association, New York.

Poppen, R. (1998). *Behavioral relaxation training and assessment* (2nd ed.). New York: Sage.

Prabhavananda, S. (1963). *The spiritual heritage of India*. Garden City, NY: Doubleday.

Qualls, P. J., & Sheehan, P. W. (1981). Electromyographic biofeedback as a relaxation training technique: A critical appraisal and reassessment. *Psychological Bulletin, 90,* 21–42.

Ritchie, T., Holmes, R., & Allen, D. (in press). Relaxation states and relaxation activities. In J. C. Smith (Ed.), *ABC relaxtion research*. New York: Springer.

Russel, R. K., & Matthews, C. O. (1975). Cue-controlled relaxation *in vivo* desensitization of a snake phobia. *Journal of Behavior Therapy and Experimental Psychiatry, 6,* 49–51.

Schultz, J. H. (1932). Das autogene Training: Konzentrative selbstent Spannung (12th ed.). Stuttgart: Georg Thieme.

Schultz, J. H., & Luthe, W. (1959). *Autogenic training: A psychophysiologic approach in psychotherapy*. New York: Grune & Stratton.

Schwartz, M. S. (1995). *Biofeedback: A practitioner's guide* (2nd ed.). New York: Guilford.

Simonton, O. C., Matthews-Simonton, S., & Creighton, J. (1978). *Getting well again*. Los Angeles: J. P. Tarcher.

Smith, J. C. (1985). *Relaxation dynamics: Nine world approaches to self-relaxation*. Champaign, IL: Research Press.

Smith, J. C. (1990). *Cognitive-behavioral relaxation training: A new system of strategies for treatment and assessment*. New York: Springer.

Smith, J. C. (1993a). *Creative stress management*. Englewood Cliffs, NJ: Prentice-Hall.

Smith, J. C. (1993b). *Understanding stress and coping*. Englewood Cliffs, NJ: Prentice-Hall.

Smith, J. C. (1999). *ABC relaxation training: An attentional behavioral cognitive approach*. New York: Springer.

Smith, J. C. (in press). *ABC relaxation research*. New York: Springer.

Smith, J . C. (in press-a). Yoga, meditation, and prayer: Differences in relaxation dispositions, motivations, beliefs, and practice patterns. In J. C. Smith (Ed.), *ABC relaxation research*. New York: Springer.

Smith, J. C. (in press-b). The factor structure and correlates of claimed benefits of relaxation. In J. C. Smith (Ed.), *ABC relaxation research*. New York: Springer.

Smith, J. C. (in press-c). Stress and relaxation. In J. C. Smith (Ed.), *ABC relaxation research*. New York: Springer.

Smith, J. C., Amutio, A., Anderson, J., & Aria, L. P. (1996). Relaxation: Mapping an uncharted world. *Biofeedback and Self-Regulation, 21,* 63–90.

Smith, J. C., McDuffie, S. R., Ritchie, T., Holmes, R., III, & Anderson, K. (in press). Racial and religious differences in relaxation states and beliefs. In J. C. Smith (Ed.), *ABC relaxation research*. New York: Springer.

Smith, J. C., Rice, S., Cucci, L., III, & Williams, J. (in press). Practice variables as predictors of stress and relaxation dispositions for yoga and meditation. In J. C. Smith (Ed.), *ABC relaxation research*. New York: Springer.

Smith, J. C., & Seidel, M. M. (1982). The factor structure of self-reported physical stress reactions. *Biofeedback and Self-Regulation, 7,* 35–47.

Smith, J. C., & Siebert, J. R. (1984). Self-reported physical stress reactions: First- and second-order factors. *Biofeedback and Self-Regulation, 9,* 215–227.

Sohnle, S. J. (in press). Relaxation dispositions and the Millon index of personality styles. In J. C. Smith (Ed.), *ABC relaxation research*. New York: Springer.

Stigsby, B., Rodenberg, J., & Moth, H. (1981). Electroencephalographic findings during mantra meditation (transcendental meditation): A controlled quantitative study of experienced meditators. *Electroencephalography and Clinical Neurophysiology, 51,* 434–442.

Wallace, R. K., & Benson, H. (1972). The physiology of meditation. *Scientific American, 226,* 84–90.

Wallace, R. K., Benson, H., & Wilson, K. (1971). A wakeful hypometabolic physiologic state. *American Journal of Physiology, 221,* 795–799.

Weinstein, M., & Smith, J. C. (1992). Isometric squeeze relaxation (progressive relaxation) vs. meditation: Absorption and focusing as predictors of state effects. *Perceptual and Motor Skills, 75,* 1263–1271.

Wiggins, J. S. (Ed.). (1996). *The five-factor model of personality*. New York: Guilford.

Wolpe, J. (1958). *Psychotherapy by reciprocal inhibition*. Stanford, CA: Stanford University Press.

Appendix A
Development of Relaxation State Inventories

Decades ago I began the task of developing a comprehensive relaxation questionnaire. My first job was to collect and catalog words used to describe the subjective relaxation states. Such a strategy is not new. "Five-factor model" personality researchers (Wiggins, 1996) have proposed that everyday "natural language" of personality terms reflects how most people conceptualize personality attributes. Similarly, I propose that the natural language of relaxation may well reflect an underlying pattern of relaxation states. The preferred empirical strategy of five-factor model personality researches has been to look for dimensions of personality by factor-analyzing (primarily principal components analysis with varimax rotation) comprehensive catalogs of personality words. I deployed the same strategy. But simply collecting and sorting words was not enough; what is the best way of presenting relaxation words in meaningful phrases and sentences?

Anyone who has taught relaxation knows that, after a practice session, clients are often quite nonverbal, not particularly likely to talk at length about their experiences. Verbal descriptions of relaxation use few, simple words. In terms of ABC theory, this is a consequence of the very nature of relaxation. A relaxed person has entered a state of sustained passive simple focus. He or she is less likely to engage in any planful or effortful analytic activity, including thinking about what words best describe relaxation.

Given the passive and simple nature of relaxation, I decided to strive for verbal descriptions that are also passive and simple, requiring little thought for response. To this end, I experimented with three levels of item construction. The simplest is the single word; here, an item is nothing more than a single descriptive word, perhaps introduced by the preface "I feel." Slightly more complex is the word cluster, where an item contains several key words, again introduced by "I feel." Most complex is the statement in which a process or activity is described. To illustrate these three levels of item complexity, consider these single-word items on an early questionnaire: "Silent," "Simple," "Speechless." The entire questionnaire was prefaced by instructions that ask one to rate "how you feel" on an appropriate scale for each item.

In a later questionnaire (not discussed in this book), we combined these words into a cluster item: "I feel silent, simple, and speechless." And in a more recent relaxation questionnaire, we used this item: "I feel an inner stillness, not thinking about anything."

My strategy has been to first deploy items at the simplest level and then increase complexity only if required to increase clarity. In the above example, words or word clusters proved to be too ambiguous, requiring use of a complex statement.

THE 230- AND 82-ITEM LISTS

I have revised my relaxation inventories seven times. Some have included only R-State items, whereas others have also included stress-related items. In an attempt to keep things clear, I designate each inventory by the number of relaxation/stress items it includes. For example, the current "18/6b" inventory includes 18 relaxation items, 6 stress items, and is the second form with this ratio. In the tables at the end of this appendix I explain each inventory; here I report on only the highlights.

I began by constructing a comprehensive lexicon of words used to describe the experiences people have while practicing or engaging in activities generally accepted as "relaxation." I examined over 200 texts and manuals of a wide range of approaches, including progressive muscle relaxation (PMR), yoga, breathing exercises, imagery, creative visualization, tai chi, self-hypnosis, meditation, contemplation, and prayer. My first relaxation dictionary contained over 400 words. I then speculated (Smith, 1990) that relaxation states reflect five categories: focusing, passivity, receptivity to unfamiliar experiences, relaxation reinforcements, and somatic sensations associated with relaxation. I sorted my list into category groups (a classification I subsequently abandoned in light of results of factor-analytic research on relaxation). The next step involved removing redundant and rarely applied words and adding words that had been overlooked. The final product was a comprehensive list of 230 relaxation-related words (Tables A.1 and A.2 at end of Appendix A; see also Smith, 1990).

Because it is not feasible to measure relaxation with a 230-item questionnaire, it became imperative to screen items. One strategy could have been to give the list to a group of five or so relaxation trainers who would select which should be included, a strategy often applied in psychology. However, rather than generating a list colored by my own bias or those of a handful of raters, I enlisted the help of 282 raters (Alexander, 1991). Each person was given these instructions:

Think of a time over the last seven days when you were very relaxed. For example, you may have been engaged in any of a number of passive activities, such as

Breathing exercises

Daydreaming

Imagery

Meditation

Prayer

Progressive relaxation

Self-hypnosis

TM

Visualization

Watching a sunset

Yoga

Zen

Please do not include active forms of relaxation, such as

Dancing

Doing puzzles

Drawing

Drinking

Eating

Jogging

Listening to music

Napping

Reading

Sex

Sleeping

Socializing

Taking drugs

Talking on the phone

Talking to others

Watching TV

Writing

To control for order effects, each participant was given one of three randomly organized lists of 230 relaxation words and asked to rate how well each "fit or described how you felt while relaxing this week." In all, participants rated a diverse array of passive activities, including daydreaming, prayer, imagery, breathing exercises, meditation, visualization, PMR, self-hypnosis, taking a bath, watching a sunset, and yoga. Through an initial factor analysis and item screening (Alexander, 1991), I reduced the list to 82 words. (See Table A.2 at the end of Appendix A).

THE 45/27 AND 25/3 ITEM LISTS

In an extensive study (Smith et al., 1996), Alberto Amutio and I asked 940 practitioners about various relaxation techniques (massage, PMR, yoga stretching, breathing, imagery, meditation, and various combination treatments) to rate their technique experiences on the 82-item list. We identified 10 interpretable factors (Table A.3 at the end of Appendix A).

At this point two issues became clear. A radically shortened item list could greatly facilitate research on relaxation states; such a form could be given to large numbers of individuals and repeated during the course of a relaxation activity or exercise. Although pervious research traditionally has assessed self-reported relaxation through a single item ("Are you relaxed?" or "Are you anxious?"), our research had used lists of considerable length. How short can a list of relaxation items get and remain reliable and valid? The second issue was that our research had focused exclusively on R-States, rather than arousal symptoms. Given that most professionals have defined relaxation as reduction of worry (cognitive arousal), negative emotion (affective arousal), or physical symptoms (somatic arousal), I decided to incorporate a quick measure of these dimensions. Previous research (chapter 2) had suggested items for assessing accessible self-report manifestations of arousal. Worry could be tapped rather directly through expressions of worry and troublesome and intrusive thoughts (Weinstein & Smith, 1992). Similarly, negative emotions are typically assessed through reports of anxiety, depression, irritation, and anger (Smith, 1990). The assessment of self- reported somatic arousal is a bit more problematic. I chose to include four global factors of somatic symptoms identified in extensive previous research of hundreds of symptoms reported by over 1,000 participants (Smith & Seidel, 1982; Smith & Siebert, 1984). These included Discomfort and Pain (fatigue, backache, skin problems), Muscle (skeletal) Tension (tight, tense, clenched, restless, fidgety, uncoordinated), Autonomic Arousal (rapid, irregular, pronounced heartbeat, nervous breathing, perspiration, dry mouth), and Digestive Problems.

I constructed two item lists, a long form and a short form. The long form consisted of 45 R-State items selected from each major relaxation factor identified in Smith et al. (1996) plus 27 stress items reflecting the stress categories just described. R- State and stress items were randomly distributed. The short form consisted of 25 R-State items and 3 stress items, one each for somatic stress, worry, and negative emotion. I created two short versions, one with items grouped according to R-State content and presented in this sequence: Disengagement,

Physical Relaxation, Mental Relaxation, Strength and Awareness, Joy, Love and Thankfulness, Prayerfulness, and Speechlessness (a precursor to what I now term Mental Quiet). In the second short form, items were presented in random order. To thoroughly control for possibly confounding order effects, six versions of the randomized form were developed, each using a different random order of items. I decided it was time to transform relaxation words into complete sentences, in both long and short forms, to increase meaningfulness. See Table A.4 at end of Appendix A.

Holmes, Ritchie, and Allen (in press) presented the grouped 25/3 form to 436 subjects and the random item form to 306 subjects. Analysis of the grouped-item version revealed five relaxation factors: Spiritual, Joy/Fun, Distant, Aware, and Calm; analysis of the randomized item version revealed six factors: Spiritual, Calm, Aware, Distant, Drowsy, and Joy/Fun.

THE 18/6 ITEM LIST AND THE SMITH RELAXATION STATES INVENTORY

Drawing on four factor analyses (Alexander, 1991; Holmes, Ritchie, and Allen, in press; Smith et al., 1996), combined with my clinical experience with the short form, I compiled three additional item lists (19/3, 18/6a, and 18/6b; Tables A.5–A.7 at the end of Appendix A). At the time of this writing, the 18/6b list is our most recent product, one I have formally named the Smith Relaxation States Inventory (SRSI). It taps my current conceptualization of nine R-States and forms the basis of most of the research referred to in this book.

TABLE A.1   Partial List of Items Suggesting Relaxation Dimensions of Somatic Sensations, Focusing, Passivity, Receptivity, and Relaxation Reinforcements

Somatic Sensations Associated with Relaxation

Bathed, caressed, cool, dissolving, drowsy, elastic, flexible, floating, flowing, heavy, high, light, limber, limp, liquid, loose, massaged, mellow, melting, sedate, sinking, slack, sleepy, slow, smooth, soft, supple, throbbing, tingling, warm

Focusing

Deployment of attention toward a target stimulus: Attentive, concentrated, fascinated, focused, interested, one-pointed, single-minded

Absence of distraction: Cleansed, clear, distant, far away, pure, quiet, silent, still, transparent, undistracted

The degree to which a target stimulus is the sole object of attention, subjectively experienced as "absorbing": Absorbed, at one, captivated, centered, charmed contemplative, deeply engrossed, entranced, meditative, mindful

The subjective experience of increased alertness that one might presume to contribute to increased attentiveness: Alert, awake, aware, bright, conscious, glowing, lucid, radiant, stimulated

Passivity

Reduced effort: At ease, easy, gentle, laid back, leisurely, listless, motionless, patient, settled, unforced, unhurried

The act of ceasing goal-directed or analytic activity: Detached, forgetting, escaped, indifferent, letting be, letting go, passive, pausing, released, relieved, surrendering

Experienced contentment associated with reduced striving: Contented, gratified, satisfied

Activity unencumbered by needless goal-directed or analytic striving: Carefree, free, playful, selfless, simple, spontaneous, unbothered, unencumbered, untroubled, unworried

Receptivity

Positive experiences beyond what one appraises to be predictable, familiar, and easily understood: Amazed, awe, boundless, cosmic, ecstatic, elated, enraptured, eternal, glorious, immortal, infinite, mysterious, mystical, new, prayerful, profound, reverent, speechless, spiritual, timeless, transcendent, wonder, wordless, worshipful

Openness to new experiences and insights: Accepting, childlike, creative, dreamy, expansive, innocent, insightful, inspired, intuitive, loving, open, receptive

Experienced change or transformation: Liberated, reborn, rejuvenated, renewed, touched, transformed

Reduced level of experienced threat that one might presume to be associated with increased receptivity: Assured, confident, encouraged, hopeful, optimistic, reassured, safe, secure, thankful, trusting, unafraid

TABLE A.1 *(continued)*

Reinforcements Associated with Relaxation

> *General relaxation*: Calm, comfortable, peaceful, relaxed, rested, tranquil
>
> *Increased self-acceptance/harmony*: Adjusted, at home, balanced, belonging, collected, complete, composed, even, harmonious, integrated, poised, stable, unified, whole
>
> *Increased sense of health and well-being*: Alive, healing, healthy, invigorated, natural, recovered, restored
>
> *Feelings of increased understanding (not necessarily associated with new insight)*: Answered, in touch, knowing, meaning, perceptive, understanding, wise
>
> *Increased self-efficacy*: Able, actualized, capable, competent, controlled, coordinated, coping, effective, energized, in control, steady, strengthened, strong, vigorous, vitalized
>
> *General positive states*: Beautiful, blessed, blissful, cheerful, cozy, delighted, enjoyable, exhilarated, exultant, fresh, fun, good, great, happy, joyful, pleasant, pleased, pleasured, positive, refreshed, rewarded, sensuous, serene, soothed, uplifted, wonderful

TABLE A.2   Items Retained and Excluded from 230-item Relaxation List after Factor Analysis

230-Item List Organized by Factors	Excluded/Included Items for 82-Item List
Aware/strengthened	
Assured[*****]	Assured
Strong[*****]	(R, Strengthened)[1]
Attentive[****]	(R, Aware
Confident[****]	Confident
Capable[****]	(R, Strengthened)
Whole[****]	Whole
Perceptive[** **]	(NR, R, Aware, Insightful)
Aware[****]	Aware
Reassured[****]	(R, Confident)
In control[****]	(NR)
Interested[****]	(A, R, Fascinated)
Balanced[****]	(A, R, Whole)
Knowing[****]	Knowing
Wise[****]	(A, R, Knowing)
Effective[****]	(R, Strengthened)
Inspired[****]	Inspired
Coordinated[****]	(NR)
Strengthened[****]	Strengthened
Meaningful[****]	(R, Knowing)
Focused[****]	Focused
Intuitive[***]	(R, Knowing)
Alert[***]	(R, Aware)
Stable[***]	(A)
Mindful[***]	(A, R, Aware, Focused, Knowing)
Poised[***]	(A)
Able[***]	(R, Strengthened)
Uplifted[***]	(R, Assured, Strengthened)
Secure[***]	(A)
Clear[***]	Clear
Positive[***]	(A)
Invigorated[***]	(R, Strengthened)
Recovered[***]	(R, Strengthened, Restored)
Complete[***]	Complete
Open[***]	(A)
Composed[***]	(A)
Unified[***]	(A, R, Whole)
Understanding[***]	(R, Knowing)
Insightful[***]	(R, Knowing)
Hopeful[***]	Hopeful

TABLE A.2   *(continued)*

Awake***	Awake
In touch	(A)
Centered***	(LL, A)
Trusting***	Trusting
Unafraid**	Unafraid
	Accepted (added to complement Accepting)
Accepting**	Accepting
Encouraged**	(LL, R, Optimistic)
Rewarded**	(R, Joyful, Happy)
Vigorous**	(R, Energetic)
Integrated**	(R, Whole, Harmonious)
Steady**	(R, Strengthened)
Flexible**	(R, Loose)
Alive**	(R, Aware, Strengthened)
Optimistic**	Optimistic
Satisfied**	(R, Complete)
Receptive**	(A, DL)
Renewed**	(A, R, Strengthened, Restored)
New**	(A, R, Strengthened, Restored)
Healthy**	(NR, R, Strengthened)
Belonging**	(A)
Liberated**	(A, DL)
Restored**	Restored
Unforced**	(NR)
Even**	(A)
Profound*	(A, LL, R, Knowing)
Released*	(A, LL, DL)
Contemplative*	(A, LL, DL, R, Knowing)
At home*	(A, LL)
Safe*	(A, LL, R, Unafraid)
Natural*	(A, LL)
Gratified*	(LL, R, Complete, Assured)
Elated*	(LL, R, Joyful)
High*	(LL, A, R, Joyful)
Touched*	(LL, A)
Limp	
Dissolving*****	Dissolving
Listless***	(A, DL)
Slack***	(DL)
Sinking***	Sinking
Elastic***	(DL)
Liquid***	Liquid
Slow***	(A)
Supple***	(DL)

(continued)

TABLE A.2 *(continued)*

Limp**	Limp
Motionless**	(ML with Factor 11)
Throbbing**	(DL)
Melting**	(A)
Simple*	Simple
Tingling*	Tingling
Forgetting*	Forgetting
Massaged*	(LL, A, R, Tingling, Limp)
Joyful/Fun	
Fun*****	Fun
Joyful*****	Joyful
Enjoyable*****	(R, Joyful)
Cheerful*****	(R, Joyful)
Delighted*****	Delighted
Happy*****	Happy
Pleased*****	Pleased
Wonderful *****	Wonderful
Pleasured****	(R, Joyful, Sensuous)
Charmed****	(A)
Glorious***	Glorious
Beautiful***	Beautiful
Playful***	Playful
Pleasant***	(R, Happy)
Great***	(R, Happy)
Glowing***	Glowing
Amazed***	(R, Glorious, Wonderful)
Soft**	(A)
Fascinated**	Fascinated
Exhilarated**	(R, Refreshed, Joyful, Energized)
Fresh**	(LL, R, Refreshed, Energized)
Stimulated**	(LL, R, Energized)
Easy**	(LL, R, At ease)
Radiant**	(LL, A, DL)
Blissful**	(LL, A, DL)
Smooth*	(LL, A, DL)
Innocent*	(LL, A, DL)
Gentle*	(LL)
Cool*	(LL, A)
Calm	
Relaxed*****	Relaxed
Rested*****	Rested
Tranquil****	(R, Relaxed)
Calm****	Calm
Unbothered***	(R, Untroubled)
At ease***	At ease

TABLE A.2   *(continued)*

Peaceful***	Peaceful
Leisurely***	(R, At ease, Relaxed)
Refreshed***	Refreshed
Soothed***	Soothed
Mellow**	(LL, R, Warm, Relaxed)
Still**	(LL, R, Calm, Untroubled, Silent)
Serene**	(LL, DL)
Comfortable**	(LL, R, At ease)
Undistracted**	(R, Focused)
Unhurried**	(R, At ease)
Letting go*	(R, At ease)
Meditative*	(LL)
Untroubled*	Untroubled (retained because of prevalence in relaxation literature)
Limber*	(DL)
Warm*	Warm (retained because of prevalence in relaxation literature)
At one*	(A)
Timeless/Infinite/Boundless	
Timeless ****	Timeless
Infinite****	Infinite
Boundless***	(A, DL)
Eternal*	(LL, A, DL)
Transcendent*	(LL, A, DL)
Cosmic*	(LL, A, DL)
Prayerful	
Worshipful*****	(R, Prayerful)
Prayerful*****	Prayerful
Spiritual* ***	Spiritual
Blessed****	Blessed
Reverent***	Reverent
Thankful***	Thankful
Answered**	(LL, A)
Reborn**	(LL, A)
Cleansed*	(LL, A)
Surrendering*	(LL, A)
	Loved (added to complement "loving")
Loving*	Loving (retained because of prevalence in relaxation literature)
Distant	
Distant*****	Distant
Escaped***	(A)
Far away**	(R, Distant)

(continued)

TABLE A.2   *(continued)*

Coping
  Coping***   (NR)
Patient
  Patient****   Patient
  Bathed*   (A, LL)
Silent/Speechless
  Silent*****   Silent
  Quiet**   (R, Silent)
  Speechless**   Speechless
  Wordless*   (LL, R, Speechless)
Caressed
  Caressed***   (A)
  Relieved*   (LL, R, At ease, Soothed)
Sensuous
  Sensuous*****   Sensuous
Cozy
  Cozy*   (LL, A)
  Letting be*   (LL, R, At ease, Relaxed)
Contented
  Contented*****   Contented
Indifferent
  Indifferent*****   Indifferent
Energized
  Vitalized****   (DL, R, Energized)
  Energized**   Energized
  Rejuvenated**   (LL, DL, R, Restored)
  Transformed*   (LL, DL, R, Restored)
Settled
  Settled**   (LL, R, At ease, Silent)
  Unencumbered*   (LL, R, Untroubled)
Pausing/Wonder
  Pausing**   (A, LL)
  Wonder*   (R, Prayerful, Spiritual, Reverent, Timeless Infinite)
Floating
  Floating***   Floating
  Flowing*(.3)   (LL, A)
Absorbed
  Absorbed****   Absorbed
  Engrossed****   (A, DL, R, Absorbed, Focused)
  Captivated**   (A, DL, R, Absorbed, Focused)
  Enraptured   (LL, A, DL)
Controlled
  Controlled*****   (NR)
Healing
  Healing****   Healing

TABLE A.2 *(continued)*

Adjusted	
Adjusted***	(R, Healing, A)
Unworried	
Unworried*	(LL, R, Untroubled)
Ecstatic	
Ecstatic****	(A, R, Joy)
Sleepy	
Sleepy****	Asleep (item rewritten to complement Drowsy)
Drowsy****	Drowsy
Dreamy*	(LL, R, Drowsy, ML)
Actualized	
Actualized***	(A)
Laid back	
Laid back***	Laid back
Carefree***	Carefree
Collected	
Collected**	(LL, A)
Deep*	(LL, A, ML)
Concentrated*	(LL, A, ML, R, Focused)
One-pointed	
One-pointed****	(R, Focused, Aware)
Single-minded**	(LL, R, Focused, A)
Expansive*	(DL, A)
Immortal	
Immortal***	(DL, A)
Eternal*	(LL, A)
Exultant*	(LL, R, Joyful, Glorious)
Childlike	
Childlike*****	Childlike
Loose	
Loose****	Loose
Good	
Good***	(A, R, Happy)
Creative*	Creative (retained because of prevalence in relaxation literature)
Free	
Free**	Free
Spontaneous	
Spontaneous****	Spontaneous
Mystical/Mysterious	
Mysterious****	Mysterious
Mystical***	Mystical
Selfless	
Selfless****	Selfless

(continued)

TABLE A.2 *(continued)*

Harmonious
   Harmonious****   Harmonious
Conscious
   Conscious***   (R, Aware, Focused)
Passive
   Passive****   Passive
Entranced
   Entranced***   (DL, A, R, Focused, Joyful)
Light
   Light****   Light
   Bright **   (LL, A)
Transparent
   Transparent****   (DL, A)
   Awe*   (LL, R, Spiritual, Prayerful, Reverent)
   Pure*   (LL, A)
Lucid
   Lucid**   (A, R, Aware, Knowing)
Heavy
   Heavy*****   Heavy
Detached
   Detached*****   Detached
Sedate
   Sedate***   (DL)
Competent
   Competent****   (NR, R, Strengthened, Energized)

---

[1] Excluded

R = Redundant with another item (listed)

DL = Item deleted because author judged reading difficulty level to be high

LL = Item's loading on factor is low

A = Meaning of item is ambiguous (could mean several things) or too general

ML = Item loads on more than one factor

NR = Not a relaxation item; perhaps a relaxation aftereffect, belief, or supporting activity

Item Loadings
* ≥ .30
** ≥ .40
*** ≥ .50
**** ≥ .60
***** ≥ .70

From Alexander (1991). Used with permission.

TABLE A.3   82-Item List and 45/27-Item List

SRI 82-Item List Factors	Excluded/Included Items for 45/27-Item List
Joyful	
Joyful[*****]	I feel joyful.
Happy[*****]	I feel happy.
Glorious[*****]	(R, Joyful)[1]
Fun[*****]	I am having fun.
Playful[****]	(R, Fun)
Delighted[****]	I feel delighted.
Loved[****]	(R, Loving)
Glowing[****]	I feel glowing.
Fascinated[****]	(DL, R, Aware, Inspired)
Spontaneous[***]	(DL)
Wonderful[***]	I feel a sense of wonder.
Pleased[***]	(R, Joyful)
Beautiful[***]	Things seem beautiful.
Optimistic[***]	I feel optimistic.
Hopeful[***]	I feel hopeful.
Creative[***]	I feel creative.
Inspired[***]	I feel inspired.
Sensuous[***]	(NR)
Blessed[***]	(DL, R, Joyful)
Trusting[***]	(NR)
Knowing[***]	I feel a deep sense of knowing and understanding.
Harmonious[**]	Things seem harmonious.
Childlike[**]	(LL, ML)
Whole[**]	(LL, A)
Warm[**]	(LL, A)
Free[**]	(LL, A)
Complete[*]	(LL)
Healing[*]	(LL)
Timeless[*]	(LL, A)
Infinite[*]	(LL)
Loving[*]	I feel loving.
Thankful[*]	I feel thankful (prevalence in relaxation literature)
Distant	
Distant[*****]	Some things seem far away and distant.
Dissolving[***]	I feel my concerns and tensions dissolving way.
Detached[***]	I feel passively detached.
Passive[**]	(*See* I feel passively detached)
Indifferent[**]	I feel passively indifferent.
Heavy[***]	(*See* I feel heavy and limp)
Drowsy[**]	(NR)
Sinking[**]	I have a sensation of physically "sinking."

(continued)

TABLE A.3   *(continued)*

Forgetting**	I find myself forgetting things that do not matter.
Calm	
Relaxed*****	I feel relaxed.
Calm*****	I feel calm.
Rested****	I feel rested.
At ease****	I feel at ease.
Peaceful***	I feel peaceful.
Restored***	I feel restored.
Refreshed***	(R, Restored)
Soothed***	I feel soothed.
Contented**	I feel contented.
Carefree**	(R, At ease)
Laid back*	(LL)
Aware	
Awake****	I feel awake.
Aware****	I feel aware.
Focused***	I feel focused.
Clear***	My mind feels clear.
Energized***	I feel energized.
Confident**	I feel confident.
Strengthened**	I feel strengthened.
Asleep**	(NR)
Prayerful	
Prayerful****	I feel prayerful.
Spiritual****	I feel spiritual.
Reverent***	I feel reverent.
Selfless*	(LL)
Acceptance	
Accepted****	(NR)
Accepting****	(NR)
Limp	
Liquid****	My body feels limp or "liquid."
Loose***	My body feels loose and limp.
Limp***	I feel heavy and limp.
	My body feels limp.
Light*	(LL)
Tingling*	(LL)
Untroubled	
Unafraid***	(R, At peace)
Untroubled***	(R, At peace)
None	
Carefree*	(LL)
Childlike *	(LL)
Free*	(LL)

TABLE A.3 *(continued)*

Silent
    Silent[***]   (A)
    Simple[***]   (A)
    Speechless [*]   (LL, A)
Mystery
    Mystical[****]   I have mystical feelings.
    Mysterious[***]   I feel the mystery of things beyond my understanding.
Loads on no factor
    Absorbed

        Somatic stress—Discomfort and pain
           I feel fatigued.
           I am troubled by a backache.
           My skin condition seems worse (blemishes, oiliness).
        Somatic stress—Muscle tension
           My muscles feel tight, tense, or clenched up (furrowed brow, making fist, clenched jaws, etc.).
           I feel restless and fidgety.
           I feel uncoordinated.
           My shoulders, neck, or back feel tense.
        Somatic stress—Autonomic arousal
           My heart beats fast, hard, or irregularly.
           I breathe nervously (hurried, shallow, or uneven).
           I perspire or feel too warm.
           My mouth feels dry.
         Somatic stress—Digestive
           I have little appetite even if it is time to eat.
           I have a nervous or upset stomach.
           I feel the need to go to the rest room unnecessarily.
        Worry
           I worry too much.
           I have difficulty keeping troublesome thoughts out of mind.
           I think unimportant, bothersome thoughts.
        Negative emotion—Anxiety
           I feel anxious.
           I feel fearful.
         Negative emotion—Depression
           I feel sad or discouraged.
           I feel depressed or "blue."
         Negative emotion—Hostility
           I feel irritated or angry.
           I have feelings of contempt for something or someone.

(continued)

TABLE A.3   *(continued)*

I have feelings of distaste or disgust.
General Negative Emotion
I am troubled by negative thoughts.
I'm frustrated.
I feel shy.

---

[1] Excluded
R = Redundant with another item (listed)
DL = Item deleted because author judged reading difficulty level to be high
LL = Item's loading on factor is low
A = Meaning of item is ambiguous (could mean several things) or too general
ML = Item loads on more than one factor
NR = Not a relaxation item. Perhaps a relaxation aftereffect, belief, or supporting activity

Item Loadings
* $\geq .30$
** $\geq .40$
*** $\geq .50$
**** $\geq .60$
***** $\geq .70$

TABLE A.4   45/27-Item List and 25/3-Item List

45/27-Item List	25/3-Item List
Joyful	Joyful
I feel joyful.	I feel happy, joyful.
I feel happy.	(Included in above item)
I am having fun.	I am having fun, feeling playful.
I feel delighted.	(R, Fun, Joyful)
I feel glowing.	(A, R, Joyful)
Things seem beautiful.	Things seem beautiful.
I feel optimistic.	I feel optimistic, hopeful.
I feel hopeful.	(Included in above item)
I feel creative.	I feel creative, full of ideas.
I feel inspired.	(R, Creative, Full of ideas)
I feel a deep sense of knowing and understanding.	I have a deeper understanding (of life's meaning or purpose, what truly matters, etc.).
Things seem harmonious.	Things seem in harmony.
I feel loving.	I feel loving, caring.
I feel thankful.	I feel thankful.
Distant	Distant
Some things seem far away and distant.	I feel distant (far away; sensation of falling, sinking; moving deeper)
I feel my concerns and tensions dissolving away.	(A, Possible somatic content with "dissolving")
I feel passively detached.	I feel indifferent (detached, unconcerned, nothing matters)
I feel passively indifferent.	(Included in above item)
I find myself forgetting things that do not matter.	I find myself forgetting what I am doing, where I am (what was being said, going on around me.)
Calm	Calm
I feel relaxed.	I feel calm, at ease (relaxed, at peace, relieved, soothed, contented).
I feel calm.	(Included in above item)
I feel rested.	(Included in above item)
I feel at ease.	(Included in above item)
I feel peaceful.	(Included in above item)
I feel restored.	(R, Renewed, refreshed, New Item)
I feel soothed.	(Included in above item)
I feel contented.	(Combined in above item)
Aware	Aware
I feel awake.	I feel aware, awake, clear.
I feel aware.	(Included in above item)

(continued)

TABLE A.4 *(continued)*

45/27-Item List	25/3-Item List
I feel focused.	I feel focused (effortless, single-pointed, undistracted attention)
My mind feels clear.	(Included in above item)
I feel energized.	I feel energized, confident, strengthened.
I feel confident.	(Included in above item)
I feel strengthened.	(Included in above item)
Prayerful	Prayerful
I feel prayerful.	I feel spiritual (reverent, prayerful, selfless, filled with awe).
I feel spiritual.	(Included in above item)
I feel reverent.	(Included in above item)
I feel a sense of wonder.	(R, Spiritual, Filled with awe)
Limp	Limp
My body feels limp or "liquid."	I feel limp (loose, heavy, warm, dissolving).
My body feels loose and limp.	
I feel heavy and limp.	(Included in above item)
My body feels limp.	(Included in above item)
I have a sensation of physically "sinking."	(A, Cognitive component of distancing)
Mystery	Mystery
I have mystical feelings.	(A)
I have feelings of mystery (of the unknown, things beyond my understanding, etc.).	I feel the mystery of things beyond my understanding.
Somatic stress—Discomfort and pain	Somatic stress
I feel fatigued.	I have physical problems (body symptoms, discomfort, aches, tension).
I am troubled by a backache.	(Included in above item)
My skin condition seems worse (blemishes, oiliness).	(Included in above item)
Somatic stress—Muscle tension	
My muscles feel tight, tense, or clenched up (furrowed brow, making fist, clenched jaws, etc.).	(Included in above item)
I feel restless and fidgety.	(Included in above item)
I feel uncoordinated.	(Included in above item)
My shoulders, neck, or back feel tense.	(Included in above item)
Somatic stress—Autonomic arousal	
My heart beats fast, hard, or irregularly.	(Included in above item)
I breathe nervously (hurried, shallow, or uneven).	(Included in above item)
I perspire or feel too warm.	(Included in above item)

TABLE A.4 *(continued)*

45/27-Item List	25/3-Item List
My mouth feels dry.	(Included in above item)
Somatic stress—Digestive	
I have little appetite even if it is time to eat.	(Included in above item)
I have a nervous or upset stomach.	(Included in above item)
I feel the need to go to the rest room unnecessarily.	(Included in above item)
Worry	Worry
I worry too much.	Troublesome thoughts go through my mind.
I have difficulty keeping troublesome thoughts out of mind.	(Included in above item)
I think unimportant, bothersome thoughts.	(Included in above item)
Negative emotion—Anxiety	Negative emotion
I feel anxious.	I experience negative emotions (anger, anxiety, irritation, sadness, depression, frustration).
I feel fearful	(Included in above item)
Negative emotion—Depression	
I feel sad or discouraged.	(Included in above item)
I feel depressed or "blue."	(Included in above item)
Negative emotion—Hostility	
I feel irritated or angry.	(Included in above item)
I have feelings of contempt for something or someone.	(Included in above item)
I have feelings of distaste or disgust.	(Included in above item)
General negative emotion	
I am troubled by negative thoughts.	(Included in above item)
I'm frustrated.	(Included in above item)
I feel shy.	(Included in above item)
	New items
	I feel drowsy, sleepy.
	I find myself losing sensation in parts of my body (hands, feet, etc.).
	My breathing is relaxed (easy, unhurried, even).
	I feel safe, secure, protected.
	I felt speechless (beyond words, silent).
	I felt renewed, refreshed.

(continued)

TABLE A.4 *(continued)*	
45/27-Item List	25/3-Item List

	Rationales for New Items

I feel drowsy, sleepy. (I have been ambivalent about whether to include sleep-related experience as part of relaxation. For this inventory, I decided to include not sleep proper but experiences that precede sleep.)

I find myself losing sensation in parts of my body (hands, feet, etc.). (I hypothesize a differentiation of disengagement: attitudinal/cognitive (indifferent), memory/attentional (forgetting), spatial/cognitive (distant, far away), and somatic (losing sensation). Item added for exploratory purposes.)

My breathing is relaxed (easy, unhurried, even). (I added this on a hunch. Relaxed breathing had been the only easily reported sign of somatic relaxation not included in my previous listings.)

I feel safe, secure, protected. (Experience with clients and students suggested that this item may reflect a common relaxation experience not detected in our previous research.)

I feel renewed, refreshed. (Although renewed/refreshed appears to load on Aware, I decided to separate it from other aware items because of clinical experience.)

I felt speechless (beyond words, silent). (This emerged as a separate factor in both the Alexander [1991] and Smith et al. [1996] factor analyses. However, in the past I have deleted the word because it also tends to correlate with more than one factor [also with Distant] and because of item ambiguity. I decided to reintroduce the item, rewritten in the hope of enhancing precision of meaning.)

I have a deeper understanding (of life's meaning or purpose, what truly matters, etc.). (Understanding loaded with Joy in

TABLE A.4 *(continued)*

45/27-Item List	25/3-Item List
	both the Alexander [1991] and Smith et al. [1996] factor analyses. However, I had excluded it because of item ambiguity. I included a rewritten item.)

R = Redundant with another item (listed)
DL = Item deleted because author judged reading difficulty level to be high
LL = Item's loading on factor is low
A = Meaning of item is ambiguous (could mean several things) or too general
ML = Item loads on more than one factor
NR = Not a relaxation item. Perhaps a relaxation aftereffect, belief, or supporting activity

TABLE A.5 The 25/3-Item List and 19/3-Item List

25/3-Item List	19/3-Item List
Joyful	Joyful
I feel happy, joyful.	I feel happy, joyful.
I am having fun, feeling playful.	I am having fun, feeling playful.
Things seem beautiful.	Things seem beautiful.
I feel optimistic, hopeful.	I feel optimistic, hopeful.
I feel creative, full of ideas.	I feel creative, full of ideas.
I have a deeper understanding (of life's meaning or purpose, what truly matters, etc.).	(A)
Things seem in harmony.	Things seem in harmony.
I feel loving, caring.	I feel loving, caring.
I feel thankful.	I feel thankful.
Distant	Distant
I feel indifferent (detached, unconcerned, nothing matters).	I feel indifferent (detached, unconcerned, nothing matters).
I find myself losing sensation in parts of my body (hands, feet, etc.).	I find myself losing sensation in parts of my body (hands, feet, etc.).
I feel distant (far away; sensation of falling, sinking; moving deeper).	I feel distant (far away; sensation of falling, sinking; moving deeper).
I find myself forgetting what I am doing, where I am (what was being said, going on around me).	I find myself forgetting what I am doing, where I am (what was being said, going on around me).
Sleepiness	
I feel drowsy, sleepy.	(Undecided as to status of sleep as R-State)
Calm	Calm
My breathing is relaxed (easy, unhurried, even).	(ML)
I feel safe, secure; protected.	(ML, LL)
I feel calm, at ease (relaxed, at peace, relieved, soothed, contented).	I feel calm, at ease (relaxed, at peace, relieved, soothed, contented).
I feel renewed, refreshed.	(ML, LL)
Aware	Aware
I feel focused (effortless, single-pointed, undistracted attention).	I feel focused (relatively effortless, single-pointed, undistracted attention).
I feel aware, awake, clear.	I feel aware, awake, clear.
I feel energized, confident, strengthened.	I feel energized, confident, strengthened.
Prayerful	Prayerful
I feel spiritual (reverent, prayerful, selfless, filled with awe).	I feel spiritual (reverent, prayerful, selfless, filled with awe).

TABLE A.5 *(continued)*

25/3-Item List	19/3-Item List
Limp	Limp
I feel limp (loose, heavy, warm, dissolving).	I feel limp (loose, heavy, warm, dissolving).
Mystery	Mystery
I feel the mystery of things beyond my understanding.	I have feelings of mystery (of the unknown, things beyond my understanding, etc.).
Speechless	
I felt speechless (beyond words, silent).	(A)
Somatic stress	Somatic stress
I have physical problems (body symptoms, discomfort, aches, tension).	I have physical problems (body symptoms, discomfort, aches, tension).
Worry	Worry
Troublesome thoughts go through my mind.	Troublesome thoughts go through my mind.
Negative emotion	Negative emotion
I experience negative emotions (anger, anxiety, irritation, sadness, depression, frustration).	I experience negative emotions.

R = Redundant with another item (listed)
DL = Item deleted because author judged reading difficulty level to be high
LL = Item's loading on factor is low
A = Meaning of item is ambiguous (could mean several things) or too general
ML = Item loads on more than one factor
NR = Not a relaxation item. Perhaps a relaxation aftereffect, belief, or supporting activity

TABLE A.6   19/3-Item List and 18/6a-Item List

19/3-Item list	18/6a-Item List
Joyful	Joy
I feel happy, joyful.	I feel happy and joyful.
I am having fun, feeling playful.	I am having fun.
Things seem beautiful.	(ML with Joy and Spiritual)
I feel optimistic, hopeful.	(ML with Aware and Joy)
I feel creative, full of ideas.	(ML with Aware and Joy)
Things seem in harmony.	(ML with Joy and Spiritual)
	Love and Thankfulness
I feel loving, caring.	I feel loving.
I feel thankful.	I feel thankful.
Distant	Disengagement
I feel distant (far away; sensation of falling, sinking; moving deeper).	I feel distant and far away from my cares and concerns.
I feel indifferent (detached, unconcerned, nothing matters).	I feel indifferent and detached from my cares and concerns.
I find myself forgetting what I am doing, where I am (what was being said, going on around me).	(R, Distant)
I find myself losing sensation in parts of my body (hands, feet, etc.).	(A, with Physical Relaxation, Symptoms)
Calm	Mental Relaxation
I feel calm, at ease (relaxed, at peace, relieved, soothed, contented).	I feel at ease, at peace.
	I feel contented.
Aware	Strength and awareness
I feel aware, awake, clear.	I feel aware, focused, and clear (others deleted as redundant)
I feel focused (relatively effortless, single-pointed, undistracted attention)	(Combined with above item 1)
I feel energized, confident, strengthened.	I feel energized, confident, or strengthened.
Prayerful	Prayerfulness
I feel spiritual (reverent, prayerful, selfless, filled with awe).	I feel timeless, infinite, and boundless.
	I feel prayerful, reverent, or spiritual.
Limp	Physical relaxation
I feel limp (loose, heavy, warm, dissolving)	My body feels relaxed, warm and heavy.
	My muscles feel relaxed and limp.
Mystery	
I have feelings of mystery (of the unknown, things beyond my understanding, etc.).	(A, ML on Spiritual and Distant)

TABLE A.6   *(continued)*

19/3-Item list	18/6a-Item List

Somatic stress
  I have physical problems (body symptoms, discomfort, aches, tension).
	Somatic stress
	  My muscles feel tight, tense (clenched fist or jaws, furrowed brow).
	
	  I feel physical discomfort, pain (backaches, headaches, fatigue).
	  My breathing is nervous, uneven (shallow, hurried).

Worry
  Troublesome thoughts go through my mind.
	Worry
	  I am worrying (troublesome thoughts go through my mind).

Negative emotion
  I experience negative emotions (anger, anxiety, irritation, sadness, depression, frustration).
	Negative emotion
	  I feel sad, depressed, "blue."
	  I feel irritated, angry.
	  I feel anxious.
	Sleepiness
	  I am dozing off or napping.
	  I feel drowsy or sleepy.
	Mental quiet
	  My mind is quiet, without thought.
	  I feel an inner stillness, not thinking about anything.
	Rationales for additions:
	  I feel timeless, infinite, and boundless. Appeared as separate factor for both Alexander (1991) and Smith et al. (1996). Further clinical and instructional experience with this item suggests it may have meaning to a specific subset of relaxation practitioners. Included on an experimental basis.
	  I am dozing off or napping. I feel drowsy or sleepy. Decided to include sleep-related items because of importance in relaxation literature. I differentiated preliminary feelings (drowsy/sleepy) from feelings more associated with the actual event of beginning to fall asleep.
	  My mind is quiet, without thought. I feel an inner stillness, not thinking about anything. These items appeared as a separate factor in both the Alexander (1991)

(continued)

TABLE A.6 *(continued)*

19/3-Item list	18/6a-Item List
	and Smith et al. (1996) factor analyses. However, in the past I have deleted these items because they tend to correlate with more than one factor (also with Distant) and because of item ambiguity. I finally decided that "silent, simple, speechless" could mean several things: (1) a relatively quiet relaxation environment, (2) speechlessness as in awestruck, (3) a state of lassitude and inertia in which one has little motivation to engage in any verbal activity, and (4) speechlessness as in "mind is quiet, without thought." Meaning 1, the assessment of a quiet environment, is perhaps not an appropriate item for a questionnaire of relaxation states. Such a variable instead reflects relaxation technique and external environment. Meaning 2, "speechless, awestruck," is perhaps fully conveyed by the dimension Prayerful. Meaning 3, low-motivation inertia, is perhaps conveyed by detachment and drowsiness. I decided to generate items to reflect Meaning 4: "My mind is quiet, without thought" and "I feel an inner stillness, not thinking about anything." *I feel at ease, at peace, contented.* I decided no longer to use "calm" because of conceptual similarity to Inner Silence. I also decided against "soothed" because its range of meaning is very restricted ("soothed headache, soothed burn, soothed nerves"). "Relaxed" was deleted because it is too general. I wanted this dimension to reflect an absence of tension, conflict, frustration, and mental discomfort but not necessarily the absence of thought itself. "At ease" seems to reflect the absence of effort and striving common to tension, conflict, frustration, and discomfort. "At peace" clearly

TABLE A.6 *(continued)*

19/3-Item list	18/6a-Item List
	depicts the absence of conflict. "Contentment" refers more to the absence of frustration.
	Differentiated stress items included. Each somatic stress item reflects a somatic stress factor identified by Smith and Siebert (1984) and Smith and Seidel (1982) and three major aspects of negative emotion commonly reported in the stress literature (Smith, 1993b).

R = Redundant with another item (listed)
DL = Item deleted because author judged reading difficulty level to be high
LL = Item's loading on factor is low
A = Meaning of item is ambiguous (could mean several things) or too general
ML = Item loads on more than one factor
NR = Not a relaxation item. Perhaps a relaxation aftereffect, belief, or supporting activity

TABLE A.7   The 18/6a-Item List and 18/6b-Item List

The 18/6a Item List	The 18/6b Item List
Sleepiness	Sleepiness
I am dozing off or napping.	I am dozing off or napping
I feel drowsy or sleepy.	I feel drowsy or sleepy.
Disengagement	Disengagement
I feel distant and far away from my cares and concerns.	I feel distant and far away from my cares and concerns.
I feel indifferent and detached from my cares and concerns.	I feel indifferent and detached from my cares and concerns.
Physical Relaxation	Physical Relaxation
My body feels relaxed, warm, and heavy.	My hands, arms, and legs feel relaxed, warm, and heavy.
My muscles feel relaxed and limp.	My muscles feel relaxed and limp.
Mental Quiet	Mental Quiet
My mind is quiet, without thought.	My mind is calm, quiet, and still.
I feel an inner stillness, not thinking about anything.	My mind is silent and calm, not thinking about anything.
Mental Relaxation	Mental Relaxation
I feel at ease, at peace.	I feel at ease.
	I feel at peace.
I feel contented.	(See note)
Strength and Awareness	Strength and Awareness
I feel aware, focused, and clear.	I feel aware, focused, and clear.
I feel energized, confident, or strengthened.	I feel energized, confident, or strengthened.
Joy	Joy
I feel happy and joyful.	I feel happy.
I am having fun.	I feel joyful. (See note)
Love and Thankfulness	Love and Thankfulness
I feel thankful.	I feel thankful
I feel loving.	I feel loving.
Transcendence	Prayerfulness
I feel timeless, infinite, and boundless.	(See note)
I feel prayerful, reverent, or spiritual.	I feel prayerful and reverent.
	I feel spiritual.
	Timeless
	I feel "timeless, infinite, or boundless."
Stress Items Unchanged	(Stress Items Unchanged)
	Added: *My mind is quiet and still. My mind is silent and calm, not thinking about any-thing.* Changed "inner" because of ambiguous referent; could refer to "physical," "emotional," or "cognitive." I added "calm" to the descriptors, "silent," "quiet," and

TABLE A.7 *(continued)*	
The 18/6a Item List	The 18/6b Item List
	"still" to emphasize an absence of thought not resulting from distress or effort ("I was so shocked and upset, I couldn't think of anything; I was dumbfounded").
	Deleted: "I feel contented" deleted because of relatively low correlation with "at ease, at peace." "I am having fun" deleted because of low loading; too active a word for passive relaxation.
	Timeless, infinite, boundless. Included as separate, experimental scale.

Appendix B
Development of Relaxation Beliefs Inventory

INITIAL FACTOR ANALYSIS

I first incorporated an initial list of 34 R-Beliefs into a questionnaire. A team of student researchers presented this questionnaire to 350 participants, mostly college students from Roosevelt University and local Chicago-area junior colleges. About 80 questionnaires were distributed to various yoga and meditation training centers. Initial factor analysis yielded five orthogonal factors with eigenvalues of at least 1. We then specified five factors, using the varimax rotation and principal components procedure. Seventeen items loaded at least .60 on at least one factor. We repeated the factor analysis on the remaining 17 items, again specifying five factors. See Table B.1 at end of Appendix B.

Examination of item content appears to suggest the following factor dimensions:

Deeper perspective (detachment from life's problems in light of some unspecified, larger positive perspective)

Positive self-acceptance (acceptance of oneself and acceptance of relaxation enjoyment)

God's love

Inner forces

Neutral detachment (acceptance of the world as it is, without reference to any positive perspective)

I used this factor analysis as a very tentative heuristic tool, to suggest what patterns might be merging and to highlight R-Beliefs that might be missed. The next step was to delete low-loading items for each factor, items that load on

171

multiple factors, and conceptually redundant items. I then generated additional items so that each factor category had roughly an equal number of items. Questionnaires were distributed to a group of 314 college students and some yoga trainees and factor analyzed. Initial factor analysis suggested eight factors with eigenvalues of 1 or more. I then repeated the analysis, specifying the eight factors. The factor solution and inventory content are reported in Table B.2 at the end of Appendix B.

I repeated this process, again looking for categories of R-Beliefs that may have been missed. After extensive discussions with six graduate research assistants, three PhD psychology faculty members, and several hundred relaxation trainees, I generated a final list of R-Belief item candidates, specifying two items for each belief (Table B.3 at the end of Appendix B). I tentatively postulated three groups of R-Beliefs: *Spiritual Living* ("God loves you" "You are part of a larger universe," "There are sources of strength and healing deep within you," "Joyfully celebrate the gifts of life," and "Life has a purpose greater than your personal wants and desires"), *Positive Living with Oneself and the World* ("Love and respect everyone," "See things as they are," "Be honest with your feelings," "Live in the present," "Accept yourself as you are," and "Be optimistic"), and *Living with Problems*, including thoughts that might enable a relaxer to temporarily put concerns about external problems aside during the course of relaxation ("There is more to life than your everyday hassles," "Acknowledge your mistakes and be willing to change," "Put aside what may feel temporarily pleasant or comfortable," "Accept things as the are, " "Stop trying and relax," "Slow down and take it easy," "It can be important to put aside and forget your cares").

FINAL FACTOR ANALYSES AND SCALE DEVELOPMENT

A team of student researchers and I conducted two factor analyses on the above belief scale. Our goal was to maximize differentiation of factors whenever they are highly interpretable with simple meaning. Mui (in press) gave this scale to two groups of college students, again supplemented by about 10% yoga participants.

Principal components analysis (our default choice in all past relaxation research) failed to produce a solution for either sample. We then attempted a principal axis factor analysis, again specifying a varimax rotation. Factor analysis of sample 1 yielded 7 interpetable factors, and sample 2 yielded 10. See Tables B.4 and B.5 at the end of Appendix B.

I deployed several strategies for screening items from both factor analyses. My first step was to identify those factors that appeared in both analyses. Designated by their top two loading items, they included the following four factors:

Life has a purpose greater than my personal wants and desires.
There's more to life than my personal concerns and worries.

God guides, loves, and comforts me.
I put myself in God's hands.

Sometimes it is important to simply take it easy.
It is important to know when to stop trying for a while and let go and relax.

I trust the body's wisdom and healing powers.
There are sources of strength and healing deep within me.

Factor analysis of Sample 2 yielded a separate factor, with clear and distinct meaning. I chose to include that factor in our final listing. Item content included

It is important to show love and respect for all.
It is important to treat people with compassion.

Two factors emerged for Sample 2 that appeared to have similar content and clear meaning. Their emergence as separate factors did not appear justified.

I believe in being direct and clear in what I say, think, and do.
It is important to understand the world clearly, without bias and distortion.
I believe in being honest and open with my feelings.

All three of these items loaded highly on a global undifferentiated Factor 1 for Sample 1. I decided to treat these three items as a single provisional scale for both Sample 1 and Sample 2, and conduct alpha reliability analyses of the same group of items for each sample. In both samples, the items "I believe in being direct and clear in what I say, think, and do" and "I believe in being honest and open with my feelings" were retained; "It is important to understand the world clearly, without bias and distortion" could be removed with virtually no reduction in alpha. Thus, our next isolated factor dimension included

I believe in being direct and clear in what I say, think, and do.
I believe in being honest and open with my feelings.

The following six items divided into different factors for samples 1 and 2, presenting us with a dilemma.

I'm optimistic about how well I will deal with my current hassles.
I believe in being optimistic.
I can accept things as they are.
I accept myself as I am.
There's no need to try to change things that simply can't be changed.
I believe in fully enjoying every moment.

I isolated these six items and conducted a factor analysis for on each group for samples 1 and 2. Both yielded two factors, and for each the top two loading items were the same:

I'm optimistic about how well I will deal with my current hassles.
I believe in being optimistic.

and

I can accept things as they are.
There's no need to try to change things that simply can't be changed.

I retained these as our final two dimensions.

For exploratory purposes I then attempted a different strategy in factor-analyzing items. I selected the specific items designated for the eight dimensions just defined, and factor-analyzed them, combining the Mui sample. Both analyses yielded four global factors in common: Acceptance of Things as They Are, Love for Others, Trust in God, and Optimism. It remains for future research to determine whether the differentiated model or the global model of relaxation philosophies is more useful.

TABLE B.1 Initial Factor Analysis of 34 Relaxation Belief Items

Factor 1 (15.49, 45.6)[a]

There are more important things than my everyday hassles.***
I can accept that I am not in control of some things in my life.**
There is more to life than my worries and problems.** (.405 on Factor 2)
It is OK if I do not get exactly what I want.**
Selfish worries distract from a deeper reality.**
My desires are not as urgent as I sometimes feel.**
Love is what really matters.**
Live simply.**
My concerns seem less urgent when seen in true perspective.** (.436 on Factor 2)
I need not strive so much for perfection.*
Be not too concerned with things that do not matter.*
It time, my troubles will pass.*
Be open to my feelings.*
Let answers come from deep within.* (.401 on Factor 2)
Not everything is my responsibility.*

Factor 2 (1.38, 49.7)

At the deepest level "I feel at peace with myself—I am an OK person." **
I am on earth to enjoy the gift of life.**
I accept myself as I am.**
Enjoy deeply every moment.**
It is good for me to let go and relax.**
It is good to be alive.** (.412 on Factor 1)
Inside, I am a beautiful person.* (.499 on Factor 4)
I trust that things will work out OK.* (.516 on Factor 3)

Factor 3 (1.32, 53.6)

God's will be done.***
God loves me and has a plan for my life.***
I trust that things will work out OK.* (.511 on Factor 2)
If it is meant to be, it will happen.**

Factor 4 (1.284, 57.4)

Do not worry about things that cannot be changed.**
Live with things as they are, even if they are not exactly as I desire.**

Factor 5 (1.101, 60.7)

Let the healing forces of life within do their work.***

Note: Only highest loading items are reported. Participants are a subsample from Holmes, Ritchie, & Allen, D. (in press).
$N = 350$ (M = 112, F = 238), ave. age = 35.12 (SD = 8.23).
[a]Eigenvalue, cumulative percentage of variance accounted for.
* Factor loadings ≥ .50.
** Factor loadings ≥ .60.
*** Factor loadings ≥ .70.
**** Factor loadings ≥ .80.

TABLE B.2 Factor Analysis of 30 Belief Items

Factor 1 (6.904, 23.012)[a]
  God guides and comforts me.[*****]
  God's will be done.[****]
  God loves me.[****]
  God has a plan for my life.[****]
  Let God be the center of my life.[****]
  God forgives me.[****]
Factor 2 (3.754, 35.524)
  Trust the body's wisdom and healing powers.[***]
  Healing forces exist deep within me.[***]
  I have inner sources of strength and wisdom.[**]
Factor 3 (1.915, 41.908)
  There is more to life than my worries and concerns.[***]
  There are more important things than my everyday hassles.[***]
  My hassles seem insignificant when I remember what really matters.[**]
  When I see things in perspective, my problems do not seem so bad.[**]
Factor 4 (1.633, 47.35)
  It is OK if I do not get exactly what I want.[***]
  I accept that some things may not change.[***]
Factor 5 (1.500, 52.35)
  At the deepest level I feel at peace with myself—I am an OK person.[**]
  I accept myself as I am.[**]
  I can live with things as they are.[**]
Factor 6 (1.364, 56.838)
  It is good for me to let go and relax.[***]
  Sometimes it is best to be detached from life's hassles.[**]
Factor 7 (1.117, 60.56)
  What will be, will be.[***]
  I don't have to take things so seriously.[**]
Factor 8 (1.057, 64.084)
  Enjoy deeply every moment.[***]

Note: Only highest loading items are reported. Participants are a subsample from Holmes, Ritchie, & Allen, D. (in press).

$N = 314$ (M = 103, F = 202), ave. age = 23.28 (SD = 7.75).

[a]Eigenvalue, cumulative percentage of variance accounted for.

[*] Factor loadings $\geq$ .50.
[**] Factor loadings $\geq$ .60.
[***] Factor loadings $\geq$ .70.
[****] Factor loadings $\geq$ .80.
[*****] Factor loadings $\geq$ .90.

TABLE B.3   Interim Catalog of R-Belief Item Candidates

Spiritual Living

God's World
 God guides, loves, and comforts me.
 I put myself in God's hands.
Deeper Reality
 I believe I am part of a larger universe.
 I believe there is a deeper reality beyond my comprehension.
Inner Strength
 There are sources of strength and healing deep within me.
 I trust the body's wisdom and healing powers.
Celebration
 I believe in joyfully celebrating the gifts of life.
 Worship, devotion, and giving thanks are an important part of life.
Purpose
 Life has a purpose greater than my personal wants and desires.
 I believe it is important to live for something larger than oneself.

Positive Living with Oneself and the World

Love and Respect
 It is important to show love and respect for all.
 It is important to treat people with compassion.
Clear Understanding
 It is important to see things as they really are.
 It is important to understand the world clearly, without bias and distortion.
Honesty
 I believe in being honest and open with my feelings.
 I believe in being direct and clear in what I say, think, and do.
Full Living
 Live fully in the present.
 I believe in fully enjoying every moment.
Self-Acceptance
 I accept myself as I am.
 At the deepest level, I'm an OK person.
Optimism (dispositional vs. situational)
 I believe in being optimistic.
 I'm optimistic about how well I will deal with my current hassles.

Living with Problems

Perspective
 There are more important things in life than my everyday hassles.
 There's more to life than my personal concerns and worries.
Forgiveness and Change
 It is important to acknowledge mistakes and be willing to change.
 Sometimes it is best to forgive and go on with life.

(continued)

TABLE B.3   *(continued)*

Detachment
  Sometimes it is best to let go of habits and attachments.
  Sometimes one should put aside what seems pleasant or comfortable.
Situational Acceptance
  It's OK if I don't have exactly what I want.
  I can accept things as they are.
Letting Go
  There's no need to try to change things that simply can't be changed.
  It's important to know when to stop trying for a while and let go and relax.
Taking It Easy
  Sometimes it is important to simply take it easy.
  Sometimes it is important to take time for quiet relaxation.
Getting Away from It All
  It is important to get away from it all.
  Sometimes one should put aside and forget one's cares and concerns.

TABLE B.4 Factor Solution for Final Belief Statements: Mui Sample #1

Factor	1	2	3	4	5	6	7
1							
It is important to acknowledge mistakes and be willing to change.	.637	.350	.122	.245	.139	.002	.002
I believe in being direct and clear in what I say, think, and do.	.592	.105	-.001	.115	.006	.007	.160
It is important to treat people with compassion.	.591	.383	.179	.148	.158	-.001	-.003
I believe in being honest and open with my feelings.	.582	.132	.007	.178	.168	.111	.110
It is important to show love and respect for all.	.533	.347	.299	.008	.213	-.001	.002
It is important to see things as they really are.	.499	.202	.008	.283	.104	.295	.006
It is important to understand the world clearly, without bias and distortion.	.488	.268	.004	.005	.221	.138	.124
I believe in joyfully celebrating the gifts of life.	.465	.249	.305	.227	.266	.112	.198
At the deepest level, I'm an OK person.	.446	.149	.108	.256	.256	.006	.151
Live fully in the present.	.313	.132	-.002	.233	.296	.291	.128
Sometimes it is best to forgive and go on with life.	.320	.257	.004	.149	.145	-.006	.004
2							
There's more to life than my personal concerns and worries	.365	.577	.008	.259	.003	.006	.001
I believe I am part of a larger universe.	.186	.559	.007	.153	.148	.001	.311
Life has a purpose greater than my personal wants and desires.	.277	.553	.303	.164	.003	.003	.108
I believe it is important to live for something larger than oneself.	.286	.526	.341	.150	.002	.008	.189
I believe there is a deeper reality beyond my comprehension.	.335	.524	.229	.115	-.004	.003	.241
There are more important things in life than my everyday hassles.	.252	.481	.004	.221	.004	.007	.002
It's OK if I don't have exactly what I want.	.178	.423	.163	.131	.116	.200	-.003
Sometimes one should put aside and forget one's cares and concerns.	-.005	.419	.004	.253	.236	.251	.004
Sometimes one should put aside what seems pleasant or comfortable.	.005	.299	.002	-.006	.121	.112	.003
Sometimes it is best to let go of habits and attachments.	.259	.291	.144	.281	.242	.266	-.002

(continued)

179

TABLE B.4 (continued)

Factor	1	2	3	4	5	6	7
3							
God guides, loves, and comforts me.	.006	.145	.852	.004	.00	.002	.008
I put myself in God's hands.	.007	.105	.889	.000	.109	.007	.007
Worship, devotion, and giving thanks are an important part of my life	.147	.170	.772	.009	.009	.002	.006
4							
Sometimes it is important to simply take it easy.	.323	.147	.111	.582	.165	.006	.009
It's important to know when to stop trying for a while and let go and relax.	.350	.259	.008	.566	.120	.223	.005
It is important to get away from it all.	.164	.243	-.002	.540	.112	.118	.005
Sometimes it is important to take time for quiet relaxation.	.471	.205	.125	.495	.106	.007	.009
5							
I'm optimistic about how well I will deal with my current hassles.	.172	.144	.149	.160	.621	.007	.241
I accept myself as I am.	.346	.007	.128	.007	.529	.199	-.001
I believe in being optimistic.	.380	.183	.006	.257	.474	.000	.220
I believe in fully enjoying every moment.	.389	.006	.150	.215	.395	.109	.193
6							
There's no need to try to change things that simply can't be changed.	.001	.008	.009	.139	.003	.512	.154
I can accept things as they are.	.190	.255	.123	.003	.396	.493	-.008
7							
I trust the body's wisdom and healing powers.	.224	.175	.008	.005	.221	.381	.563
There are sources of strength and healing deep within me.	.234	.196	.268	.150	.219	.009	.570

N = 496 (M = 204, F = 285), ave. age = 22.70; SD = 842

Initial eigenvalues and cumulative percent of variance accounted for: Factor 1 = 11.813, 32.813; Factor 2 = 2.400, 39.480; Factor 3 = 1.749, 44.338; Factor 4 = 1.560, 48.672; Factor 5 = 1.202, 52.011; Factor 6 = 1.132, 52.155; Factor 7 = 1.030, 58.017.

From Mui (in press).

TABLE B.5 Factor Solution for Final Belief Statements: Mui Sample #2

Factor	1	2	3	4	5	6	7	8	9	10
1										
There are more important things in life than my everyday hassles.	.591	.004	.180	.189	.003	.004	.009	.004	−.009	.009
Life has a purpose greater than my personal wants and desires.	.585	.267	.110	.006	.003	.009	.189	.003	.008	.000
There's more to life than my personal concerns and worries.	.564	.007	.108	.118	.003	.009	.003	.000	.006	.176
I believe it is important to live for something larger than oneself.	.504	.276	.153	.007	.005	.002	.006	.003	.339	−.172
I believe there is a deeper reality beyond my comprehension.	.433	.119	.102	−.001	.007	.342	.002	−.002	.242	.008
I believe I am part of a larger universe.	.432	.007	.187	.003	.006	.324	.174	−.001	.008	−.003
Sometimes one should put aside what seems pleasant and comfortable.	.414	.004	.116	−.001	.009	.101	−.005	.192	.134	.000
It's OK if I don't have exactly what I want.	.403	.001	.005	.010	.004	.005	.195	.306	−.009	.112
Sometimes it is best to let go of habits and attachments.	.313	.007	.134	.134	.110	.155	.191	.270	.282	.004
Sometimes it is best to forgive and go on with life.	.288	.210	.248	.208	.008	.136	.187	−.005	.211	.117
2										
God guides, loves, and comforts me.	.131	.889	.003	.005	−.005	.009	.005	.003	−.003	.111
I put myself in God's hands.	.103	.856	−.001	.004	−.003	.009	.111	.106	.006	.006
Worship, devotion, and giving thanks are an important part of life.	.180	.749	.001	.009	.004	.151	.144	.006	.008	−.001

(continued)

181

TABLE B.5 *(continued)*

Factor	1	2	3	4	5	6	7	8	9	10
3										
Sometimes it is important to simply take it easy.	.217	-.004	.609	.174	.006	.009	.005	-.005	.134	.127
Sometimes it is important to take time for quiet relaxation.	.212	.006	.601	.005	.000	.009	.173	.002	.140	.142
It is important to know when to stop trying for a while and let go and relax.	.153	.005	.555	.004	.007	.158	.002	.173	.178	-.002
It is important to get away from it all.	.161	-.005	.419	.003	.005	-.001	.106	.108	-.005	.000
Live fully in the present.	-.002	.003	.419	.134	.004	.006	.005	.193	.118	.151
I believe in fully enjoying every moment.	.006	.137	.388	.320	.003	.143	.172	.137	-.002	.278
4										
I'm optimistic about how well I will deal with my current hassles.	.009	.006	.007	.767	.004	.109	-.001	.008	.194	-.002
I believe in being optimistic.	.204	.006	.108	.641	.005	.009	.107	.006	.006	.106
At the deepest level I'm an OK person.	.004	.153	.238	.266	-.002	.208	.138	.133	.117	.005
5										
It is important to acknowledge mistakes and be willing to change.	.009	.007	.008	.006	.828	.000	.106	-.004	.006	.010
Sometimes one should put aside and forget one's cares and concerns.	.114	-.004	.009	.001	.928	.007	-.005	.162	-.003	-.005

TABLE B.5 (continued)

Factor	1	2	3	4	5	6	7	8	9	10
6										
I trust the body's wisdom and healing powers.	.112	.120	.134	.009	.006	.666	.000	.195	.009	.008
There are sources of strength and healing deep within me.	.235	.175	.008	.214	.001	.588	.105	-.004	.008	.009
7										
It is important to show love and respect for all.	.126	.240	.180	.009	.004	.009	.686	.107	.113	.130
It is important to treat people with compassion.	.341	.166	.269	.010	.007	.003	.515	.009	.123	.128
8										
I can accept things as they are.	.102	-.003	.007	.194	.004	.004	.165	.614	.129	.135
I accept myself as I am.	-.003	.109	.142	.342	.000	.006	.215	.438	.146	.229
There's no need to try to change things that simply can't be changed.	.007	.130	.194	-.008	.005	.006	-.008	.400	.002	-.107
9										
I believe in being direct and clear in what I say, think, and do.	.007	.009	.271	.188	.001	.007	-.005	.007	.494	.402
It is important to understand the world clearly, without bias and distortion.	.119	.006	.009	.162	-.001	.276	.273	.183	.318	.004
It is important to see things as they really are.	.007	.008	.007	.008	.002	.004	.008	.006	.272	.005

(continued)

TABLE B.5 *(continued)*

Factor	1	2	3	4	5	6	7	8	9	10
10										
I believe in being honest and open with my feelings.	.163	.007	.127	.005	.005	.119	.201	.009	.151	.481
I believe in joyfully celebrating the gifts of life.	.279	.295	.257	.252	.008	.237	.154	−.003	.008	.330

N = 1,167 (M = 461, F = 698) ave. age = 22.92, SD = 7.90

Initial eigenvalues and cumulative percent of variance accounted for: Factor 1 = 8.314, 23.093; Factor 2 = 2.423, 29.824; Factor 3 = 1.955, 35.255; Factor 4 = 1.581, 49.647; Factor 5 = 1.448, 43.670; Factor 6 = 1.372, 47.482; Factor 7 = 1.331, 51.179; Factor 8 = 1.154, 54.179; Factor 9 = 1.22, 57.504; Factor 10 = 1.012, 60.316.

From Mui (in press).

Appendix C

Smith Relaxation
Inventory Series

I am making available six inventories that tap the relaxation variables introduced in this book. The Smith Relaxation States Inventory (SRSI) measures one's immediate level of relaxation and stress. It is appropriate for process studies examining immediate changes during the course of a relaxation activity. The Smith Post Relaxation Inventory (SPRI) measures the immediate effects of a relaxation activity. The Smith Recalled Relaxation Activity Inventory (SRRAI) asks participants to recall and describe relaxation states associated with a relaxation activity. Much of the research in this book is based on the SRRAI, which is proving to be a highly sensitive measure. The Smith Relaxation Dispositions/ Motivations Inventory (SRDMI) measures one's propensity to be relaxed over a 2-week period (disposition) as well as one's desire to be more relaxed (motivation). Both are appropriate outcome measures for treatment intervention. The Smith Relaxation Beliefs Inventory (SRBI) measures beliefs hypothesized to be conducive to deeper and more generalized relaxation. The Smith Relaxation Concern's Inventory (SRCI) assesses the most frequent goals people have for learning relaxation.

Please note that all Smith Relaxation Inventories are under development. The versions included here are current as of April, 1999. If you wish to use any inventory in this series, including those not yet developed, please contact the publisher for the most current version.

INSTRUCTIONS FOR OBTAINING
PERMISSION TO USE

The Smith Relaxation Inventory Series is owned by Springer Publishing Company. It is illegal to use any inventory from this series without prior written permission from the publisher. To acquire permission to copy and use and to receive a scoring key and manual, contact the publisher.

BACKGROUND INFORMATION

Your Gender: ❑ M ❑ F   **Your Age:** _____

Your Annual Income (closest amount):
  ❑ $10,000 ❑ $20,000 ❑ $30,000 ❑ $40,000 ❑ $50,000 ❑ $60,000 ❑ $70,000
  ❑ $80,000 ❑ $90,000

Check if you are: ❑ Currently in any type of psychotherapy.

Check if you are taking a prescription psychiatric medication for:
  ❑ Anxiety ❑ Depression ❑ Other _____

Highest Level of Education:
  ❑ Some high school ❑ Finished high school ❑ Some college ❑ Finished undergrad
  ❑ At least some grad school

Are you (optional):
  ❑ Gay/Lesbian ❑ Bisexual ❑ Heterosexual ❑ Transgendered

Religious Affiliation:
  ❑ Buddhist ❑ Catholic ❑ Hindu ❑ Jewish ❑ Muslim/Islamic ❑ Protestant
  ❑ New Age/Yoga/Meditation ❑ None

Family Background:
  ❑ Upper Class ❑ Middle Class ❑ Blue Collar/Working Class ❑ Poor

Are you:
  ❑ African American ❑ Hispanic ❑ Caucasian ❑ Native American
  ❑ Asian/Pacific Islander

How well does the term you chose in the above question describe you?
  ❑ Not at All ❑ A Little ❑ Moderately ❑ A Lot ❑ Totally

Which best describes your ethnic and cultural heritage?

❑ Africa	❑ South American	❑ Native North American Indian
❑ Chinese	❑ Caribbean Islands	❑ Middle Eastern
❑ Indian/India	❑ Pacific Islands	❑ European
❑ North American	❑ Japanese	❑ Korean ❑ Other Asian

How well does what you chose in the above Question describe you?
  ❑ Not at All ❑ A Little ❑ Moderately ❑ A Lot ❑ Totally

Were one or both of your parents born in the U.S.?
  ❑ One ❑ Both ❑ Neither ❑ Don't Know

(continued)

SRRAI

RELAXATION ACTIVITY

PEOPLE DO MANY THINGS FOR *RELAXATION AND RENEWAL*. WE ARE INTER-
ESTED IN WHAT CAN BE DONE *PASSIVELY* IN A RELAXED STANDING,
SEATED, OR RESTING POSITION (*This* **excludes** *hobbies, camping, hiking, taking
trips, dancing, movies, TV, parties, sports, fitness exercises, forms of recreation, sex,
eating, drugs, alcohol, tobacco. We are also excluding activities that involve talking to
or interacting with other people.*) BELOW ARE EXAMPLES OF PASSIVE FORMS
OF RELAXATION AND RENEWAL. PLEASE CHECK HOW MANY **TIMES A
WEEK** you do each activity. Please write your answers in the blanks.

I DO THIS ACTIVITY ___ TIMES A WEEK (FILL IN BLANK BY ITEM)

1. _____ Art / Pictures (Looking at, appreciating)

2. _____ Audio relaxation tapes

3. _____ Breathing exercises

4. _____ Church / synagog, temple (attending)

5. _____ Daydreaming

6. _____ Hatha yoga stretches

7. _____ Hot tubs / baths

8. _____ Hypnosis (self)

9. _____ Imagery / visualization

10. _____ Massage

11. _____ Meditation (TM)

12. _____ Meditation (mantra, not TM)

13. _____ Meditation (breathing, Zen, Mindfulness)

14. _____ Music (Playing for self)

15. _____ Music (Listening to)

16. _____ Nature appreciation

17. _____ Petting pets

18. _____   Prayer (alone, not in group)

19. _____   Prayer (with others, in group)

20. _____   Progressive muscle relaxation

21. _____   Radio, listening to

22. _____   Reading the Bible/Koran

23. _____   Reading Fiction

24. _____   Reading (inspirational – not Bible/Koran)

25. _____   Reading Nonfiction

26. _____   Reading Poetry

27. _____   Progressive muscle relaxation

28. _____   Resting in bed

29. _____   Showers, baths

30. _____   Steam baths

31. _____   Sunbathing

32. _____   TV, watching (including video tapes)

33. _____   Yoga (hatha)

34. _____   Walking (leisurely)

(continued)

RELAXATION ACTIVITY
(continued)

Please think about the past two weeks. What was the single MOST REWARDING AND EFFECTIVE passive thing you did for relaxation and renewal? It doesn't have to be any of those listed above. Please describe this in the box below. As much as possible, be specific and detailed:

MY PASSIVE FORM OF RELAXATION AND RENEWAL (DONE IN A RELAXED STANDING, SEATED, OR RESTING POSITION)

How often do you engage in this activity alone, by yourself? How many days out of the week?
   ❑ Less than 1 day a week ❑ 1 day a week ❑ 2 days ❑ 3 days
   ❑ 4 days ❑ 5 days ❑ 6 days ❑ 7 days

How often do you engage in this activity in a group, with others?
   ❑ Less than 1 day a week ❑ 1 day a week ❑ 2 days ❑ 3 days
   ❑ 4 days ❑ 5 days ❑ 6 days ❑ 7 days

For about how many years and/or months have you engaged in this activity?
   _____ Years _____ Months

How skilled are you at this activity? (Skip if not applicable)
   ❑ 1. Not at all ❑ 2. Slightly ❑ 3. Moderately ❑ 4. Very much

Now, please close your eyes and recall what you've just described in the above box. What was this activity like? What did you experience? On the next page are some phrases that describe experience people often have. Please recall how you felt while engaged in the activity you put in the above box and answer the questions provided.

SRRAI

PLEASE CHECK TO WHAT EXTENT YOU FELT EACH OF THE FOLLOWING DURING OR JUST AFTER THE ACTIVITY YOU DESCRIBED IN THE BOX ON THE OTHER PAGE.

1. **I felt AT EASE ...**
   ❏ 1. Not at all ❏ 2. A little ❏ 3. Moderately ❏ 4. Very much
2. **I felt AWARE, FOCUSED, and CLEAR ...**
   ❏ 1. Not at all ❏ 2. A little ❏ 3. Moderately ❏ 4. Very much
3. **My mind was CALM, QUIET, AND STILL.**
   ❏ 1. Not at all ❏ 2. A little ❏ 3. Moderately ❏ 4. Very much
4. **My hands, arms, or legs felt relaxed, WARM and HEAVY ...**
   ❏ 1. Not at all ❏ 2. A little ❏ 3. Moderately ❏ 4. Very much
5. **I was HAPPY ...**
   ❏ 1. Not at all ❏ 2. A little ❏ 3. Moderately ❏ 4. Very much
6. **I was DOZING OFF or NAPPING ...**
   ❏ 1. Not at all ❏ 2. A little ❏ 3. Moderately ❏ 4. Very much
7. **I felt THANKFUL ...**
   ❏ 1. Not at all ❏ 2. A little ❏ 3. Moderately ❏ 4. Very much
8. **I felt DISTANT and FAR AWAY from my cares and concerns ...**
   ❏ 1. Not at all ❏ 2. A little ❏ 3. Moderately ❏ 4. Very much
9. **I felt JOYFUL ...**
   ❏ 1. Not at all ❏ 2. A little ❏ 3. Moderately ❏ 4. Very much
10. **I felt "TIMELESS," "INFINITE," and "BOUNDLESS" ...**
    ❏ 1. Not at all ❏ 2. A little ❏ 3. Moderately ❏ 4. Very much
11. **My muscles felt relaxed and LIMP ...**
    ❏ 1. Not at all ❏ 2. A little ❏ 3. Moderately ❏ 4. Very much
12. **I felt LOVING ...**
    ❏ 1. Not at all ❏ 2. A little ❏ 3. Moderately ❏ 4. Very much
13. **I felt INDIFFERENT and DETACHED from my cares and concerns ...**
    ❏ 1. Not at all ❏ 2. A little ❏ 3. Moderately ❏ 4. Very much
14. **I felt AT PEACE ...**
    ❏ 1. Not at all ❏ 2. A little ❏ 3. Moderately ❏ 4. Very much
15. **My mind was SILENT AND CALM, not thinking about anything ...**
    ❏ 1. Not at all ❏ 2. A little ❏ 3. Moderately ❏ 4. Very much
16. **I felt PRAYERFUL and REVERENT ...**
    ❏ 1. Not at all ❏ 2. A little ❏ 3. Moderately ❏ 4. Very much
17. **I felt DROWSY and SLEEPY ...**
    ❏ 1. Not at all ❏ 2. A little ❏ 3. Moderately ❏ 4. Very much
18. **I felt ENERGIZED, CONFIDENT, or STRENGTHENED ...**
    ❏ 1. Not at all ❏ 2. A little ❏ 3. Moderately ❏ 4. Very much

(continued)

PLEASE CHECK TO WHAT EXTENT YOU FELT
EACH OF THE FOLLOWING DURING OR JUST AFTER
THE ACTIVITY YOU DESCRIBED IN THE BOX ON THE OTHER PAGE.
(continued)

19. **I felt SPIRITUAL ...**
    ❏ 1. Not at all ❏ 2. A little ❏ 3. Moderately ❏ 4. Very much
20. **My muscles felt TIGHT, TENSE • Clenched fist or jaws • Furrowed brow**
    ❏ 1. Not at all ❏ 2. A little ❏ 3. Moderately ❏ 4. Very much
21. **I felt SAD, DEPRESSED, "BLUE"**
    ❏ 1. Not at all ❏ 2. A little ❏ 3. Moderately ❏ 4. Very much
22. **I felt PHYSICAL DISCOMFORT, PAIN • Backaches • Headaches • Fatigue**
    ❏ 1. Not at all ❏ 2. A little ❏ 3. Moderately ❏ 4. Very much
23. **I was WORRYING • Troublesome thoughts went through my mind**
    ❏ 1. Not at all ❏ 2. A little ❏ 3. Moderately ❏ 4. Very much
24. **I felt IRRITATED, ANGRY**
    ❏ 1. Not at all ❏ 2. A little ❏ 3. Moderately ❏ 4. Very much
25. **My BREATHING was NERVOUS, UNEVEN • Shallow • Hurried**
    ❏ 1. Not at all ❏ 2. A little ❏ 3. Moderately ❏ 4. Very much
26. **I felt ANXIOUS.**
    ❏ 1. Not at all ❏ 2. A little ❏ 3. Moderately ❏ 4. Very much

SRDMI

THINK BACK OVER THE PAST TWO WEEKS. TO WHAT EXTENT DID YOU EXPERIENCE THE FOLLOWING?

1. I felt AT EASE ...
❑ 1. Not at all ❑ 2. A little ❑ 3. Moderately ❑ 4. Very much
■ Would you like to feel this more ? ❑ 1. No ❑ 2. A Little ❑ 3. Somewhat more
❑ 4. Much more

2. I felt AWARE, FOCUSED, and CLEAR ...
❑ 1. Not at all ❑ 2. A little ❑ 3. Moderately ❑ 4. Very much
■ Would you like to feel this more ? ❑ 1. No ❑ 2. A Little ❑ 3. Somewhat more
❑ 4. Much more

3. My mind was CALM, QUIET AND STILL.
❑ 1. Not at all ❑ 2. A little ❑ 3. Moderately ❑ 4. Very much
■ Would you like to feel this more ? ❑ 1. No ❑ 2. A Little ❑ 3. Somewhat more
❑ 4. Much more

4. My hands, arms, or legs felt relaxed, WARM and HEAVY ...
❑ 1. Not at all ❑ 2. A little ❑ 3. Moderately ❑ 4. Very much
■ Would you like to feel this more ? ❑ 1. No ❑ 2. A Little ❑ 3. Somewhat more
❑ 4. Much more

5. I was HAPPY ...
❑ 1. Not at all ❑ 2. A little ❑ 3. Moderately ❑ 4. Very much
■ Would you like to feel this more ? ❑ 1. No ❑ 2. A Little ❑ 3. Somewhat more
❑ 4. Much more

6. I was DOZING OFF or NAPPING ...
❑ 1. Not at all ❑ 2. A little ❑ 3. Moderately ❑ 4. Very much
■ Would you like to feel this more ? ❑ 1. No ❑ 2. A Little ❑ 3. Somewhat more
❑ 4. Much more

7. I felt THANKFUL ...
❑ 1. Not at all ❑ 2. A little ❑ 3. Moderately ❑ 4. Very much
■ Would you like to feel this more ? ❑ 1. No ❑ 2. A Little ❑ 3. Somewhat more
❑ 4. Much more

8. I felt DISTANT and FAR AWAY from my cares and concerns ...
❑ 1. Not at all ❑ 2. A little ❑ 3. Moderately ❑ 4. Very much
■ Would you like to feel this more ? ❑ 1. No ❑ 2. A Little ❑ 3. Somewhat more
❑ 4. Much more

9. I felt JOYFUL ...
❑ 1. Not at all ❑ 2. A little ❑ 3. Moderately ❑ 4. Very much
■ Would you like to feel this more ? ❑ 1. No ❑ 2. A Little ❑ 3. Somewhat more
❑ 4. Much more

(continued)

**THINK BACK OVER THE PAST TWO WEEKS. TO WHAT EXTENT
DID YOU EXPERIENCE THE FOLLOWING?**
(continued)

10. I felt "TIMELESS," "INFINITE," or "BOUNDLESS" . . .
  ❏ 1. Not at all ❏ 2. A little ❏ 3. Moderately ❏ 4. Very much
  ■ Would you like to feel this more ? ❏ 1. No ❏ 2. A Little ❏ 3. Somewhat more
  ❏ 4. Much more

11. My muscles felt relaxed and LIMP . . .
  ❏ 1. Not at all ❏ 2. A little ❏ 3. Moderately ❏ 4. Very much
  ■ Would you like to feel this more ? ❏ 1. No ❏ 2. A Little ❏ 3. Somewhat more
  ❏ 4. Much more

12. I felt LOVING . . .
  ❏ 1. Not at all ❏ 2. A little ❏ 3. Moderately ❏ 4. Very much
  ■ Would you like to feel this more ? ❏ 1. No ❏ 2. A Little ❏ 3. Somewhat more
  ❏ 4. Much more

13. I felt INDIFFERENT and DETACHED from my cares and concerns . . .
  ❏ 1. Not at all ❏ 2. A little ❏ 3. Moderately ❏ 4. Very much
  ■ Would you like to feel this more ? ❏ 1. No ❏ 2. A Little ❏ 3. Somewhat more
  ❏ 4. Much more

14. I felt AT PEACE . . .
  ❏ 1. Not at all ❏ 2. A little ❏ 3. Moderately ❏ 4. Very much
  ■ Would you like to feel this more ? ❏ 1. No ❏ 2. A Little ❏ 3. Somewhat more
  ❏ 4. Much more

15. My mind was SILENT AND CALM, not thinking about anything . . .
  ❏ 1. Not at all ❏ 2. A little ❏ 3. Moderately ❏ 4. Very much
  ■ Would you like to feel this more ? ❏ 1. No ❏ 2. A Little ❏ 3. Somewhat more
  ❏ 4. Much more

16. I felt PRAYERFUL or REVERENT . . .
  ❏ 1. Not at all ❏ 2. A little ❏ 3. Moderately ❏ 4. Very much
  ■ Would you like to feel this more ? ❏ 1. No ❏ 2. A Little ❏ 3. Somewhat more
  ❏ 4. Much more

17. I felt DROWSY and SLEEPY . . .
  ❏ 1. Not at all ❏ 2. A little ❏ 3. Moderately ❏ 4. Very much
  ■ Would you like to feel this more ? ❏ 1. No ❏ 2. A Little ❏ 3. Somewhat more
  ❏ 4. Much more

18. I felt ENERGIZED, CONFIDENT, or STRENGTHENED . . .
  ❏ 1. Not at all ❏ 2. A little ❏ 3. Moderately ❏ 4. Very much
  ■ Would you like to feel this more ? ❏ 1. No ❏ 2. A Little ❏ 3. Somewhat more
  ❏ 4. Much more

19. I felt SPIRITUAL . . .
  ❏ 1. Not at all ❏ 2. A little ❏ 3. Moderately ❏ 4. Very much

■ Would you like to feel this more ? ❏ 1. No ❏ 2. A Little ❏ 3. Somewhat more ❏ 4. Much more

20. My muscles felt TIGHT, TENSE • Clenched fist or jaws • Furrowed brow
❏ 1. Not at all ❏ 2. A little ❏ 3. Moderately ❏ 4. Very much
■ Would you like to feel this less ? ❏ 1. No ❏ 2. A Little ❏ 3. Somewhat less ❏ 4. Much less

21. I felt SAD, DEPRESSED, "BLUE"
❏ 1. Not at all ❏ 2. A little ❏ 3. Moderately ❏ 4. Very much
■ Would you like to feel this less ? ❏ 1. No ❏ 2. A Little ❏ 3. Somewhat less ❏ 4. Much less

22. I felt PHYSICAL DISCOMFORT, PAIN • Backaches • Headaches • Fatigue
❏ 1. Not at all ❏ 2. A little ❏ 3. Moderately ❏ 4. Very much
■ Would you like to feel this less ? ❏ 1. No ❏ 2. A Little ❏ 3. Somewhat less ❏ 4. Much less

23. I was WORRYING • Troublesome thoughts went through my mind
❏ 1. Not at all ❏ 2. A little ❏ 3. Moderately ❏ 4. Very much
■ Would you like to feel this less ? ❏ 1. No ❏ 2. A Little ❏ 3. Somewhat less ❏ 4. Much less

24. I felt IRRITATED, ANGRY
❏ 1. Not at all ❏ 2. A little ❏ 3. Moderately ❏ 4. Very much
■ Would you like to feel this less ? ❏ 1. No ❏ 2. A Little ❏ 3. Somewhat less ❏ 4. Much less

25. My BREATHING was NERVOUS, UNEVEN • Shallow • Hurried
❏ 1. Not at all ❏ 2. A little ❏ 3. Moderately ❏ 4. Very much
■ Would you like to feel this less ? ❏ 1. No ❏ 2. A Little ❏ 3. Somewhat less ❏ 4. Much less

26. I felt ANXIOUS
❏ 1. Not at all ❏ 2. A little ❏ 3. Moderately ❏ 4. Very much
■ Would you like to feel this less ? ❏ 1. No ❏ 2. A Little ❏ 3. Somewhat less ❏ 4. Much less

SPRI

How does this exercise make you feel?
Please check every statement.

1. I feel AT EASE ...
   ❏ 1. Not at all ❏ 2. A little ❏ 3. Moderately ❏ 4. Very Much
2. I feel AWARE, FOCUSED, and CLEAR ...
   ❏ 1. Not at all ❏ 2. A little ❏ 3. Moderately ❏ 4. Very Much
3. My mind is CALM, QUIET, AND STILL.
   ❏ 1. Not at all ❏ 2. A little ❏ 3. Moderately ❏ 4. Very Much
4. My hands, arms, or legs feel relaxed, WARM and HEAVY ...
   ❏ 1. Not at all ❏ 2. A little ❏ 3. Moderately ❏ 4. Very Much
5. I am HAPPY ...
   ❏ 1. Not at all ❏ 2. A little ❏ 3. Moderately ❏ 4. Very Much
6. I am DOZING OFF or NAPPING ...
   ❏ 1. Not at all ❏ 2. A little ❏ 3. Moderately ❏ 4. Very Much
7. I feel THANKFUL ...
   ❏ 1. Not at all ❏ 2. A little ❏ 3. Moderately ❏ 4. Very Much
8. I feel DISTANT and FAR AWAY from my cares and concerns ...
   ❏ 1. Not at all ❏ 2. A little ❏ 3. Moderately ❏ 4. Very Much
9. I feel JOYFUL ...
   ❏ 1. Not at all ❏ 2. A little ❏ 3. Moderately ❏ 4. Very Much
10. I feel "TIMELESS," "INFINITE," or "BOUNDLESS" ...
    ❏ 1. Not at all ❏ 2. A little ❏ 3. Moderately ❏ 4. Very Much
11. My muscles feel relaxed and LIMP ...
    ❏ 1. Not at all ❏ 2. A little ❏ 3. Moderately ❏ 4. Very Much
12. I feel LOVING ...
    ❏ 1. Not at all ❏ 2. A little ❏ 3. Moderately ❏ 4. Very Much
13. I feel INDIFFERENT and DETACHED from my cares and concerns ...
    ❏ 1. Not at all ❏ 2. A little ❏ 3. Moderately ❏ 4. Very Much
14. I feel AT PEACE ...
    ❏ 1. Not at all ❏ 2. A little ❏ 3. Moderately ❏ 4. Very Much
15. My mind is SILENT AND CALM, not thinking about anything ...
    ❏ 1. Not at all ❏ 2. A little ❏ 3. Moderately ❏ 4. Very Much
16. I feel PRAYERFUL or REVERENT ...
    ❏ 1. Not at all ❏ 2. A little ❏ 3. Moderately ❏ 4. Very Much
17. I feel DROWSY and SLEEPY ...
    ❏ 1. Not at all ❏ 2. A little ❏ 3. Moderately ❏ 4. Very Much
18. I feel ENERGIZED, CONFIDENT, or STRENGTHENED ...
    ❏ 1. Not at all ❏ 2. A little ❏ 3. Moderately ❏ 4. Very Much
19. I feel SPIRITUAL ...
    ❏ 1. Not at all ❏ 2. A little ❏ 3. Moderately ❏ 4. Very Much
20. My muscles feel TIGHT, TENSE • Clenched fist or jaws • Furrowed brow
    ❏ 1. Not at all ❏ 2. A little ❏ 3. Moderately ❏ 4. Very Much
21. I feel SAD, DEPRESSED, "BLUE"
    ❏ 1. Not at all ❏ 2. A little ❏ 3. Moderately ❏ 4. Very Much

22. **I feel PHYSICAL DISCOMFORT, PAIN • Backaches • Headaches • Fatigue**
    ❏ 1. Not at all ❏ 2. A little ❏ 3. Moderately ❏ 4. Very Much

23. **I am WORRYING • Troublesome thoughts go through my mind**
    ❏ 1. Not at all ❏ 2. A little ❏ 3. Moderately ❏ 4. Very Much

24. **I feel IRRITATED, ANGRY**
    ❏ 1. Not at all ❏ 2. A little ❏ 3. Moderately ❏ 4. Very Much

25. **My BREATHING IS NERVOUS, UNEVEN • Shallow • Hurried**
    ❏ 1. Not at all ❏ 2. A little ❏ 3. Moderately ❏ 4. Very Much

26. **I feel ANXIOUS**
    ❏ 1. Not at all ❏ 2. A little ❏ 3. Moderately ❏ 4. Very Much

SRSI

Please check to what extent you are
feeling each of the following
RIGHT NOW, AT THE PRESENT MOMENT.
Please check every statement.

1. **I feel AT EASE ...**
    ❏ 1. Not at all ❏ 2. A little ❏ 3. Moderately ❏ 4. Very Much
2. **I feel AWARE, FOCUSED, and CLEAR ...**
    ❏ 1. Not at all ❏ 2. A little ❏ 3. Moderately ❏ 4. Very Much
3. **My mind is CALM, QUIET, AND STILL.**
    ❏ 1. Not at all ❏ 2. A little ❏ 3. Moderately ❏ 4. Very Much
4. **My hands, arms, or legs feel relaxed, WARM and HEAVY ...**
    ❏ 1. Not at all ❏ 2. A little ❏ 3. Moderately ❏ 4. Very Much
5. **I am HAPPY ...**
    ❏ 1. Not at all ❏ 2. A little ❏ 3. Moderately ❏ 4. Very Much
6. **I am DOZING OFF or NAPPING ...**
    ❏ 1. Not at all ❏ 2. A little ❏ 3. Moderately ❏ 4. Very Much
7. **I feel THANKFUL ...**
    ❏ 1. Not at all ❏ 2. A little ❏ 3. Moderately ❏ 4. Very Much
8. **I feel DISTANT and FAR AWAY from my cares and concerns ...**
    ❏ 1. Not at all ❏ 2. A little ❏ 3. Moderately ❏ 4. Very Much
9. **I feel JOYFUL ...**
    ❏ 1. Not at all ❏ 2. A little ❏ 3. Moderately ❏ 4. Very Much
10. **I feel "TIMELESS," "INFINITE," or "BOUNDLESS" ...**
    ❏ 1. Not at all ❏ 2. A little ❏ 3. Moderately ❏ 4. Very Much
11. **My muscles feel relaxed and LIMP ...**
    ❏ 1. Not at all ❏ 2. A little ❏ 3. Moderately ❏ 4. Very Much
12. **I feel LOVING ...**
    ❏ 1. Not at all ❏ 2. A little ❏ 3. Moderately ❏ 4. Very Much
13. **I feel INDIFFERENT and DETACHED from my cares and concerns ...**
    ❏ 1. Not at all ❏ 2. A little ❏ 3. Moderately ❏ 4. Very Much
14. **I feel AT PEACE ...**
    ❏ 1. Not at all ❏ 2. A little ❏ 3. Moderately ❏ 4. Very Much
15. **My mind is SILENT AND CALM, not thinking about anything ...**
    ❏ 1. Not at all ❏ 2. A little ❏ 3. Moderately ❏ 4. Very Much
16. **I feel PRAYERFUL or REVERENT ...**
    ❏ 1. Not at all ❏ 2. A little ❏ 3. Moderately ❏ 4. Very Much
17. **I feel DROWSY and SLEEPY ...**
    ❏ 1. Not at all ❏ 2. A little ❏ 3. Moderately ❏ 4. Very Much
18. **I feel ENERGIZED, CONFIDENT, or STRENGTHENED ...**
    ❏ 1. Not at all ❏ 2. A little ❏ 3. Moderately ❏ 4. Very Much
19. **I feel SPIRITUAL ...**
    ❏ 1. Not at all ❏ 2. A little ❏ 3. Moderately ❏ 4. Very Much

20. **My muscles feel TIGHT, TENSE • Clenched fist or jaws • Furrowed brow**
  ❏ 1. Not at all ❏ 2. A little ❏ 3. Moderately ❏ 4. Very Much

21. **I feel SAD, DEPRESSED, "BLUE"**
  ❏ 1. Not at all ❏ 2. A little ❏ 3. Moderately ❏ 4. Very Much

22. **I feel PHYSICAL DISCOMFORT, PAIN • Backaches • Headaches • Fatigue**
  ❏ 1. Not at all ❏ 2. A little ❏ 3. Moderately ❏ 4. Very Much

23. **I am WORRYING • Troublesome thoughts go through my mind**
  ❏ 1. Not at all ❏ 2. A little ❏ 3. Moderately ❏ 4. Very Much

24. **I feel IRRITATED, ANGRY**
  ❏ 1. Not at all ❏ 2. A little ❏ 3. Moderately ❏ 4. Very Much

25. **My BREATHING IS NERVOUS, UNEVEN • Shallow • Hurried**
  ❏ 1. Not at all ❏ 2. A little ❏ 3. Moderately ❏ 4. Very Much

26. **I feel ANXIOUS**
  ❏ 1. Not at all ❏ 2. A little ❏ 3. Moderately ❏ 4. Very Much

SRBI

WHAT DO YOU BELIEVE?
People have many beliefs and philosophies, like those below.
To what extent do you agree with each statement?
Rate each item by checking the appropriate boxes.

1. Life has a purpose greater than my personal wants and desires
   ❑ 1. Do not agree ❑ 2. Agree a little ❑ 3. Agree moderately ❑ 4. Agree very much
2. I can accept things as they are.
   ❑ 1. Do not agree ❑ 2. Agree a little ❑ 3. Agree moderately ❑ 4. Agree very much
3. God guides, loves, and comforts me.
   ❑ 1. Do not agree ❑ 2. Agree a little ❑ 3. Agree moderately ❑ 4. Agree very much
4. I believe in being direct and clear in what I say, think, and do.
   ❑ 1. Do not agree ❑ 2. Agree a little ❑ 3. Agree moderately ❑ 4. Agree very much
5. I trust the body's wisdom and healing powers.
   ❑ 1. Do not agree ❑ 2. Agree a little ❑ 3. Agree moderately ❑ 4. Agree very much
6. Sometimes it is important to simply take it easy.
   ❑ 1. Do not agree ❑ 2. Agree a little ❑ 3. Agree moderately ❑ 4. Agree very much
7. I'm optimistic about how well I will deal with my current hassles.
   ❑ 1. Do not agree ❑ 2. Agree a little ❑ 3. Agree moderately ❑ 4. Agree very much
8. It is important to love and respect others.
   ❑ 1. Do not agree ❑ 2. Agree a little ❑ 3. Agree moderately ❑ 4. Agree very much
9. There's more to life than my personal concerns and worries.
   ❑ 1. Do not agree ❑ 2. Agree a little ❑ 3. Agree moderately ❑ 4. Agree very much
10. There's no need to try to change what can't be changed.
   ❑ 1. Do not agree ❑ 2. Agree a little ❑ 3. Agree moderately ❑ 4. Agree very much
11. I put myself in God's hands.
   ❑ 1. Do not agree ❑ 2. Agree a little ❑ 3. Agree moderately ❑ 4. Agree very much
12. I believe in being honest and open with my feelings.
   ❑ 1. Do not agree ❑ 2. Agree a little ❑ 3. Agree moderately ❑ 4. Agree very much
13. There are sources of strength and healing deep within me.
   ❑ 1. Do not agree ❑ 2. Agree a little ❑ 3. Agree moderately ❑ 4. Agree very much
14. It is important to know when to stop trying, let go, and relax.
   ❑ 1. Do not agree ❑ 2. Agree a little ❑ 3. Agree moderately ❑ 4. Agree very much
15. I believe in being optimistic.
   ❑ 1. Do not agree ❑ 2. Agree a little ❑ 3. Agree moderately ❑ 4. Agree very much
16. It is important to treat people with compassion and understanding.
   ❑ 1. Do not agree ❑ 2. Agree a little ❑ 3. Agree moderately ❑ 4. Agree very much

SRCI

WHAT ARE YOUR CONCERNS?

People have many different difficulties, problems, and unmet desires. What are your concerns? In what areas are you doing OK? In what areas could you do better? Below is a list of common concerns. Please indicate the extent to which each has been a concern for you over the past two weeks. Do so by checking the appropriate box under each statement.

1. **Preparing for or recovering from surgery**
   ❏ 1. I'm doing OK ❏ 2. I could do a little better ❏ 3. I could do moderately better
   ❏ 4. I could do much better
2. **Artistic work**
   ❏ 1. I'm doing OK ❏ 2. I could do a little better ❏ 3. I could do moderately better
   ❏ 4. I could do much better
3. **Reducing my pain and discomfort**
   ❏ 1. I'm doing OK ❏ 2. I could do a little better ❏ 3. I could do moderately better
   ❏ 4. I could do much better
4. **Spiritual growth**
   ❏ 1. I'm doing OK ❏ 2. I could do a little better ❏ 3. I could do moderately better
   ❏ 4. I could do much better
5. **Managing my depression**
   ❏ 1. I'm doing OK ❏ 2. I could do a little better ❏ 3. I could do moderately better
   ❏ 4. I could do much better
6. **Enhancing my physical health**
   ❏ 1. I'm doing OK ❏ 2. I could do a little better ❏ 3. I could do moderately better
   ❏ 4. I could do much better
7. **Dealing with interpersonal conflict**
   ❏ 1. I'm doing OK ❏ 2. I could do a little better ❏ 3. I could do moderately better
   ❏ 4. I could do much better
8. **Enhancing my creativity**
   ❏ 1. I'm doing OK ❏ 2. I could do a little better ❏ 3. I could do moderately better
   ❏ 4. I could do much better
9. **Controlling my tobacco use**
   ❏ 1. I'm doing OK ❏ 2. I could do a little better ❏ 3. I could do moderately better
   ❏ 4. I could do much better
10. **Increasing personal strength or stamina**
    ❏ 1. I'm doing OK ❏ 2. I could do a little better ❏ 3. I could do moderately better
    ❏ 4. I could do much better
11. **Managing my physical symptoms**
    ❏ 1. I'm doing OK ❏ 2. I could do a little better ❏ 3. I could do moderately better
    ❏ 4. I could do much better
12. **Dealing with my insomnia**
    ❏ 1. I'm doing OK ❏ 2. I could do a little better ❏ 3. I could do moderately better
    ❏ 4. I could do much better

(continued)

WHAT ARE YOUR CONCERNS?
(continued)

13. **Developing my ability to pray**
    ❏ 1. I'm doing OK ❏ 2. I could do a little better ❏ 3. I could do moderately better
    ❏ 4. I could do much better
14. **Managing my anxiety over medical / dental procedures**
    ❏ 1. I'm doing OK ❏ 2. I could do a little better ❏ 3. I could do moderately better
    ❏ 4. I could do much better
15. **Enhancing personal alertness and energy**
    ❏ 1. I'm doing OK ❏ 2. I could do a little better ❏ 3. I could do moderately better
    ❏ 4. I could do much better
16. **Coping with others**
    ❏ 1. I'm doing OK ❏ 2. I could do a little better ❏ 3. I could do moderately better
    ❏ 4. I could do much better
17. **Enhancing my personal insight**
    ❏ 1. I'm doing OK ❏ 2. I could do a little better ❏ 3. I could do moderately better
    ❏ 4. I could do much better
18. **Controlling my use of illegal substances**
    ❏ 1. I'm doing OK ❏ 2. I could do a little better ❏ 3. I could do moderately better
    ❏ 4. I could do much better
19. **Enhancing my sleep**
    ❏ 1. I'm doing OK ❏ 2. I could do a little better ❏ 3. I could do moderately better
    ❏ 4. I could do much better
20. **Controlling my eating problems**
    ❏ 1. I'm doing OK ❏ 2. I could do a little better ❏ 3. I could do moderately better
    ❏ 4. I could do much better
21. **Enhancing sex**
    ❏ 1. I'm doing OK ❏ 2. I could do a little better ❏ 3. I could do moderately better
    ❏ 4. I could do much better
22. **Enhancing my resistance to disease**
    ❏ 1. I'm doing OK ❏ 2. I could do a little better ❏ 3. I could do moderately better
    ❏ 4. I could do much better
23. **Preparing for or recovering from exercise workouts**
    ❏ 1. I'm doing OK ❏ 2. I could do a little better ❏ 3. I could do moderately better
    ❏ 4. I could do much better
24. **Managing the side effects of prescription medication**
    ❏ 1. I'm doing OK ❏ 2. I could do a little better ❏ 3. I could do moderately better
    ❏ 4. I could do much better
25. **Enhancing my performance at sports**
    ❏ 1. I'm doing OK ❏ 2. I could do a little better ❏ 3. I could do moderately better
    ❏ 4. I could do much better
26. **Managing my anxiety, worry, and frustration**
    ❏ 1. I'm doing OK ❏ 2. I could do a little better ❏ 3. I could do moderately better
    ❏ 4. I could do much better
27. **Enhancing my ability to meditate**
    ❏ 1. I'm doing OK ❏ 2. I could do a little better ❏ 3. I could do moderately better
    ❏ 4. I could do much better

Index*

---

*Entries in italics indicate Relaxation Words
(R-Words)

203